The Origin of Christology

The Origin of Christology

C. F. D. MOULE

FELLOW OF CLARE COLLEGE
EMERITUS LADY MARGARET'S PROFESSOR OF DIVINITY
IN THE UNIVERSITY OF CAMBRIDGE

CAMBRIDGE UNIVERSITY PRESS

CAMBRIDGE

LONDON · NEW YORK · MELBOURNE

Published by the Syndics of the Cambridge University Press
The Pitt Building, Trumpington Street, Cambridge CB2 1RP
Bentley House, 200 Euston Road, London NW1 2DB
32 East 57th Street, New York, NY 10022, USA
296 Beaconsfield Parade, Middle Park, Melbourne 3206, Australia

First published 1977

Reprinted 1978

Printed in Great Britain
at the
University Press, Cambridge

Library of Congress cataloguing in publication data
Moule, Charles Francis Digby.
The origin of Christology.
Includes bibliographical references and indexes.
1. Jesus Christ – History of doctrines – Early
church, ca. 30–600 – Addresses, essays, lectures.
I. Title.
BT198.M68   232'.09'015   76-11087
ISBN 0 521 21290 1

Contents

Acknowledgements

If anything at all in this book is of value, nobody could be more conscious than I am of the countless friends to whom credit is due. Indebted to generations of students on whom – poor victims! – some of the ideas have been tried, and with many of whom they have been profitably discussed, I owe much also to various bodies whose invitations to lecture have given me the incentive to put some thoughts on paper and the opportunity to ventilate them. In particular, I must thank the President and staff of Asbury Theological Seminary, at Wilmore in Kentucky, for the invitation to lecture there at the fiftieth anniversary of the Seminary in March 1974. On the same trip, I was kindly welcomed by certain colleges and universities in North Carolina also. Further, I owe thanks to the Council of the University of Otago for the invitation to deliver lectures in the same year at Knox College, Dunedin, as the Thomas Burns Visiting Professor in the Faculty of Theology, and to the Archbishop of Melbourne for the invitation, also in 1974, to deliver the Moorhouse Lectures; and I must thank the University of Aberdeen and several South African universities for invitations to lecture in 1975, enabling me to revise and add to certain parts of the material. I am grateful, also, for permission to reprint here two sections that have appeared in academic journals in South Africa. It is because acceptance of the Moorhouse Lectureship is conditional on the intention to publish the lectures that I have plucked up courage to get them into book-form; and it is thanks to the Syndics of the Cambridge University Press that the book has been accepted for publication. But if I were to give an adequate list of names, those to whom I am particularly indebted would include not only many persons in each of the bodies just named, but a host of others who heard the lectures, in all sorts of different places and contexts, and who helped me with lavish hospitality, kindly attention, and useful debate. To all these I must express deep gratitude, yet without naming them, because to name any would mean naming all, and that would make the acknowledgements longer than the book. If I have been stubborn in sticking to some of the ideas when perhaps I ought to have listened harder to adverse criticism, that is my fault. But certainly the fact that the book has taken shape, and is in better shape than it might have been, is thanks to countless friends. I am truly grateful for the honour done me by the invitations to lecture and for all the help afforded me in the process; grateful also to those whose patience and skill have got me into print – Mrs Ann Abraham and Mrs Paula Arfield at typewriters, and all who have been involved in the production at the University Press. I regret that Greek and Hebrew appear in English letters; it looks unscholarly and unsightly; but it is in the interests of economy. I have kept the direct address of lecture style, but considerably rearranged and added to the material. It seemed best to make a chapter out of each main theme. This has led to unevenness in the length of the chapters, but not, I hope, to inconvenience for the reader.

C. F. D. MOULE

Clare College, Cambridge
December 1975

Abbreviations

Aust. Bib. Review	*Australian Biblical Review*
BJRL	*The Bulletin of the John Rylands University Library of Manchester* (Manchester)
CBQ	*The Catholic Biblical Quarterly* (Washington)
CD	The Damascus Document (Zadokite Fragments), mss. from the Cairo Geniza. See index of references.
ET	*The Expository Times* (Birmingham)
EvQ	*The Evangelical Quarterly* (London)
HTR	*The Harvard Theological Review* (Cambridge, Mass.)
Interp	*Interpretation* (Richmond)
JBL	*The Journal of Biblical Literature* (Missoula, Mont.)
JBR	*The Journal of Bible and Religion* (Wolcott, N.Y.)
JSS	*The Journal of Semitic Studies* (Manchester)
JTS	*The Journal of Theological Studies* (Oxford)
LXX	The Septuagint
MT	The Massoretic Text
Nov Test	*Novum Testamentum* (Leiden)
NTS	*New Testament Studies* (Cambridge)
OS	The Old Syriac version
Q	1 etc. Q = documents from the first etc. cave at Qumran. See index of references.
RB	*Revue Biblique* (Jerusalem)
RGG	*Die Religion in Geschichte und Gegenwart* (Tübingen: Mohr ³1957–)
RHPR	*Revue d'Histoire et de Philosophie Religieuses* (Strasbourg)

RHR	*Revue d'Histoire des Religions* (Paris)
S-B	H. L. Strack und P. Billerbeck, *Kommentar zum Neuen Testament aus Talmud und Midrasch* (München: C. H. Beck 1922–8)
SBL	The Society of Biblical Literature
SJT	*The Scottish Journal of Theology* (Edinburgh)
Stud Evang	*Studia Evangelica,* papers presented at international congresses on N.T. Studies at Oxford, in *T und U.*
ThLz	*Theologische Literaturzeitung* (Leipzig)
T und U	*Texte und Untersuchungen zur Geschichte der altchristlichen Literatur* (Berlin: Akademie-Verlag)
TWNT	G. Kittel und G. Friedrich, Herausg., *Theologisches Wörterbuch zum Neuen Testament* (Stuttgart: Kohlhammer 1933–74). Eng. trans., G. W. Bromiley, ed., *Theological Dictionary of the New Testament* (Grand Rapids: Eerdmans 1965–74)
VT	*Vetus Testamentum* (Leiden)
ZAW	*Zeitschrift für die Alttestamentliche Wissenschaft* (Berlin)
ZNW	*Zeitschrift für die Neutestamentliche Wissenschaft* (Berlin)
ZThK	*Zeitschrift für Theologie und Kirche* (Tübingen)

Introduction

The scope of this book is strictly limited, and so is the equipment of the writer, as no one knows better than he. The inquiry is limited almost entirely to the New Testament documents, and the instruments employed are only those of ordinary New Testament investigation. But if anything that is cogent emerges from the argument, it will have an importance in the wider field of systematic theology, and so, ultimately, in the presentation and application of the Christian gospel. Therefore, although so far 'behind the lines', and although deliberately refraining from the discussion of recent work on Christology beyond the New Testament period, I refuse to believe that this activity has nothing to do with matters of contemporary urgency.

Indeed, it is, in a sense, a reply to a contemporary challenge. Apart from the more immediate incentive provided by sundry invitations to lecture, for which I have already expressed my gratitude, the main impetus behind these studies is the conviction, slowly generated over the years, that there are unexamined false assumptions behind a good deal of contemporary New Testament scholarship. Of these, the one I have particularly in mind is the assumption that the genesis of Christology – the coming into existence, that is, of the descriptions and understandings of Jesus which emerge in the course of Christian history – can be explained as a sort of evolutionary process, in the manner of the so-called 'history of religions school' of thought (*die religionsgeschichtliche Schule*).[1] If one were to

---

[1] For descriptions and criticisms of this approach, see J. Hempel in *RGG* (^{3}1961), *s.v.* (attributing the name to A. Jeremias, 1904), and C. Colpe, *Die religionsgeschichtliche Schule: Darstellung und Kritik ihres Bildes vom gnostischen Erlösungsmythes* (Göttingen: Vandenhoeck und Ruprecht 1961), 9; and M. Hengel, *Der Sohn Gottes: die Entstehung der Christologie und die jüdisch-historische Religionsgeschichte* (Tübingen: Mohr 1975), Eng. trans. *The Son of God* (London: SCM

caricature this assumption – grossly and unfairly, no doubt – one might say that it starts with a Palestinian Rabbi and ends with the divine Lord of a Hellenistic Saviour-cult, and that it explains the transition from the one to the other in much the same way as popular science may exhibit (probably quite correctly) the evolution of *homo sapiens* from lemur or ape in a diagrammatic tree, marking the emergence of each new species and assigning successive periods to them. In reaction against applying this type of assumption to the genesis of Christology – though of course it is never presented with so little finesse and sophistication as that – I find my own reading of the evidence leading me to the view that development is a better analogy for the genesis of Christology than evolution. This is only an analogy, of course: I am in no way concerned to deny evolution in the biological field. But if, in my analogy, 'evolution' means the genesis of successive new species by mutations and natural selection along the way, 'development', by contrast, will mean something more like the growth, from immaturity to maturity, of a single specimen from within itself.

The analogy is a rough and ready one of course, and it soon breaks down. But it serves to define the difference between two tendencies in the presentation of Christology. The tendency which I am calling 'evolutionary' and which I want to challenge, is the tendency to explain the change from (say) invoking Jesus as a revered Master to the acclamation of him as a divine Lord by the theory that, when the Christian movement spread beyond Palestinian soil, it began to come under the influence of non-Semitic Saviour-cults and to assimilate some of their ideas; and also by appeal to the effect of lapse of time, which may itself lead to the intensification of terms of adoration. It is like the so-called Euhemeristic theory of how Greek mythology found its gods.[2]

By contrast, the tendency which I am advocating as closer to the evidence, and which I call 'developmental', is to explain all the various estimates of Jesus reflected in the New Testament as,

1976), 17ff.; see also *idem*. 'Christologie und neutestamentliche Chronologie', in H. Baltensweiler and B. Reicke, edd., *Neues Testament und Geschichte* (Zürich: Theol. Verlag/Tübingen: Mohr 1972), 43ff.
[2] Euhemerus is said to have been a member of Cassander's court in Macedonia, in the fourth century B.C., and is associated with the rationalist theory that the gods were simply men who, after their death, had come to be worshipped.

in essence, only attempts to describe what was already there from the beginning. They are not successive additions of something new, but only the drawing out and articulating of what is there. They represent various stages in the development of perception, but they do not represent the accretion of any alien factors that were not inherent from the beginning: they are analogous not so much to the emergence of a new species, as to the unfolding (if you like) of flower from bud and the growth of fruit from flower. Moreover, when once one assumes that the changes are, in the main, changes only in perception, one is at the same time acknowledging that it may not be possible, *a priori*, to arrange such changes in any firm chronological order. In evolution, the more complex species generally belong to a later stage than the more simple; but in development, there is nothing to prevent a profoundly perceptive estimate occurring at an early stage, and a more superficial one at a later stage: degrees of perception will depend upon individual persons and upon circumstances which it may be impossible to identify in any intelligibly chronological sequence.

This is not, of course, to deny that certain sorts of language and expression may become available only in certain contexts and at certain periods. It is certainly not to eliminate the chronological factor altogether. But if the 'model' of development is nearer to the truth, then less confidence can be placed in a clear-cut chronological sequence such as the series commonly assumed in New Testament studies: early Palestinian Jewish Christianity, early diaspora Jewish Christianity, pre-Pauline Gentile Christianity, Pauline Christianity, post-Pauline developments.[3]

I said that the analogy soon broke down; and it goes without saying that even in so continuous a process as the opening of a bud into a flower, plenty of extraneous matter is absorbed. Metabolism in a living thing is never a completely self-contained process, like the mere springing open of a Japanese paper flower when it is dropped into water. But even if the edges of these two

[3] For criticism of the assumption that there is sufficient evidence, in any case, to establish these stages, see I. H. Marshall, 'Palestinian and Hellenistic Christianity. Some Critical Comments', *NTS* 19.3 (April 1973), 271ff.; M. Hengel, 'Christologie und neutestamentliche Chronologie', as in n. 1, and G. B. Caird, 'The Development of the Doctrine of Christ in the New Testament', in N. Pittenger, ed., *Christ for Us today* (London: SCM 1968), 66ff.

'models', evolution and development, are necessarily blurred, and even if there comes a point when one merges into the other, they nevertheless serve their purpose. To abandon the analogy and speak plain prose, what I am saying is that the evidence, as I read it, suggests that Jesus was, *from the beginning,* such a one as appropriately to be described in the ways in which, sooner or later, he did come to be described in the New Testament period – for instance, as 'Lord' and even, in some sense, as 'God'. Whether such terms in fact began to be used early or late, my contention is that they are not evolved *away,* so to speak, from the original, but represent the development of true insights into the original.[4] In a word, I am concerned to challenge, in the name of the evidence, such a statement as that 'the fundamental problem of a Christology of the NT...was that the view of Jesus found in NT Christology was *not historically true of Jesus himself*' (my italics).[5]

Clearly, the attempt to fault this statement is going to encounter formidable problems of definition, and will always be in danger of becoming a circular argument. For instance, can it seriously be maintained that it is 'historically true of Jesus himself' to attribute preexistence to him? M. J. Suggs finds reason to believe that, whereas 'Q' saw Jesus as only an *envoy* of Wisdom, 'Matthew' (the evangelist) saw Jesus as Wisdom itself, and as Torah itself, and altered Q-sayings accordingly.[6] Does not this look like a case of 'evolution' from the correct estimate of Jesus as a highly inspired prophet to a myth of the preexistent Agent in creation? Can it possibly be said that the latter estimate of Jesus is true of the historical Jesus himself? Is it not more reasonable to believe that the former is nearer to a sober estimate of the man of Nazareth, whereas the latter is an estimate evolved through contact with alien cults and alien worlds of thought, in a period when the real Jesus of history was beginning to be

---

[4] What affinities such a thesis may have with Roman Catholic doctrines of 'development' must be for historians of doctrine to decide. See, for instance, W. O. Chadwick, *From Bossuet to Newman: the Idea of Doctrinal Development* (Cambridge: University Press 1957).

[5] H. Boers, 'Jesus and the Christian Faith: New Testament Christology since Bousset's *Kyrios Christos*', *JBL* 89.4 (Dec. 1970), 450ff. (452).

[6] *Wisdom, Christology, and Law in Matthew's Gospel* (Cambridge, Mass.: Harvard 1970).

magnified in the imagination of a generation remote from his own?

Or, again, how 'true to the historical Jesus' is the story of the virginal conception of Jesus?[7] Can we say that it is a way of expressing a true insight that, from the beginning, Jesus was such a one as cannot adequately be described as only human? Or is it not simpler, once again, to say that the virginal conception is a myth evolved in the processes of accommodating Christian thought to current ideas? One of the attractive features of the latter view is that it seems to escape from the transcendental into the safer territory of the rational and intelligible.

My reason for putting a query against this type of assumption, despite its attractiveness, is that it seems to me simply not to do justice to the evidence. I am not concerned in this book to discuss this particular question of the virginal conception, and I am not prepared to take sides in that debate. But I am prepared to believe that the stories in Matthew and Luke represent one way (whether adequate or not for the modern mind) of express-ing the inadequacy of a one-sided understanding of the Person of Christ. My main point is not that all Christological expressions in the New Testament are adequate for modern statements of Christology, but that they are all more successfully accounted for as insights, of varying depth, into what was there in Jesus, than as the result of increasing distance from him.

I must make it clear that, in using such an expression as 'what was there in Jesus', I am not implying a naïve belief that all the *sayings* attributed to Jesus in the Gospels can be used as evidence. I am not speaking, primarily at least, of the *teaching* of Jesus. I am speaking, rather, of the impact made by him on those who knew him during his ministry, as this may be deduced from the traditions of his deeds as well as of his words, and the impact made by him after the resurrection, as this may be deduced from the religious experience reflected in the New Testament.

And here, manifestly, the danger of circularity in the argument

[7] See R. E. Brown, *The Virginal Conception and Bodily Resurrection of Jesus* (London: Geoffrey Chapman 1973; the first part is a revised form of an inaugural lecture published in *Theological Studies* 33 (1972), 3ff.); J. A. Fitzmyer, 'The Virginal Conception of Jesus in the New Testament', *Theol. Stud.* 34.4 (Dec. 1973), 541ff. (560, 563f., 572); and J. A. Saliba, 'Virgin Birth and Anthropology', *Theol. Stud.* 36 (1975), 428ff.

arises. By what criterion is one to judge whether a religious experience is 'historically true of Jesus himself', rather than derived from extraneous sources? What can 'historically' true mean when it is applied to an alleged experience of one who had long before been put to death? The answer, in my belief, is a cumulative one. Partly, it is in the discovery that certain titles of 'high' Christology, such as 'Lord', exhibit more continuity than is often allowed with the earliest, Palestinian Church's estimate. Partly, it is in the discovery that it is among the earliest datable parts of the New Testament (the most widely acknowledged Pauline epistles) that experiences of Christ are reflected which are unprecedented in pre-Christian religious experience and which it is difficult to explain as borrowings from the Gentile world and which indicate nothing short of divine status for him. Partly it is in the congruity between the traditions of Jesus' ministry and these religious experiences of subsequent days.

I am certainly not concerned to defend all estimates of Jesus within the New Testament as equally valid or equally profound. My point is only that the evidence does not support the assumption that a 'high' Christology evolved from a 'low' Christology by a process of borrowing from extraneous sources, and that these Christologies may be arranged in an evolutionary sequence from 'low' to 'high'. For instance, there is a tendency in the Acts to portray the wonder-working power of the name of Jesus as evidence of his 'superiority' to rival wonder-workers (see below, pp. 45f.). Is this a primitive view which was corrected in time as Christian thought developed? Or is it not, rather, simply less profound than a great deal that one finds in Mark, which is generally deemed earlier than Luke–Acts, and in Paul, who is earlier still? And are not the profoundest estimates most naturally explained as due to the actual impact of the person of Jesus?

When one asks, Who could Jesus have been, to affect his disciples and their successors in the ways in which he did?[8] the 'evolutionary' type of answer, plausible though it may seem at first, seems less than adequate. More adequate is an answer which finds, from the beginning, a Person of such magnitude that, so

---

[8] Cf. the much-quoted question posed by Leonard Hodgson: 'What must the truth have been if it appeared like this to men who thought like that?', *For Faith and Freedom*, Gifford Lectures for 1955–7, i (Oxford: Blackwell 1956), 87f.

far from pious imagination's embroidering and enlarging him, the perennial problem was, rather, how to reach any insight that would come near to fathoming him, or any description that was not pitifully inadequate. Successive attempts at word-painting are (as I read the evidence) not evolving away from the original. They are all only incomplete representations of the mighty Figure that has been there all the time.

In particular, I want to ask whether New Testament scholarship has paid enough attention to the strange fact that Paul, at any rate, seems to reflect an experience of Christ which implies such dimensions as any theist would ascribe to God himself: that is to say, Christ is, for Paul, personal, indeed, but more than individual. A more than individual personality is a perplexing enough notion; yet it is this and nothing less that seems to attach to Christ in our very earliest documents of Christian experience, the early and authentic Pauline epistles. In this study I do not ignore the titles of Christ: I begin by trying to show, by select examples, that a fresh examination of the facts about them endorses my claim for 'development' as against 'evolution'. But I regard that other evidence as even more significant: quite independently of any titles, who, I ask, can this be who, although a vividly known individual of recent history, is experienced by Paul in this 'theistic' dimension?

Of course, a prior question is, How was it that the friends of Jesus came to be convinced that he was alive, after his death on the cross, with an absolute and ultimate life? But I have attempted to discuss that elsewhere,[9] and in the present study it is the subsequent Christian experience that must occupy our attention.

Although I must not saddle others with my own views, I believe that I may claim O. Cullmann as, in many respects at least, an advocate of what I am labelling a developmental, as against an evolutionary view of the genesis of Christology. It is basically for this (although the terms are not used) that Cullmann incurs criticism from Hendrikus Boers: 'By assuming', Boers writes,

that the foundation of NT Christology was the activity of Jesus in these four areas [Boers is referring to Cullmann's division of his field into the

---

[9] E.g. *The Phenomenon of the New Testament* (London: SCM 1967), and *Theology* 75. 628 (Oct. 1972), 507ff.

earthly, the future, the present, and the preexistent], he interprets the primitive Christian formulations of faith in Christ as merely the articulation of (what must be considered) an already underlying Christology. Thus, even Cullmann's discussion of the historical development in the use of the various titles becomes the mere explicating of the details of an already presupposed Christology.[10]

Precisely! And, for my part I do not believe that this assumption of Cullmann's has yet been proved wrong, or even implausible. There are *details* of Cullmann's work with which I venture to disagree; but this basic assumption seems to me to fit the evidence positively better than the assumption of what Boers calls 'the generating power of the religious environment',[11] which he accuses even F. Hahn of under-estimating, although Hahn's magnificent and learned study of Christology[12] tends to make what I am calling 'evolutionary' assumptions.

Cullmann is right, in my opinion, in allowing for the sheer originality of Jesus himself, in which I would wish, for myself, to include not merely the originality of what Jesus may have said, but also of what he was. 'One must certainly react from the very beginning', wrote Cullmann,

against the erroneous notion lying behind many representations of early Christian Christology, that this Christology had necessarily to conform to the conceptual scheme already present in Judaism or Hellenism. Although the viewpoint of comparative religions is justified in itself, an exaggeration of it undoubtedly leads to such a way of thinking. But as scholars we simply cannot neglect to take Jesus' own self-consciousness into consideration. For one must reckon *a priori* with the possibility – even with the probability – first, that in his teaching and life *Jesus accomplished something new from which the first Christians had to proceed in their attempt to explain his person and work*; second, that their experience of Christ exhibited special features not present in every obvious analogy to related religious forms. It is simply unscholarly prejudice methodically to exclude from the beginning this possibility – this probability.[13] [italics mine]

[10] Hendrikus Boers, as in n. 5 above, 455.
[11] *Loc. cit.*, 456.
[12] F. Hahn, *Christologische Hoheitstitel: Ihre Geschichte im frühen Christentum* (Göttingen: Vandenhoeck und Ruprecht 1963); abridged Eng. trans., *The Titles of Jesus in Christology* (London: Lutterworth 1969).
[13] *Die Christologie des Neuen Testaments* (Tübingen: Mohr 1957); Eng. trans., *Christology of the New Testament* (London: SCM 1959), 5.

Many scholars have, rightly or wrongly, criticized Cullmann's use of the idea of *Heilsgeschichte* in his Christology; but his refusal to assume that the Christological processes may all be explained from analogies in other religions is independent of this, and is undeniably sound.

Like Cullmann to this extent, R. H. Fuller emphatically affirms 'a direct line of continuity between Jesus' self-understanding and the church's christological interpretation of him'. Fuller says even of the preexistence of the Redeemer, articulated, as he believes, in the Gentile mission, that, although it 'looks like a tremendous advance on the more primitive Christologies', it was really implicit all along.[14] Fuller's account of how the various stages of Christology arose seems to me, like Cullmann's, at certain points to rest on speculation. But both these writers take seriously the originality of Christ himself and the continuity between New Testament Christology and the initial datum in Jesus, and in this I believe they are close to the evidence. The same must be said, I believe – and I hope I am not misrepresenting them – of W. Kümmel, in his various publications, and of Martin Hengel, whose small but weighty book, *Der Sohn Gottes*,[15] based on his inaugural lecture at Tübingen in May 1973, is, in my opinion, of outstanding importance in this connexion, as are certain essays by the same writer.[16]

Here, then, is the main thrust of this inquiry. It is an attempt, without prejudging the issue in favour of more 'conservative' or more 'orthodox' Christologies, simply to ask whether a 'developmental' account of the genesis of Christology does not do better justice to the evidence than an 'evolutionary' account; and, especially, to ask whether, when we have finished asking about the '*titles*' of Jesus, there is not something even more basic, of which any description of the genesis of Christology must take account, namely, the *experience* of him reflected in the New Testament.

What I have called 'evolutionary' accounts of the genesis of

---

[14] *The Foundations of New Testament Christology* (London: Lutterworth 1965; Collins, Fontana Library, 1969), 15, 254.

[15] As in n. 1.

[16] See in particular, 'Christologie und neutestamentliche Chronologie', in H. Baltensweiler and Bo Reicke, edd., *Neues Testament und Geschichte, Oscar Cullmann zum 70. Geburtstag* (Zürich: Theologischer Verlag 1972), 43ff.

Christology offer a great deal of circumstantial detail by way of supporting their contention. If one makes the counter-claim that 'development' is a better model, to what may one appeal by way of supporting evidence? If the case is to be made, the detailed evidence must be seen to be sound. By way of testing the thesis, then, I propose to start by considering four well-known terms – 'the Son of Man', 'the Son of God', 'Christ', and 'Lord' – in order to see what evidence emerges as to their origins.

1

Four well-known descriptions of Jesus

I. THE SON OF MAN[1]

It is held by many scholars that the term, 'the Son of Man', meant a supernatural, apocalyptic figure and was first applied, as a title, to Jesus by the early Palestinian communities, who signified by

[1] I have told this story dozens of times now, and the fact that I am still in a small minority makes me wonder what is wrong with it. But I can, so far, not find the flaw; and the fact that most writers still ignore the definite article in 'the Son of Man' demonstrates that they have not taken account of this remarkable phenomenon. M. Hengel very correctly and exactly notes the phenomenon, but draws from it different conclusions. Discussing Hellenistic communities of the stage between the early Palestinian communities and Paul, he writes: Ein Indiz für einen festen Ort der Übertragung der Jesustradition bietet weiter die sonderbare, im Neuen Testament völlig einheitliche Übersetzung des bᵉrā [dc'našā odcr bar] 'ᵃnaš(ā) [I give the text as filled out in his own hand in my copy: printed is only bᵉrā 'ᵃnaš(ā)] mit *ho huios tou anthrōpou* bei klarer messianischer Bedeutung. Sie muss an *einem* bestimmten Ort erfolgt sein, denn nur auf diese Weise konnte sic sich so durchsetzen, dass andere Übertragungsmöglichkeiten wie das – näherliegende – *anthrōpos* oder *huios anthrōpou* nicht mehr aufkommen konnten. Hinter dieser ungewohnten Übersetzung muss eine eindeutige christologische Konzeption stehen, die vielleicht in dem Menschensohn der Stephanusvision ihren Niederschlag gefunden hat ('Zwischen Jesus und Paulus', *ZThK* 72.2 (June 1975), 151ff. (202f.)).
In a footnote, he refers to an unpublished Tübingen dissertation by R. Kearns, 'Der Menschensohn. Morphologische und semasiologische Studien zur Vorgeschichte eines christologischen Hoheitstitels', 1973. B. Lindars, 'Re-Enter the Apocalyptic Son of Man', *NTS* 22.1 (Oct. 1975), 52ff. (cf. *idem*. 'The Apocalyptic Myth and the Death of Christ', *BJRL* 57.2 (Spring 1975), 366ff.), alludes to my essay (n. 5 below), but seems to think that the special form of the Greek phrase somehow represents an Aramaic phrase 'already laden with a specialized meaning', and that it is used only when 'it is felt to be a self-reference on the part of Jesus' (p. 65). This seems to me rather vague, and less simple or satisfactory than tracing the Greek phrase to a straightforward Aramaic demonstrative phrase. See below. Since this note was written I have seen R. Pesch and R. Schnackenburg, edd., *Jesus und der Menschensohn, für Anton Vögtle* (Freiburg/Basel/Wien: Herder 1975), in which the phenomenon of the definite article is taken careful account of by E. Schweizer, 'Menschensohn und eschatologischer Mensch im Frühjudentum' (100ff.), and by E. Grässer, 'Beobachtungen zum Menschensohn in Hebr 2,6' (404ff.).

its use their belief that Jesus was the dominant figure of an imminent apocalyptic climax.[2] If Jesus used it himself at all, it was only – so this theory goes – with reference to a figure other than himself. It was not by Jesus himself but by Christians in the earliest period after the first Easter that it began to be used to designate Jesus.

Others hold that Jesus did apply the Semitic equivalent of this expression to himself, but only in certain limited connexions, whether as an oblique, idiomatic alternative simply for the first person pronoun – 'I' or 'me' – or as a more specific indication of himself as a frail mortal. Professor J. W. Bowker of the University of Lancaster, in particular, emphasizes the latter.[3] He observes that, in the Old Testament, 'Son of man' occurs mainly in three contexts: in the vocative, as an address to Ezekiel; in Dan. 7, in the special context of that vision; and in a 'scatter' of texts such as Num. 23: 19 and Ps. 8: 4, which emphasize the contrast between frail mortal man and the angels, or God himself. This latter sense he is also able to illustrate impressively from Jewish literature outside the Old Testament.[4] He holds, therefore, that, even if Dan. 7 may well have been used by Jesus himself to introduce the further dimension of the paradoxical vindication of frail, mortal man in the heavenly court, the mortality and frailness are necessary ingredients and Dan. 7 cannot alone account for the Gospel usage.

While not quarrelling at all with the illuminating suggestion that the phrase carries in it all the overtones of this frailty motif, I am among those who still believe that it is Dan. 7 that gives it, in the Gospel tradition, its decisive colour.[5] And what confirms

---

[2] P. Vielhauer, 'Gottesreich und Menschensohn in der Verkündigung Jesu' and 'Jesus und der Menschensohn', in *Aufsätze zum Neuen Testament* (München: Kaiser Verlag 1965), 55ff.

[3] In lectures when he was a University Lecturer at Cambridge, and in the Wilde Lectures at Oxford.

[4] In the Targums there is a strong tendency (Professor Bowker tells me) to substitute 'son of man' for other terms for man, where the context suggests frailty and mortality.

[5] See my essay, 'Neglected Features in the Problem of "the Son of Man"', in J. Gnilka, ed., *Neues Testament und Kirche* (für Rudolf Schnackenburg) (Freiburg/Basel/Wien: Herder 1974), 413ff. See also certain features of F. Neugebauer, 'Die Davidssohnfrage (Mark xii, 35–57 parr.) und der Menschensohn', *NTS* 21.1 (Oct. 1974), 81ff. There are others who share this view to some extent: see I. H. Marshall, 'The Synoptic Son of Man Sayings in Recent Discussion', *NTS* 12 (1965–6), 327ff., and 'The Son of Man in Contemporary

me in this conclusion is, among other things, the fact that, almost invariably in the Gospel tradition, the phrase is not, in fact, 'Son of Man' but '*the* Son of Man', with the definite article. This leads me to believe that what lies behind the Greek, *ho huios tou anthrōpou*, must be some Aramaic expression that meant, unequivocally, not just 'Son of Man' but '*the* Son of Man' or '*that* Son of Man', and that this phrase was thus demonstrative because it expressly referred to Daniel's 'Son of Man'. In the Aramaic of Daniel 7 it is without the definite article: *kᵉ bar ᵉnāš*, 'like a son of man'. This figure that looked to the seer like a human being evidently represents, in Dan. 7 as it now stands, the devout Jews who, in the days of Antiochus Epiphanes' persecution, had remained resolutely loyal. I say 'in Dan. 7 as it now stands', because Old Testament scholars postulate a long redaction history for it, and it may well have grown out of a very different scene – one, for instance, in which one dominant deity asserted his sway over other, vanquished deities.[6] It is argued by some that even 'the people of the saints of the Most High' in Dan. 7 means not the Israelite loyalists but a host of angels, or heavenly beings of some sort; and it is well known, of course, that the adjective 'holy', used as a noun, 'holy one', is, indeed, far easier to illustrate from the Old Testament in its angelic than in its human connotation (see, e.g. Noth and Colpe, article '*hagios*', in *TWNT*). But it is, to me at least, very difficult to believe that in Dan. 7 as it now stands it does not mean human persons – the persecuted loyalists who are afflicted by the 'horn' that represents Antiochus Epiphanes, and who are brought very low; and there are some other examples of 'holy one' apparently meaning a human person, for instance in Deut. 33: 3, Pss. 16: 3, 34: 9 (MT 10), and in 1QM 10. 10, where it is difficult to deny it a human

Debate', *EvQ* 42.2 (April–June 1970), 67ff., and the extensive bibliography in those articles.

[6] J. A. Emerton, 'The Origin of the Son of Man Imagery', *JTS* n.s. 9 (1958), 225ff. W. J. Dumbell, 'Daniel 7 and the Function of Old Testament Apocalyptic', *The Reformed Theological Review* 34.1 (Jan.–April 1975), 16ff., alludes to this and other theories of this chapter's origin; and himself concludes (20) that 'The Son of Man figure in the vision is a heavenly being...and certainly not in the vision the representative of a specific people or kingdom'. But I do not think that, even if he is right, this tells us much about what subsequent interpreters – Jesus, the writer of Enoch, and others – made of it. In any case, he seems to jump to unwarranted conclusions about the human figure even within the setting of Dan. 7.

connotation.[7] If, then, the human figure of Dan. 7 stands not for some angelic host but for God's loyal people vindicated in the heavenly court after tribulation, what more appropriate symbol could be found for the vocation which Jesus saw to be his own, and which Jesus called his disciples also to share, as T. W. Manson constantly maintained, and, I think, with reason?[8] The precise relation of the 'human figure' to the collective body it is not necessary to determine. Whether the 'human figure' is an angelic being or a personification or simply a symbol, in any case, in Dan. 7 as it stands, he represents 'the saints'. It is often pointed out that the Danielic vision constitutes a meditation on the supremacy of Adam over the rest of nature in the Genesis creation stories. Perhaps it is even more apposite to recall that Ps. 8 expresses surprise and admiration that God has exalted frail man to this position of supremacy. All in all, then, the human figure in Dan. 7 is highly appropriate to the ministry of Jesus. On this showing, it is not a *title* for Jesus, but a symbol of a vocation to be utterly loyal, even to death, in the confidence of ultimate vindication in the heavenly court. Jesus is alluding to '*the* (well known, Danielic)[9] Son of Man' in this vein. As Dr Morna Hooker has shown,[10] this makes good sense of the Marcan sayings about the Son of Man's authority: it is the authority (whether in heaven or on earth) of true Israel, and so, of authentic Man, obedient, through thick and thin, to God's design.

But, say the Aramaists (or, at least, some of them),[11] there was

---

[7] Even J. J. Collins, 'The Son of Man and the Saints of the Most High', *JBL* 93.1 (March 1974), 50ff., who argues for the view that the figure in Dan. 7 represents 'primarily the angelic host and its leader' (though *also* 'the faithful Jews in so far as they are associated with the heavenly host in the eschatological era' (66)), allows (52, n. 17) that 'at least... 1QM 10. 10... '*am qᵉdôŝê bᵉrît* must refer to human beings'. See further (?)CD 20.8, 4QpsDanª (with J. T. Milik, *RB* 63 (1956), 407ff.); and O. E. Evans, 'New Wine in Old Wineskins. XIII. The Saints', *ET* 86.7 (April 1975), 196ff., quoting C. H. W. Brekelmans, 'The Saints of the Most High and their Kingdom', in *Oudtestamentische Studien*, XIV (Leiden 1965), 305ff.

[8] E.g. in *The Teaching of Jesus* (Cambridge: University Press 1935), 227.

[9] For the popularity of Daniel at this period, see Josephus *Ant.* x. 267 quoted below (cf. F. Neugebauer as in n. 5 above, 93 n. 1).

[10] M. D. Hooker, *The Son of Man in Mark* (London: SPCK 1967).

[11] E.g. G. Vermés, 'The use of *bar nāŝâ/bar nāŝ* in Jewish Aramaic', in M. Black, *An Aramaic Approach to the Gospels and Acts* (Oxford: University Press ³1967), 310ff. But *contra* J. A. Fitzmyer in *CBQ* 30 (1968), 424ff.; and see J. Jeremias, *Neutestamentliche Theologie* i (Gütersloh: Mohr 1971), Eng. trans., *New Testament Theology* i (London SCM 1971) 260ff., for a careful survey of the linguistic facts.

no distinction in meaning at this period between the emphatic
state in Aramaic (*bar-nāšâ*) and the absolute state (*bar-⁽ᵉ⁾naš*), and
it is therefore a mistake to assume that the Greek phrase with
the definite article, *ho huios tou anthrōpou*, could have reflected
a distinctively demonstrative form in the original language of
Jesus. This (though I am no Aramaist) I would venture to
challenge. I cannot believe that it was impossible to find a phrase
in Aramaic that would unequivocally mean 'that Son of Man' or
'*the* Son of Man'. It is true that the Syriac versions of the New
Testament, both Old Syriac and Peshitta, make no distinction
between *ho huios tou anthrōpou* and *huios anthrōpou*, rendering
them both alike by *bᵉrēh d'ᵉnāšâ* (or, in some places in the OS,
bᵉrēh dᵉgabrâ);[12] but it seems to me not unlikely that this uniform-
ity may be due to the fact that, by that time, these Christian
translators had made up their minds that all the occurrences of
the Greek phrase, in whatever form, applied to Christ, and
therefore rendered it (so far as their constructions went) uni-
formly. It is all the more significant that in the Similitudes of
Enoch (i.e. 1 Enoch 37–71), which most scholars regard as a
non-Christian work, even if, as I believe, it is most likely to belong
in date to a period later than the formation of the earliest Gospel
traditions, there occurs, in the Ethiopic version, which is our main
authority for its text, precisely the phenomenon which I am
conjecturing for the days of Jesus himself. That is to say, an
initial quotation of the Danielic phrase, without the article, is
followed by frequent references back to it, in phrases which are
all, in one way or another, in a definite form. The initial
formulation is in 1 Enoch 46.1: 'And with him [i.e. the aged
figure] was another being whose countenance had the appear-
ance of a man...'. Thereafter, it is always (so I am informed
by Ethiopic scholars) '*that* Son of Man' or '*the* Son of Man', or
'*this* Son of Man' (46.2, 3, 4; 48.2; 62.5, 7, 9, 14; 63.11; 69.26, 27;
70.1; 71.14 ('Thou art the Son of Man'), 17). This phenomenon
was duly noted by Wilhelm Bousset long ago,[13] but he did not,

---

[12] For further details, see my essay as in n. 5 above, 421, n. 27, with acknowledgements to Dr D. R. de Lacey.

[13] See his *Kyrios Christos. Geschichte des Christusglaubens von den Anfängen des
Christentums bis Irenaeus* (Göttingen ¹1913, ⁶1967), Eng. trans., by J. E. Steely,
*Kyrios Christos: a History of the Belief in Christ from the Beginnings of Christianity
to Irenaeus* (Nashville/New York: Abingdon 1970), 44f.

of course, exploit it, as I am doing, as an exact analogy to what I am postulating for Jesus himself – the use of the equivalent of the definite article or a demonstrative pronoun by way of allusion back to an initial mention (or an assumed knowledge among the hearers) of Daniel's human figure. (There is good reason to believe that Daniel would have been widely known and an allusion to it recognized. Josephus (*Ant.* x.267f.) says: 'the books which he [Daniel] wrote and left behind are still read by us even now...Daniel was a prophet of good tidings to them, so that through the auspiciousness of his predictions he attracted the goodwill of all...') In Dan. 7, the seer sees *a* human figure (*kᵉbar* *ᵉnāš* – 'what looked like a man'); but Jesus, referring back to this symbol, with all its associations, speaks of his own vocation and that of his friends in terms of '*the* Son of Man': it is for him and for them to be or to become that figure.

The significance of the definite article in the Greek version is further underlined by the remarkable fact that there is, to the best of my knowledge, only one instance in Hebrew literature before the New Testament of the definite article used with the singular, '*the* Son of Man' (though the plural, 'the sons of men', is, of course, found); and that, which occurs in the Qumran Manual of Discipline, 1QS 11.20, appears to be an afterthought, for the *he* (ה) of the definite article is placed above the first letter of 'Man' (that is, over the *a* (א) of *'ādām*).[14] By contrast, in the New Testament, there is only one instance, among all the sayings attributed to Jesus (and the one attributed to Stephen), of the phrase *without* the definite article. It is different when the phrase is in a quotation direct from the Old Testament. Then, it is, naturally, anarthrous. In Heb. 2: 6 it appears anarthrously in a quotation from Ps. 8: 4; and in Rev. 1: 13, 14: 14 the Aramaic of Dan. 7: 13 is literally rendered into barbarous Greek as *homoios huios anthrōpou*. But otherwise, in the Gospel traditions, only in John 5: 27 does *huios anthrōpou* (indefinite) occur.[15]

[14] See the facsimile in M. Burrows with J. C. Trever and W. H. Brownlee, *The Dead Sea Scrolls of St Mark's Monastery* (New Haven: The American Schools of Oriental Research, 1951), ii, Plate XI. E. Lohse, *Die Texte aus Qumran, hebräisch und deutsch* (München: Kösel 1964), 42, simply includes the *he* in his transcription, as though it were on the same line as *'ādām*.

[15] Dr L. L. Morris, hearing this lecture at Melbourne on 11 August 1974, was kind enough to point out that even John 5: 27, which runs *hoti huios anthrōpou estin*,

Outside the Gospel tradition of the words of Jesus, the phrase with the article occurs, as is well known, on the lips of Stephen, in Acts 7: 56, and on the lips of James the Lord's brother in the account of his death related by Eusebius from Hegesippus (*H.E.* 2.23.13). Significantly, both of these are martyr stories, and the Danielic martyr figure (as I believe it to be) is appropriate. Otherwise, it is confined to sayings attributed to Jesus; and it is, again, significant that when Justin Martyr is citing words of Jesus from the traditions he retains the definite article, whereas when alluding to Dan. 7, or in his own comments, he drops it.[16] It looks as though (like many modern commentators) Justin had not observed the force of the article, and was content, when writing freely in his own name, to use the phrase in either form, once it had become Christological.

Thus there is a strong case (or so it seems to me) for the view that the phrase belonged originally among Jesus' own words as a reference to the vindicated human figure of Dan. 7 and as a symbol for the ultimate vindication of obedience to God's design. The Similitudes of Enoch are a much less likely source, being quite possibly later than the time even of the Evangelists[17] and representing an independent interpretation of Dan. 7.[18] 2 Esdras 13: 3ff., so far as it goes (and it never uses the actual expression) may well be another independent interpretation of Dan. 7, later than the New Testament. As for Ezekiel, the rather colourless vocative, 'O son of man!' (2: 1 and *passim*), seems to provide no substantial background for the use with the definite article and in the third person.

need only be an idiomatic equivalent for *hoti estin ho huios tou anthrōpou.* (See E. C. Colwell's celebrated study of this syntactical phenomenon, 'A Definite Rule for the Use of the Article in the Greek New Testament', *JBL* 52 (1933), 12ff.; and P. B. Harner, 'Qualitative Anarthrous Predicate Nouns: Mark 15: 39 and John 1: 1', *JBL* 92.1 (March 1973), 75ff.) I think, however, that if John 5: 27 had been intended as a definite reference to '*the* (Danielic) Son of Man', in the manner I am postulating, the unambiguous order and the definite phrase would have been adopted.

[16] *Apol.* 1.51.9; *Trypho* 31.1; 32.1; 76.1; 100.3 (second occurrence), are all anarthrous; but *Trypho* 76.7; 100.3 (first occurrence) (= Mark 8: 31) are with the article. See F. H. Borsch, *The Christian and Gnostic Son of Man* (London: SCM 1970), 43ff.

[17] It is well known that, so far at least, the Similitudes have not been found, as the rest of Enoch has, at Qumran. Note also internal evidence for a later date according to J. C. Hindley, 'Towards a Date for the Similitudes of Enoch. An Historical Approach', *NTS* 14 (1967/8), 551ff.

[18] Cf. N. Perrin, *Rediscovering the Teaching of Jesus* (London: SCM 1967), 166.

But, it is objected, the human figure of Dan. 7 is brought *to* God, whereas, in the apocalyptic passages of the Gospels, the Son of Man comes *from* heaven. How, then, can the two be associated – let alone identified? It seems to me that the vindication of the son of man in the court of heaven (when he is brought *to God*) is identical in meaning with his manifestation in judgement *on* earth (or *to* the dwellers on earth), and that it is not difficult to make the link between the two. His coming to God for vindication *is* his being shown on earth in judgement. The glory of the human figure in heaven *is* his investiture as Judge of the earth. I would dare to call it prosaic and unimaginative to object that the one cannot be identical with the other. The '*coming*' of the Son of Man, precisely because it is his coming to God for *vindication*, *is* also his coming to earth in judgement and (as Dr J. A. T. Robinson has said) for '*visitation*'.[19]

The Johannine use of 'the Son of Man' is distinctive,[20] as compared with that of the Synoptists, and, in particular, it adds the dimension of preexistence (3: 13, 6: 62) which is lacking in the Synoptic tradition. Bousset, assuming that the phrase's origins are post-dominical, is driven to implausible explanations as to why the dimension of preexistence was, in that case, not attached to it from the first.[21] For my part, I am prepared to believe that the actual articulation of the idea of preexistence is post-dominical, and that, whereas it appears in an early stratum, indeed, of post-dominical thought (possibly even pre-Pauline, if, as most assume, Phil. 2: 5ff. is pre-Pauline), it did not get attached actually to sayings about the Son of Man before the level of such Johannine interpretation was reached. That the attribution of preexistence to Christ is, in the terms of my formula, a 'legitimate development' and not an evolutionary borrowing from outside the Christian data, I shall argue in another chapter. Meanwhile,

[19] *Jesus and His Coming* (London: SCM 1957); and see M. Black, 'The Maranatha invocation and Jude 14, 15 (1 Enoch 1: 9)', in B. Lindars and S. S. Smalley, edd., *Christ and Spirit in the New Testament* (Cambridge: University Press 1973), 189ff. (193f.). God himself is to come in judgement (Ps. 50: 3, Isa. 63: 19b (Eng. 64: 1)); the Kingdom of God is to come on earth; and the Son of Man, in coming to God, will come on earth.

[20] See E. Ruckstuhl, *Die johanneische Menschensohnforschung 1957–1969* = J. Pfammatter and F. Furger, edd., *Theologische Berichte* (Zürich 1972), 171ff.

[21] *Kyrios Christos*, Eng. trans. (as in n. 13 above), 48.

returning to the Son of Man traditions, what I am saying is certainly not that all the occurrences of the phrase even in the Synoptic Gospels are actual words of Jesus. Some, indeed, such as that in Matt. 16:13, are almost demonstrably additions. But the evidence does, I believe, suggest that it was Jesus himself who originated the usage; and that, interpreted in the way I am proposing, all the familiar main categories of its use – relating to present circumstances, to suffering, and to future glorification – are intelligible in the setting of the ministry of Jesus himself, as a description of his vocation and authority. Evidence for 'the Son of Man's' becoming a popular title for Christ in the early Church seems to me virtually non-existent. He is never *addressed* or *invoked* as 'the Son of Man'; never does the phrase occur in this form in any of the Epistles; and only once, at most, is there any hint of 'the Son of Man's' being used as a confessional title. This is in John 9: 35, where Jesus puts to the man born blind the question, 'Do you believe on the Son of Man?' It is true that there is a variant reading 'the Son of God', which would bring it into line with more orthodox confessions, but this is probably a scribe's adjustment;[22] and the original reading then remains as a striking exception to the rule: but it is hardly sufficient basis for the theory that 'the Son of Man' was applied to Jesus by the early Church's usage.[23]

No doubt the position I have presented would stand more securely if, in each several strand of the Gospel traditions – Mark, Q, 'L' and 'M' – 'the Son of Man' carried all the associations of suffering, vindication, and judgement simultaneously, and if Dan. 7 were more specifically cited in the Son of Man sayings. But it seems to me that all the strands of tradition are at least patient of this interpretation, and I dare to believe that it solves the problem, too long ignored, of that tenacious definite article as no other suggestion does; and that, as earlier writers such as T. W. Manson and C. H. Dodd observed, it makes excellent

---

[22] For the probable genuineness of the reading 'the Son of Man', see B. M. Metzger, *A Textual Commentary on the Greek New Testament* (London/New York: United Bible Societies 1971), *in loc.*

[23] Even if it were the Palestinian community's phrase, it might still (it was pointed out to me in conversation at Melbourne on 11 August 1974) rank as a 'legitimate development', in my terms. Perhaps: but it seems to me that, as it happens, the evidence points to dominical origins.

sense as a characterization of the vocation of Christ.[24] Among contemporary writers, Dr G. B. Caird offers a masterly summary of a similar position in his short, popular commentary on St Luke's Gospel (The Pelican Gospel Commentaries, 1963), 94f.:

> It [the phrase] enabled [Jesus], without actually claiming to be Messiah, to indicate his essential unity with mankind, and above all with the weak and humble, and also his special function as predestined representative of the new Israel and bearer of God's judgement and kingdom. Even when he used it as a title, its strongly corporate overtones made it not merely a title, but an invitation to others to join him in the destiny he had accepted. And when he spoke of the glory of the Son of man he was predicting not so much his own personal victory as the triumph of the cause he served.

This appears to me far more probable than the theory that it was first applied to Jesus by the post-resurrection Church, for which (as I say) I can find virtually no evidence. And it seems to me, therefore, that the Son of Man traditions provide a good example of material that tells against 'evolution', in the sense in which I am using that term: indeed, it represents a factor so basic and so deeply embedded in the words of Jesus himself that it does not even represent an insight that was subsequently developed: it seems to have come through virtually unmodified from Jesus himself, and scarcely to have been used except in the historical exercise of recalling his words.[25]

Perhaps it is necessary to add a few words in defence of the corporate or collective interpretation of the phrase. This is specially associated with the names of T. W. Manson and C. H. Dodd, but generally receives short shrift in current criticism, although G. B. Caird, just quoted, and Morna Hooker are ex-

[24] E.g., T. W. Manson, *The Teaching of Jesus* as in n. 8, 227f.; C. H. Dodd, *According to the Scriptures* (London: Nisbet 1952), 96, etc.

[25] It is worth while to point here to signs that the tide of opinion may be turning: R. Leivestad's two articles, 'Der apokalyptische Menschensohn ein theologisches Phantom', *Ann. of the Swedish Theol. Institute* 6 (1968), 49ff., and 'Exit the Apocalyptic Son of Man', *NTS* 18 (1972), 243ff., though by no means accepting my position, are significant and are not, in my opinion, overthrown by B. Lindars as in n. 1 above; and E. Schweizer has never conformed to precisely the 'orthodox' position. See also L. Hartman, 'Scriptural Exegesis in the Gospel of St Matthew and the Problem of Communication', in M. Didier, ed., *L'Évangile selon Matthieu* (Bibl. Theol. Lovan. 29) (Gembloux 1972), 131ff. (142f.).

ceptions. The case for Jesus' having used 'the Son of Man' as a symbol for the martyr people of God, who are ultimately to be vindicated – the martyr people of Dan. 7 – with Jesus himself as their centre and growing-point, does not rest only on the occurrences in the Gospels of the actual phrase. One has to take into account also the passages where other features in that Danielic scene are recalled, even without the phrase. This applies to the saying attributed to Jesus in Luke 22: 28–30: 'You are the men who have stood firmly by me in my times of trial; and now I vest in you the Kingship which my Father vested in me; you shall eat and drink at my table in my kingdom and sit on thrones as judges of the twelve tribes of Israel.' Now, this may or may not be nearer to the original, dominical saying than the Matthean parallel (Matt. 19: 28) in which the Son of Man is mentioned:[26] '...in the world that is to be, when the Son of Man is seated on his throne in heavenly splendour, you my followers will have thrones of your own, where you will sit as judges of the twelve tribes of Israel'; but, with or without the explicit mention of the Son of Man, it is irresistibly reminiscent of Dan. 7: 9ff., where thrones were set and sovereignty and kingly power were given to the human figure who (elsewhere in the chapter) is clearly recognized as in some sense representing God's loyal people. There, in Dan. 7, the heavenly court seems to give judgement *in favour of* the Son of Man; but it is but a short step, in interpretative exegesis, to understanding also that the power to judge is given *to* the Son of Man, so that he – or, rather, 'the saints' collectively whom he represents – become themselves judges or assessors in God's court. The same is true of 1 Cor. 6: 2f., 'It is God's people' (*hoi hagioi*, 'the saints of the Most High') 'who are to judge the world...Are you not aware that we are to judge angels?' And consider the account of the millennium, the rule of the saints, in Rev. 20. In Rev. 20: 4, Dan. 7 is actually quoted: 'Then I saw thrones, and upon them sat those to whom judgement was committed' [n.b.!, so the NEB, rightly, for *kai krima edothē autois*]...These...reigned with Christ...' The same sort of ambivalence seems to have attached to Ps. 72: 1, where the LXX (71: 1) has: *to krima sou tō(i) basilei dos.* Thus, while I see no case

---

[26] I am not convinced by J. Jeremias, 'Die älteste Schichte der Menschensohn-logien', *ZNW* 58 (1967), 159ff.

for the early Church's having invented the application of 'the Son of Man' to Jesus, there is good reason for believing that from his own use of the term they learned the function and destiny of the martyr people of God.

In this presentation of one particular interpretation of the Son of Man traditions, I have made no attempt to offer even the sketchiest survey of the long and complicated debate as a whole; nor have I so much as touched upon the part played by Ps. 80 in the development of Christological thinking – a matter which has recently been taken up in an original way by Professor O. F. J. Seitz,[27] and to which we shall be led in the next section. My sole purpose has been to offer an interpretation of the evidence sufficient to explain why I conclude that 'the Son of Man', so far from being a title evolved from current apocalyptic thought by the early Church and put by it onto the lips of Jesus, is among the most important symbols used by Jesus himself to describe his vocation and that of those whom he summoned to be with him. The early Church, pondering on the traditions of his sayings, began to see the significance of these for their own role: there was development of insight. But I see no sign of the phrase's having 'evolved' away from Jesus' own usage.

2. THE SON OF GOD

We are pursuing the question, 'How did Christians come to describe Jesus as they did?' Was it that descriptions and estimates of him 'evolved', in the sense that, as Christian groups grew up in each successive area of their expansion through the ancient world and at each successive stage in the history of the Church, their convictions were changed and moulded by the religions and cultures there and then prevailing, until a conception of Jesus was reached which could hardly be called historically true to the original? Was the process a 'Euhemeristic' one, comparable to the apotheosis of a Heracles from hero to god? Or was it, rather, that the successive descriptions and evaluations of Jesus constituted only new insights into what was there from the beginning, and new modes of expression for an original datum?

[27] O. F. J. Seitz, 'The Future Coming of the Son of Man: Three Midrashic Formulations in the Gospel of Mark', *Stud Evang* 6 = *T und U* 112 (1973), 478ff.

Obviously, it is difficult – probably impossible – to give a rigorous definition of 'what was there from the beginning'. (As we have already begun to ask ourselves, was there, 'there from the beginning', something to justify the attribution of, for instance, pre-existence to Christ?) Obviously, too, it would be uncritical and insensitive to press the contrast absolutely, as though there were no overlap or blurring of the edges between the two. But it is my thesis that, at their two poles, the two theories are significantly opposed; and I do believe that it is worth while to challenge a widespread assumption that there was, in the Christian communities, a generating and creative force such that the final product could not be said to have been 'given' from the first, but rather 'created' by the communities.

By way of testing my contention that the evidence on the whole favours 'development' (if we may accept this contrast between 'development' and 'evolution' as at least a serviceable stylization), we are looking once more at familiar instances of Christological formulation in the New Testament; and I have argued that 'the Son of Man' does not even represent a developed insight on the part of the early Christians into what was there from the first, but is a phrase applied by Jesus himself to his vocation and the vocation of those who responded to him, and scarcely used by the early Christians except in their traditions of his own words.

But this leads us naturally to the term 'the Son of God'. It is a truism for New Testament scholars that it was only after the New Testament period that use began to be made of the two phrases 'the Son of Man' and 'the Son of God' to designate the human and divine natures respectively in a 'two-nature' Christology. According to the majority opinion, indeed, 'the Son of Man', so far from connoting the 'manhood' of Christ, stands for an exalted, apocalyptic figure. But even according to the interpretation I have adopted, it stands for more than merely manhood: it symbolizes the vindication, beyond death and in the court of heaven, of the loyalists who accept martyrdom rather than surrender their faithfulness to God's design. Yet, in a roundabout way, 'the Son of Man' does turn out to be getting somewhere near to connoting manhood; and, equally, it turns out to be next door to 'the Son of God'. It does, in its roundabout way, get near to the function of denoting the humanity of Jesus,

if I am right in insisting that, in his sayings, it stands for the
martyr-loyalty of frail man in the face of bestial, persecuting
tyrannies. But it also turns out – again, by a curious route – to
be approximating to the same meaning as 'the Son of God'.

In the Synoptic accounts of the trial of Jesus before the Jewish
court, the High Priest asks him whether he is the Christ; and the
reply of Jesus, whether in the affirmative or not,[28] includes the
statement (according to Mark and Matthew) that they will see the
Son of Man seated at the right hand of the Power (that is, God),
and coming with (or on) the clouds (Mark 14: 62, Matt. 26: 64;
Luke 22: 69 omits the reference to coming with clouds).

At least two scholars independently of one another have suggested that Ps. 80, at some stage or in some way, came to be
associated with this saying. In Dan. 7, the human figure is not
explicitly said to be seated at God's right hand. This phrase is
always traced to Ps. 110: 1. How, then, did it get joined to the
Son of Man? Ps. 80 (LXX 79): 16, 18 contains phrases which may,
it has been suggested, throw light on this conjunction of 'the Son
of Man' and God's right hand. The Psalmist is expostulating with
God about Israel's plight, and pleading with him to restore his
'vine' (that is, Israel) and (apparently) its King. The Hebrew runs
(the definite articles are not in the Hebrew, but are necessary in
English because of the words which qualify them): (verse 15b)
'...look from heaven and see and visit this vine', (verse 16) 'and
the stock which your right hand planted, and upon (*sic*) the son
(*ben*) (whom) you made strong for yourself...' (verse 18) 'Let
your hand be upon (the) man of your right hand (*'îš y^emîneḵā*),
upon (the) son of man (*ben-'āḏām*) you made strong for yourself.'
The Septuagint renders the plain 'son' of verse 16 by *huios
anthrōpou*, and, in verse 18, renders 'the man of your right hand'
by *anēr dexias sou*, and correctly renders *ben-'āḏām*, by, again,
huios anthrōpou.

C. H. Dodd, in *According to the Scriptures* (London: Nisbet
1952), 101f. points out that, although this passage is not directly
quoted in the New Testament, it

combines ideas which in the New Testament are so organically united
in the person of Christ that it is impossible to suppose the parallel

[28] For a recent discussion of this much-debated question, see D. R. Catchpole,
'The Answer of Jesus to Caiaphas (Matt. xxvi. 64)', *NTS* 17.2 (Jan. 1971), 213ff.

accidental. Indeed, Ps. lxxx. 17, which identifies 'God's right-hand Man' (the one who 'sits at God's right hand') with the divinely strengthened 'Son of Man', might well be regarded as providing direct scriptural justification for the fusion of the two figures in Mk. xiv. 62.

Professor O. F. J. Seitz, in a communication contributed to a New Testament congress at Oxford (*Studia Evangelica* 6, 1973 as in n. 27 above), independently (see p. 482, n. 4) reached the conclusion that Ps. 80 was the unseen 'catalyst' (p. 481) which brought together the Son of Man and the right hand of God, and he believes that the allusion to 'the clouds' of Dan. 7 was only an afterthought: 'That the primary reference to the "son of man" was undoubtedly Ps. 80, 17, rather than Dan. 7, 13, is plainly indicated by the position assigned to him at the right hand of God' (485).

Professor Seitz's article is brilliantly worked out; and I have little doubt that both he and Dodd are right in believing that Ps. 80 played a part in Christian reflexion on Christ. I am not yet, however, fully convinced that it was as decisive or as creative as Professor Seitz holds, and this, for two reasons. My first reason – with which I think Professor Seitz would concur – concerns the passages of Scripture most likely to spring to mind upon the utterance of the words in Mark 14: 62. If due weight is given (and I must pray indulgence for harping on this theme) to the definite article in 'the Son of Man' in the trial saying, we must assume that the phrase referred back to some figure familiar to the hearers–'the Son of Man whom we all know about'. If so, which 'son of man' is more likely to spring to their minds – that of Dan. 7 or that of Ps. 80? I would say that of Dan. 7, that of Ps. 80 being less clearly defined. And again, when sitting at the right hand of God is referred to, surely Ps. 110 is a much more obvious source than the curiously indirect 'man of your right hand' in Ps. 80, which despite Dodd's paraphrase, contains no reference to any session. My second reason is that I think it is possible to suggest a more obvious 'catalyst' than Ps. 80 for bringing 'the Son of Man' into relation with the session on the right hand of God. It is that the human figure of Dan. 7 is, in fact, instated in a position of royal splendour in that very scene, and, as it seems to me, is as clearly reckoned God's Son as any statement can tell us, short of explicitly saying so. I am not denying that Ps. 80 may well have exercised an influence in Christian reflexion about Christ, and, incidentally, I welcome Dodd's interpretation of the vine as an indication of the collective associations of the Son of Man (*According to the Scriptures*, 102 and cf. n. 24 above), as well as Seitz's very persuasive and subtle analysis of the component parts of an elaborate exercise in the Christian exegesis of *testimonia*. I am only suggesting that there is a more direct route from the idea of the Son of Man to the idea of the heavenly session and, indeed, to the idea of the Son of God. The fact that in Dan. 7 the figure representing God is that of an aged person (the 'ancient of days'), and that the human figure who is vindicated in his court is given dominion and Kingship, is enough to enable us, if we wish, to see, in the aged figure the Father who says (in the words of Ps. 2) to a messianic King, 'Thou art my son'; and to see, in the human figure, the royal Son, who is thus addressed. Does not the old age stand for Fatherhood? Does not the Kingship imply Sonship? In other words, if God is seen as an aged figure and the Son of Man standing before him as a royal figure, then is not that royal figure God's Son? The messianic King is addressed by God as 'Son' in Ps. 2, and caused to sit, vindicated, at God's right hand in Ps. 110. Thus, the messianic King, God's Son, coincides in a remarkable way with the frail human figure, 'the Son of Man', whose vulnerable, martyr-loyalty has brought him through death to this position of glory and dominion before the aged 'President of the immortals'.

No doubt this association of the Son of Man of Dan. 7 with the Son of God of Ps. 2 and the royal conqueror of Ps. 110 looks like the artificial exegesis of an uncritical age; and if Ps. 80 is added to the amalgam, whether as a creative medium or merely as a further link in the sequence of thought, the process becomes all the more elaborate and, one might say, artificial. And it might be deduced that the royal conqueror seated on the right hand of God is therefore a reflexion of precisely the sort of evolutionary sequence that I am out to deny. (For good measure, we might add Professor Matthew Black's observation that there is, at some point at least, a latent pun discernible between *ben*, the Son, and *'eben* the 'stone' which the builders rejected but which was vindicated by circumstances, and, for that matter, all the other 'stones' of Christian testimonia.)[29]

But while the use of none of these exegetical devices need be denied – and undoubtedly there were those in the early Church who were much given to this occupation – there were, I believe, far profounder and more organic forces at work initially. One of the messages which emerge most clearly from Mark's Gospel is that the suffering Son of Man it is who is to be gloriously vindicated, that the meaning of greatness is service, that to be God's Son means to be dedicated unconditionally to God's purposes, even to death. It is therefore organic to the ministry of Jesus that the Son of God shows himself as the frail and vulnerable Son of Man. The two are identical in reality, long before ingenious exegetical connexions are spun round them. And it seems to me, therefore, that the saying at the trial could easily be essentially dominical. Jesus says, 'Yes, I am (if you like) Messiah'; but he then goes on to characterize the meaning of messiahship in terms of the vindication in the court of heaven, as Son of God – may we not say? – and King and Right-hand Man, of the frail and vulnerable martyr-figure, that Danielic Son of Man, who is now a prisoner before the Sanhedrin. Conversely – if you like – the one who dares to address God as his Father, with that most intimate word 'Abba!' (Mark 14: 36), turns out to be the one who cannot and will not escape the bitter cup of suffering.[30]

The term, 'the Son of God', only wins this profound meaning through the circumstances in which it emerges, and through its subtle linking with 'the Son of Man'. In itself, of course, 'the Son of God' does not necessarily carry any such profound associations. Although the earliest, Semitic-speaking communities were not unfamiliar with its use for at least angelic or supernatural persons (see Dan. 3: 25 and Job 38: 7 and Ps. 82: 6), it need be no more than a purely messianic term.[31] Whether or not 'the Son

---

[29] 'The Christological Use of the Old Testament in the New Testament', *NTS* 18.1 (Oct. 1971), 1ff. (12).

[30] I have learnt much in this connexion from a stimulating Ph.D. dissertation (Cambridge University 1975: unpublished) by E. E. Lemcio, 'Some new proposals for interpreting the Gospel of Mark'.

[31] In the Old Testament, 'son' is occasionally used as a term of submission or dutiful feeling towards a superior: Ben-hadad to Elisha, 2 Kings 8: 9; Ahaz

of God' would have been recognized at the time of Jesus as an actual synonym for the Messiah – a much debated question – it is certainly demonstrable that to be God's son was at any rate recognized as one of the Messiah's characteristics. This is sufficiently evidenced by Nathan's prophecy in 2 Sam. 7, which is quoted in the collection of testimonies from Qumran (1Q flor. 10f.). 'Son of God' is said to have come to light once or twice elsewhere in the Qumran material (4Q 243 and possibly 1QSa 2.11f.).[32] And there is Ps. 2, which was certainly interpreted messianically; and Ps. 80, which we have already considered; and Ps. 89: 26f. ('he will say to me, "Thou art my Father...",...and I will name him my firstborn'). In itself, therefore, the claim that Jesus was 'the Son of God' is not necessarily a claim to transcendental status. In Mark 14: 61 the High Priest's words, 'Are you the Christ, the son of the Blessed One?', are presumably understood by the Evangelist as a question about a Messianic claim, whatever may be intended by Jesus' reply.

But the associations of the phrase in the Gospel traditions put a different colour on it. Not only are there subtle links between 'the Son of God' and 'the Son of Man', in the manner I have described, and not only was it already possible for 'a Son of God' to mean an angelic figure, but – much more important – there is a whole network of indications that the traditions about Jesus had led to a radical reinterpretation of what it meant to be a son of God.[33]

to Tiglath-pileser, 2 Kings 16: 7 ('your servant and your son'). But this is scarcely relevant to this inquiry.

[32] 4Q243 is to be published (I understand) by J. T. Milik but has not been seen by me. 1QSa 2.11f. refers to the begetting of the Messiah, and it is probably 'God' that should be supplied in the lacuna as the begetter: *'im yôlîd* [*'êl*] *'ê* [*t*] *hammāšîaḥ.*

[33] See a careful and judicious assessment of the evidence by J. D. G. Dunn, *Jesus and the Spirit* (London: SCM 1975), 21ff. Subjoined is an analysis of significant passages:

(i) Jesus directly addresses God as Father (see J. Jeremias, *New Testament Theology* as in n. 11, 62):
Mark: 14: 36 *Q*: Matt. 6:9, Luke 11: 2; Matt. 11: 25f., Luke 10: 21.
L: Luke 23: 34, 46. *M*: Matt. 26: 42.

(ii) Other passages concerned with Jesus' thinking of God as Father:
Mark: 1: 11 (Matt. 3: 17, Luke 3: 22); 9: 7 (Matt. 17: 5, Luke 9: 35); 12: 6 (Matt. 21: 37, Luke 20: 13); 13: 32 (Matt. 24: 36); 14: 61f. (Matt. 26: 63f., Luke 22: 70). *Q*: Matt. 4: 3ff., Luke 4: 3ff.
L: Luke 2: 49.

(iii) Others think of Jesus as Son:

What I mean is best explained by considering what a startling transformation the religious meaning of water undergoes in the New Testament. Water must have been almost universally used as a religious symbol in the ancient world, as it is still: proselyte baptism, John the Baptist's baptism, other Jewish sectarian lustrations (Qumran and the rest), the lustral rites of pagan religions – one could multiply them indefinitely. But, to the best of my knowledge, there is nothing comparable to what the Pauline doctrine of baptism makes of water. It makes it far more than a cleansing symbol. It makes baptism a sacrament of death and of new life, and that, in the power of God's Spirit, which constitutes the baptizand a son of God: baptism – death – life – the Spirit – sonship: a nexus between these ideas becomes visible. Thus, Rom. 6: 3ff. links baptism with death and new life; Rom. 8: 10f. speaks of death accepted and new life entered upon through the indwelling Spirit, which (Rom. 8: 15, Gal. 4: 6) is the Spirit enabling us to become sons of God and to echo Christ's own address to him, 'Abba!' It is true that the theme of the Spirit does not actually occur in the Rom. 6 passage, nor that of baptism in Rom. 8 or Gal. 4; but death and new life, associated with baptism in Rom. 6, are associated with the Spirit bringing sonship in Rom. 8 and Gal. 4, and there seems little doubt that, for Paul at least, water baptism carries all these implications – death, life, the Spirit, sonship. The same is implicit also in 1 Peter, where the water of baptism is not only cleansing but drowning, and where the theme of invoking God as Father is clear enough (1 Pet. 1: 3, 14, 17; 3: 21–4: 2).

If one turns, now, to the Gospel traditions, the Sonship of Jesus is associated with baptism and with the coming of the Spirit in all three Synoptists; in the Q traditions, there is, immediately following the baptism, the stringent *testing* of God's Son; in Mark there is the theme of the suffering Son of Man and of the son

Mark 3: 11 (Luke 4: 41); 5: 7 (Matt. 8: 29, Luke 8: 28); 15: 39 (Matt. 27: 54).

(iv) Evidence of related themes:
The baptism of Jesus is connected with the divine address as 'Son', with the endowment by the Spirit, and with the temptation (which, in Q, is a test of Sonship). Luke 12: 50 and Mark 10: 38f. associate the metaphor of 'baptism' with death; and Mark 10: 38f. associates death also with the 'cup'; and Mark 14: 36 associates 'Abba!' with the 'cup' and with death.
Compare, then, Rom. 6: 3–14, 8: 12–17, Gal. 4: 6f., 1 Pet. 3: 18–4: 1.

crying 'Abba!' while wrestling with the temptation to escape the cup of suffering (Mark 14: 36); and, in both Mark and Luke, baptism is used as a symbol of suffering (Mark 10: 38, Luke 12: 50). Finally, through death, Jesus is vindicated, and according to the narratives of Luke and John (anticipated by the Baptist's saying in the Synoptic and Johannine traditions, Mark 1: 8 and parallels Matt. 3: 11 and Luke 3: 16; John 1: 33), there follows the bestowal of the Spirit by Jesus upon others (Luke 24: 49, Acts 2: 33, John 20: 22; cf. 7: 39).

Now, it seems to me difficult to explain whence so profound an interpretation of baptism in terms of an obedient and suffering filial vocation could have sprung, unless from the life and teaching of Jesus himself, in view of the fact that it enters so deeply and subtly into the Gospel traditions, in words which do not appear to be borrowed from the Pauline circle and which yet coincide so remarkably in meaning and intention with Pauline teachings. It seems to me to constitute a signal example of a high Christology being unobtrusively – one might almost say secretly – embedded in the traditions about Jesus. There is no case to be made, it seems to me, for these Gospel themes having been imposed on the narrative from the Pauline theology.

In a similar way, B. M. F. van Iersel has made a case for the sonship *logia* of the Gospels being prior to the preaching in Acts about Jesus as Son of God, deducing that the affirmations in the sermons are based on traditions of Jesus' own consciousness reflected in genuine sayings.[34] Again, J. D. G. Dunn, in a careful investigation of the meaning of Sonship in the consciousness of Jesus, concludes: 'In short, Spirit and sonship, sonship and Spirit, are but two aspects of the one experience of God out of which Jesus lived and ministered.'[35]

The upshot of all this is, I suggest, simply, that it is probably unrealistic to put notions of sonship into successive compartments, as though we could segregate a more or less humanistic, merely messianic use from a transcendental and theological use developing at a later stage. The indications are, rather, that the words and practices of Jesus himself, together with the fact of

[34] '*Der Sohn*' in den synoptischen Jesusworten: Christusbezeichnung der Gemeinde oder Selbstbezeichnung Jesu?, Supplements to *Novum Testamentum* III (Leiden: Brill 1961).
[35] As in n. 33 above, 67.

the cross and of its sequel, presented the friends of Jesus, from the earliest days, with a highly complex, multivalent set of associations already adhering to the single word 'Son'. No doubt there is development in perception. No doubt the famous phrase in Rom. 1: 4, 'declared Son of God by a mighty act in that he rose from the dead', reflects (whatever we make of the words *kata pneuma hagiōsunēs*, omitted from this quotation) the conviction that it was the aliveness of Jesus that had clinched a new understanding of his status. No doubt it was the earliest theologians of the New Testament who first sharpened the terminology. For instance, Paul, though using *huios* alike for Jesus and for believers, points to the uniqueness of Christ's sonship by using 'adoption' (*huiothesia*) for the status of Christians, and 'God's own Son' (*ho idios huios*) for Christ (Rom. 8: 31, etc.); while the Johannine Gospel and Epistles reserve *huios* for Christ, and use words such as *teknon* for Christians. But, although a distinctiveness of status and being begins to become explicit in these various ways, the materials for it seem to be rooted in the traditions about Jesus himself.

3. CHRIST

There is an old-fashioned view that the use of this title by Christians for Jesus goes back to the ministry and the attitude of Jesus himself. It would, of course, help to support a theory of 'development' as against 'evolution' if this turned out to be true; the reader, therefore, must judge whether the following argument is based on a sound interpretation of the evidence or on bias.

The Hebrew word 'messiah' (*māšîaḥ*) means, strictly speaking, 'an anointed person or thing'. It is a verbal adjective used as a noun, and, as such, is to be distinguished from the true passive participle *māšuaḥ*;[36] and, whereas the Septuagint correctly translates the latter by *ēleimmenos*, the perfect passive participle of the ordinary Greek word for 'to anoint' (*aleiphein*), it uses *christos* for the noun-adjective, *māšîaḥ*. The Septuagint seems,

---

[36] It is true that 2 Sam. 1: 21, referring to Saul's shield as 'anointed with oil', uses the word *māšîaḥ* as though it were the participle, *māšûaḥ*; but (if it is the correct reading) this is an exception. LXX has (*ouk*) *echristhē*.

thus, to have introduced a new technical term. More often than not, *chriein*, in secular Greek, is a simple active verb and means to 'rub or pour on' (with ointment or oil as the object), rather than to 'cover with oil', 'anoint' (with a person as object); and when biblical Greek uses *christos*, not for the ointment ('for external application') but for an anointed person or thing, this is a new usage.[37] It is a technical word for (generally) a person who has been ritually appointed by being anointed with a sacred unguent. Our own Queen is one such; and mostly, such a person is, in biblical contexts, a divinely appointed King of Israel. It is true that prophets and priests are also spoken of in Hebrew-Jewish literature as anointed.[38] But 'an anointed one', or 'the anointed one', without further designation, would almost certainly mean nothing except the divinely appointed King.[39]

How, then, did Jesus come to be known by this title? There is little doubt that there were times during Jesus' brief ministry when hope ran high that he would be the Leader who would rally his people to throw off Roman domination. A strong case can be made for his having been offered the title 'Messiah' (e.g. by Peter at Caesarea Philippi) or 'Son of David' (e.g. by Bartimaeus at Jericho). But an equally strong case can be made for Jesus' having refused to be drawn into the circle of those, such as the Zealots, who wished to use violence in support of messianic claims. Despite all efforts to prove that he was a Zealot or a

[37] The light-hearted little quip, quoted anonymously by D. E. Nineham, that '*christos* might well have been taken to mean "the person who has just had a bath"' ('A Partner for Cinderella?', in M. Hooker and C. Hickling, edd., *What about the New Testament? Essays in Honour of Christopher Evans* (London: SCM 1975), 154, n. 19), is not quite as erudite as it might be. Apart from the fact that a commoner word for this kind of anointing was *aleiphein*, there is also the fact that, in secular Greek, *christos* is applied to the ointment, never, it seems, to the one anointed: it means 'for external application' or 'externally applied', as against something that is drunk and used internally: Euripides *Hipp*, 516: *potera de christon ē poton to pharmakon*; 'Is the medicine for external or internal application?' (see *TWNT* art. *chriō*, ix. 485).

[38] Prophets: Ps. 105: 15, 1 Kings 19: 16, 1QM 11.7f., CD 2.12, 6.1 (? if *mšyhw* be emended to *mšyhy* (i.e. -*hô* to -*hê*)), 11 Q Melch 18 (*NTS* 12.4 (July 1966), 302 (= the first known instance of the word in the *singular* being applied to a prophet)); cf. Isa. 61: 1.
Priests: Exod. 40: 13, Zech. 4: 14 (lit. 'sons of oil'), Dan. 9: 25f. (if = Onias III), 1QS 9.11, etc. See F. Hahn, *The Titles of Jesus in Christology* (as in Introduction, n. 12), 36off.

[39] See G. Vermés, *Jesus the Jew* (London: Collins 1973), 132, etc.

pro-Zealot, the evidence (it seems to me) simply breaks down.[40] But, if he refused to align himself with those who wanted to fight the Romans in a messianic cause, must he not also have refused to have anything to do with a royal messiahship? This does not necessarily follow. It is frequently said, indeed, that, at Caesarea Philippi, Jesus refused the title Christ. But Mark certainly does not say so. What he does say is that on being hailed as Christ by Peter, Jesus strictly forbade his disciples to tell anybody about him (Mark 8: 30) – which suggests that he accepted the title but instructed his friends not to divulge it – at any rate for the time being. At the climax of his ministry, however, the so-called triumphal entry (Mark 11) looks uncommonly like a deliberate messianic gesture or demonstration – but there, one so staged as to say, 'If I *am* Messiah, I am not going to fight the Romans. I am going to fight abuse at the heart of Judaism.' And finally, when it is perfectly clear that no violent action is possible, because Jesus is already a prisoner, he is represented, apparently, as acknowledging messiahship before the Sanhedrin (Mark 14: 62).

Now, the crucifixion must once and for all have extinguished absolutely any literal hopes that Jesus might become the King of Israel. It put an end to any idea of his messiahship in that sense. Why, then, did his followers ultimately use the title, *māšiaḥ* or *christos* for him – so much so that it eventually became all but a proper name, like 'Jesus'?

The origin can hardly have been the title on the cross. This, in any case, seems to have been framed in secular terms, with 'King' rather than 'anointed one' (*basileus, meleḵ, rex*, not *christos, māšiaḥ, christus*).[41] Besides, even if 'Christ' had been written over the cross, Christians of the New Testament period would be unlikely to perpetuate, in a title, the idea that Jesus was crucified ostensibly as a revolutionary. They could admit this when telling the story, as they did in the Gospels; but that they should gather it up in one, unglossed term, and use that as the regular name for their Lord, could hardly be so explained. But neither are they likely to have given Jesus the title Christ by way of signifying his

[40] For a brief summary, see M. Hengel, *War Jesus Revolutionär?* (Stuttgart: Calwer 1970), Eng. trans. with introd. by J. Reumann, *Was Jesus a Revolutionist?* (Philadelphia: Fortress 1972).

[41] Cf. F. Bovon, *Les derniers jours de Jésus* (Neuchâtel etc.: Delachaux et Niestlé 1974), 37, invoking also Mara bar Sarapion.

spiritual anointing, his endowment with the Spirit, for, as I have said, *Christos*, by itself and without further qualification, would inevitably have been taken as the designation of a King rather than of a prophet or other inspired person: a 'charismatic' leader, whose 'chrism' had been 'charism', would hardly be called 'Christ' without qualification.[42] The tenacity of the usage is most plausibly explained, therefore, if Jesus himself had accepted the royal title, but, during his ministry, had so radically reinterpreted it that it became natural to his followers to use it in this new way. If he had interpreted messiahship, as we have seen him interpreting sonship, in terms of suffering and service and, only by that route and in that sense, of vindication and royal status, then it seems conceivable that the title might have been revived and perpetuated after he had been crucified. 'The early Church', Cullmann has well said, 'believed in Christ's messiahship only because it believed that Jesus believed himself to be Messiah.'[43]

Perhaps it should be mentioned that a striking comment on the problem has recently been offered by the well-known Jewish scholar Professor David Flusser.[44] He alludes to the Jewish idea that no man can claim to be Messiah until he has achieved his messianic task. In the light of this, he suggests that three phenomena in antiquity might be explained by some such authentic messianic diffidence: the alleged 'messianic secret' in the Gospels, the attitude of the Qumran Teacher, and the attitude of ben Kosebah or bar Cochba in the Murabba'at documents. In all three, he sees a high consciousness of authority that, nevertheless, stopped short of an actual claim to messiahship. But it is questionable whether the so-called 'messianic secret' of the Gospels is rightly to be interpreted along these lines;[45] and it

---

[42] *Pace* W. C. van Unnik, 'Jesus the Christ', *NTS* 8.2 (Jan. 1962), 101ff.

[43] *Christology* (as in Introduction, n. 13), 8.

[44] 'Two notes on the Midrash on 2 Sam. vii', *Israel Exploration Journal* ix (2, 1959), 99ff. (107ff.). See R. N. Longenecker, 'The Messianic Secret in the Light of Recent Discoveries', *EvQ* 41 (1969), 207ff., appealing to 1QH (if by the Teacher) over against passages which exalt the Teacher; and *idem*, *The Christology of Early Jewish Christianity* (London: SCM 1970), 107–9; and J. C. O'Neill, 'The Silence of Jesus', *NTS* 15.2 (Jan. 1969), 165ff.

[45] See my essay 'On Defining the Messianic Secret in Mark', in E. E. Ellis and E. Grässer, edd., *Jesus und Paulus: Festschrift für Werner Georg Kümmel zum 70. Geburtstag* (Göttingen: Vandenhoeck und Ruprecht 1975), 239ff., and literature there cited.

seems to be closer to the evidence to say, not that Jesus refused or even postponed the claim to be Messiah, but, rather, that, when offered the title, he reinterpreted it, and, if he ultimately claimed it, did so only in a reinterpreted form. This is an absurdly old-fashioned conclusion, but the question is whether it does not still fit the evidence. It would explain, as nothing else seems to, the ready use of the title by the Christian community, and would represent a signal triumph of 'spirituality', based on the deeds and words and attitude of Jesus himself.[46]

4. *KURIOS*[47]

Let the fourth and last 'test case' for the genesis of Christology be the prominent title 'kyrios' (*kurios*), 'Lord'. First, the vocative, *kurie*, must be cleared out of the way. Many writers on these matters make the mistake of counting instances of the vocative when they are preparing statistics for the application of *kurios* as a title to Jesus. But *kurie* is so common as a respectful address in human intercourse that it would be as truthful, statistically, to reckon a schoolboy's 'O Sir' as evidence that the schoolmaster had been knighted.[48] It is the use of the word in cases other

---

[46] Hahn, however, makes the messiahship of Jesus essentially eschatological (as in Introduction, n. 12 above, Eng. trans. 168, 171, 172; though see 188, 348).

[47] In much of what follows, I am glad to find myself in agreement with what E. Schweizer wrote in 'Jesus, the Lord of his Church', *Aust. Bib. Review* 19 (Oct. 1971), 52ff., though I part company with him over the use of *mārê*'. There is useful material on *kurios* and *despotēs* in B. A. Mastin, 'The Imperial Cult and the Ascription of the Title *Theos* to Jesus (John xx. 28)', *Stud Evang* (= *T und U* 112, 1973), 352ff.

    To my regret, J. A. Fitzmyer's important 'Der semitische Hintergrund des neutestamentlichen Kyriostitels', in G. Strecker, ed., *Jesus Christus in Historie und Theologie, für H. Conzelmann* (Tübingen: J. C. B. Mohr 1975), 267ff., reached me too late for use in this chapter.

[48] W. Heitmüller, long ago, recognized this for Marcan usage: '*kurie* in der Anrede hat bei ihn [i.e. Mark] nur den Wert der Höflichkeitswerdung', 'Zum Problem Paulus und Jesus', *ZNW* 13 (1912), 320ff. (334). So R. Bultmann, *Theologie des Neuen Testaments* (Tübingen: J. C. B. Mohr [3]1958), Eng. trans. *Theology of the New Testament* (London: SCM 1952), 51: 'The vocative "Lord" ...proves nothing.' Even so careful a review as J. D. Kingsbury, 'The Title "Kyrios" in Matthew's Gospel', *JBL* 94.2 (June 1975), 246ff, makes, to my mind, too little allowance for the neutrality of the vocative. Despite his observation that 'Matthew employs *kyrios* overwhelmingly in the vocative case' (248), he proceeds to reckon these instances in when estimating the Christological significance of the title for Matthew. Admittedly, the context sometimes enhances the meaning of the vocative (e.g. Matt. 7: 21). But it still remains precarious to reckon it in statistical counts.

than the vocative that needs to be investigated for the present purpose.

This said, we may next inquire about the origins of *kurios* as a Christological title. Since Wilhelm Bousset's magisterial *Kyrios Christos*,[49] it has been customary to make a clear distinction between *invocation* and *acclamation*. Thus, it is alleged that, whereas the early, Palestinian, Semitic-speaking communities, using the formula *marana tha, invoked* Jesus as the Master,[50] temporarily removed but destined to return as an eschatological Judge, it was not until pagan Saviour-cults had introduced a new dimension into Christian thinking that Jesus began to be *acclaimed* as Lord. Invocation as 'Master' ('Come, Master!') is thus sharply contrasted with acclamation as 'Lord' ('Jesus is Lord'), and the latter is seen as, so to speak, the evolution of a new species.

Against this view it may be urged that it is largely guess-work, and that there are facts which seem to point in a different direction. First, the semantic range of the Aramaic word *mārê'* (*mārâ'*, or such forms as *mārēh* or *mar*) is not so much narrower as used to be imagined than that of the Greek word *kurios*. I myself used to stress the difference, reminding my classes that, even if *kurios* was the natural Greek translation for *mārê'*, it did not follow that the two words were synonymous. And no doubt it is still true that they are not synonymous. But it is important to note that *mārê'* is by no means confined to address to humans, nor is it (so far as I can see) correct to call it 'decisively different' from *kurios*.[51] Long ago, it was noted by Baudissin and others that the Semitic root was used in pagan inscriptions with reference to a divine being.[52] Already, too, there were two instances in the Aramaic of Daniel (2: 47, 5: 23), which, though admittedly not

[49] As in n. 13 above.
[50] S. J. Samartha, *The Hindu Response to the Unbound Christ* (Madras: Christian Literature Society, 1974), 123, refers to Subba Rao as one to whom 'Jesus Christ is not so much a god to be worshipped as a *guru* to be followed.'
[51] H. Boers is making an incorrect statement when he says: 'What Bousset did not know, but has become clear in the meantime due [*sic*] to the availability of new materials, is that the Aramaic *mara* had a meaning which was decisively different from the Hellenistic Greek designation *kurios*', *Interp* 26.3 (July 1972), 315 (following Schulz).
[52] Wolf Wilhelm Graf Baudissin, ed. O. Eissfeldt, *Kyrios als Gottesname in Judentun und seine Stelle in der Religionsgeschichte* (Giessen: Töpelmann 1929), iii, 57ff. Further bibliography in *TWNT* article *maranatha*, iv, 471, n. 19.

an absolute use as a title, were significant.[53] But now the Qumran scrolls have added several instances at least of the descriptive use, especially in the Genesis Apocryphon.[54]

To this must be added, following M. Black, the evidence of the Aramaic Enoch, where 'the title *Mare* and *Maran*...used *simpliciter* for the Lord of the Old Testament now appears...at chapter 9, verse 6, and later 89.31, 33, 36, where the Greek, has *ho kurios*'.[55]

Therefore, it is established that the Palestinian communities of the very earliest days already had a word *mārê'*, which was capable of being used in a sense uncommonly near to that of *kurios* as a divine designation; and, even if Bultmann were right in saying that, in Jewish usage, it is unthinkable that 'the Lord', absolutely, should have been applied to Jesus,[56] it would still be significant if 'our Lord' (and comparable phrases) had already been applied in Semitic-speaking regions to a more than human being. No doubt 'Lord' with a qualification – 'my Lord', 'our Lord', 'Lord of heaven and earth', etc. – is not the same as 'the Lord' absolutely. But at least it is true that one did not need to wait for the Church to move out into the Greek world, for the bridge to be built between a 'Master' to be invoked and a 'Lord' to be worshipped and acclaimed: the necessary linguistic bridge

[53] W. Kramer, *Christos, Kyrios, Gottessohn* (Zürich: Zwingli 1963), Eng. trans. *Christ, Lord, Son of God* (London: SCM 1966), 101, n. 350, quite rightly observes (as does Bultmann, as in n. 48, *ibid.*) that 'Lord of Kings' or 'Lord of heaven' is different from 'Lord' absolutely. But that *mārê'* is applied to God is still not without significance.

[54] J. A. Fitzmyer, *The Genesis Apocryphon of Qumran Cave 1, a Commentary* (Rome: Biblical Institute Press, ²1971): 1QGen. apoc. 20.12–15 (Abraham prays: '...O God Most High, my Lord (*mry*)...For you are Lord (*mrh*) and Master over all ...my Lord (*mry*)...you are the Lord (*mrh*) of all the Kings...), 22.16 (Melchizedek said: 'Blessed be Abram by the Most High God, the Lord (*mrh*) of heaven and earth'), 21 (Abraham speaks: 'Lord (*mrh*) of heaven...'). See also Fragm. 2 (Fitzmyer p. 50), and 2.4, 7.7, 12.17; and, for *mrh* addressed to men, 2.9, 13, 24, 22.18. Also J. P. K. van der Ploeg, O.P., et A. S. van der Woude, *Le Targum de Job de la Grotte 6, XI de Qumran* (Leiden: Brill 1971): 11Q tg Job 24. 6, 7 (= MT 34: 12): *wmr'*, tr. 'le Seigneur...'. In Melchizedek's words in 1QGen. apoc. 22.16, the corresponding Hebrew in Gen. 14: 19 uses *kōnēn*, 'Maker'; the phrase in the apocryphon is exactly equivalent to 'Lord of heaven and earth' in Matt. 11: 25, Luke 10: 21. It is admittedly in the vocative, but it gains significance from the 'of heaven and earth'. (Cf. 'Lord of heaven' in Dan. 5: 23.)

[55] 'The Maranatha invocation and Jude 14, 15 (1 Enoch 1: 9)', as in n. 19 above.

[56] *Theologie des Neuen Testaments* as in n. 48, 54.

was already there. It so happens that, in the phrase *marana tha*, the *marana* is vocative, and, as such, constitutes, perhaps, as little evidence as its Greek vocative counterpart for a divine designation. My point is merely that an Aramaic word capable of designating divinity is shown to be current at the time. Incidentally, F. Hahn points out that the designation of Christ's brothers as 'the brothers of the Lord' (*tou kuriou*, 1 Cor. 9: 5, Gal. 1: 19), and later as *desposunoi*, seems to point to an application of the term 'the Lord' to the Jesus of the earthly ministry.[57] If so, here is another pointer in the same direction.

A second reason against driving a wedge between an allegedly early invocation as 'Master' and a later acclamation as 'Lord' is that, from the earliest days, there was another Semitic word-bridge, namely, the Hebrew word *âdōn*. This word, which appears strictly to mean 'Lord and Master', in the sense of 'owner' or 'overlord' (one of the conspicuous connotations also of *kurios*), was undeniably applied in a special way to God. As well as its occasional application to God almost as a metaphor for 'overlord' (e.g. Isa. 1: 24, 10: 16, 33), it was also used in a special form (if we may judge from the Massoretic Text), whenever the Hebrew Scriptures were read aloud, as a substitute for the sacred tetragrammaton. That statement is an over-simplification, for the special form needs further definition.[58] The mere plural used as an honorific is not absolutely distinctive: it is not uncommonly used in respectful reference to a human overlord (e.g. Neh. 3: 5, where versions vary as to whether 'their lords' is divine or human. The NEB renders it as 'their governor', meaning Nehemiah himself). The same mere plural is frequently, however, used also for God and it was used (as indicated by the vowel signs attached to the sacred tetragrammaton in the Massoretic Text) as a substitute, when reading aloud, for the sacred name. With the second or third person suffix ('your lords' or 'their lords') there is nothing to distinguish this from the honorific plural used for an exalted human person. But when it appears with the first person singular suffix in the form 'my lords', then the Massoretic pointing always indicates the sacred Name by using the pausal

---

[57] *The Titles of Jesus in Christology*, as in Introduction n. 12, 86.
[58] M. Delcor, 'Les diverses manières d'écrire le tetragramme sacré dans les anciens documents hébraiques', *RHR* 147 (1955), 145ff.

form with a *long* 'a ' (*qāmeṣ*) instead of the normal *short* 'a' (*pathaḥ*). Thus 'my lords', when a human lord is meant will be *'adōnăy*, but when the word represents the sacred Name it will be *'adōnāy*.[59]

On any showing, however (and this is my point), the way between *adon* used for God and *adon* used for man is quite easily traversed in either direction; and the best known example is, of course, Ps. 110: 1. In the Hebrew, this reads: *n^e'ûm YHWH l'aḏōnî*, 'an oracle of Yahweh to my lord'; but if, in the synagogue, in order to avoid uttering the Name, it was read as: *n^e'ûm 'aḏōnāy* ('my lords', plural, and with special pointing) *l'aḏōnî* ('my lord', singular), then two uses of *adon*, divine and human, come very close to each other; and when the Septuagint translates both 'Yahweh' and *'aḏonî* by *kurios*, distinguishing the divine Lord only as *ho kurios* ('the Lord', absolutely) from the human over-lord, *ho kurios mou* ('my lord') – *eipen ho kurios tō(i) kuriō(i) mou* – a linguistic bridge is built between the two ideas. Incidentally, one is reminded of the same bridge between divine and human by 1 Pet. 3: 6 (Sarah calling Abraham *kurios*, a reference to Gen. 18: 12, where it is *'adōnî*) as compared with verse 15 of the same chapter, where the readers are bidden 'sanctify Christ as *Kurios*' (or, NEB, 'hold the Lord Christ in reverence').

Thus, Jewish communities that, at the time of the rise of Christianity, still read (or heard) the Scriptures in Hebrew were conversant with a versatile word, *'âḏon*, which could be applied both to man and God. The same communities, when they spoke Aramaic (or heard a Targum in Aramaic) would know a similar word, *mārê'*. And Greek-speaking communities would be using *kurios* to translate both uses of both words, and would be particularly familiar with the use of *kurios* in the Scriptures, to represent the sacred Name of God, the tetragrammaton. It has, it is true, been pointed out[60] that nearly all surviving copies of the Scriptures in Greek are from Christian communities, and that, in the

[59] Details in *Gesenius' Hebrew Grammar as edited and enlarged by E. Kautzsch* (Eng. trans., Oxford: Clarendon Press 1898), 124 *i* (p. 419), 135 *q* (p. 463). See further *TWNT* iii, 1058f., and Baudissin (n. 52 above).

[60] S. Schulz, 'Maranatha und Kyrios Jesus', *ZNW* 53 (1962), 125ff. The same article usefully (132) gives the evidence for the earliest dateable occurrences of the substitute of another word for the tetragrammaton (Origen on Ps. 2: 2, Philo *de vita Mosis* IV. 114, Josephus *Ant.* II. 12.4, with Baudissin's summing up, ii. 235, and with the further evidence from Qumran).

few fragments of non-Christian Greek documents in which the divine tetragrammaton is represented, it is rendered not by *Kurios* but by a quasi-transliteration (ΠΙΠΙ) or by other means.[61] But it is hasty to conclude that only Christians read *kurios* for the divine Name in their Greek Scriptures, and that therefore pre-Christian Judaism would not have been familiar with that end of the 'word-bridge'. In the first place, what, if not this word *kurios*, would readers have been taught to utter when they came to some representation of the divine name (e.g. ΠΙΠΙ) in the Greek text? At the very least, *kurios* must have done duty, in Greek piety, for *'adōnāy* in Hebrew for avoiding the utterance of the sacred Name. But further, it is difficult to imagine a distinctively Christian motive, when copying the Greek Scriptures, for substituting *kurios* for some other designation of God. And, finally, there are indications that non-Christian Greek-speaking Jews used *kurios* for God. There is a tell-tale passage in Aquila's version where, finding insufficient room in his line for the tetragrammaton in archaic letters which he mostly uses, he substitutes *kū* (the abbreviation for the genitive of *kurios*).[62] Again, Philo uses *kurios* as well as *despotēs* for God (carefully defining the difference by reference to their supposed etymology in *QRDH* 23); and, although Josephus scarcely uses *kurios*,[63] it is significant that he relates how the Jews refused to call the Emperor *kurios* (*B.J.* VII. 419f.), clearly because they regarded it as reserved for God.[64] Further, the Testaments of the Twelve Patriarchs uses *kurios* for *'ēl*,[65] and the *Letter of Aristeas* 155 contains a reminis-

---

[61] By square Hebrew characters in Papyrus Fouad 266, of which the text was published in *Etudes de Papyrologie* 9 (1971), 81ff.; an introduction by Françoise Dunand, 'Papyrus Grecs Bibliques (Papyrus F.INV. 266), volumina de la Genèse et du Deuteronome', appeared in *Recherches d'Archéologie, de Philologie et d'Histoire* 27 (Cairo: Institut français d'archéologie orientale 1966), 1ff. See especially pp. 39ff. of the latter. F. Dunand is inclined to date the fragments not later than 50 B.C. (p. 12). Here, square Hebrew characters are used for the tetragrammaton, not the archaic form. I am indebted to Dr J. A. Fitzmyer for this reference.

[62] F. C. Burkitt, *Fragments of the Books of Kings according to the translation of Aquila* (Cambridge: University Press 1897), 16.

[63] A. Schlatter, 'Wie Sprach Josephus von Gott?', *Beiträge zur Forderung christlicher Theologie* (Gütersloh) 14. 1, 9–10 (not available to me, but see Bousset's *Kyrios Christos*, Eng. trans. 146, n. 101).

[64] A. Deissmann, *Licht vom Osten* (Tübingen ⁴1923), Eng. trans. (London: Hodder and Stoughton 1927), 355f.

[65] Dunand, 'Papyrus Grecs Bibliques', 52.

cence of a Pentateuchal passage with *kurios*.[66] Thus, linguistic apparatus already existed in Hebrew, Aramaic, and Greek for using almost, if not quite, the same designation for an honoured human being and for God, and one should be very chary of assuming that early Palestinian Christians are likely to have kept the human clearly segregated from the more than human in their minds when they were referring to Jesus. How far from worship can you keep invocation?

Besides, even if 'our Lord' is not the same as 'the Lord' absolutely, and even if the Aramaic *mārê'* had been used mostly for humans and not for God (which we have seen reason to question) one does not call upon a mere Rabbi, after his death, to come. The entire phrase, *Maranatha*, if it meant 'Come, our Master!', would be bound to carry transcendental overtones even if the *maran* by itself did not. It is true that there is little or no evidence for the actual *worship* of Jesus in early Palestinian traditions. The verb *proskunein*, 'to prostrate oneself', is too ambiguous in its usage to provide evidence, as an examination of its occurrences in the New Testament shows.[67]

But even in the absence of this type of evidence, the other clues make a cumulatively impressive case, as it seems to me, for the belief that the acclamation of Jesus as Lord, whenever it may have been first heard, was not necessarily an innovation, built up from material borrowed from alien sources, but could, rather, have been the articulation of an insight appropriate to what was at least implicit all along. Moreover, there is a further piece of evidence pointing in the same direction. Not only is the word *kurios* charged with overtones derived from its use for God in Greek versions of the Hebrew Scriptures. The New Testament exhibits numerous instances of the transfer to Christ of passages in the Scriptures originally relating to God – and that, at an early stage in New Testament thinking. Phil. 2: 10f. is one of the most remarkable. At latest, it represents Paul himself, or, at earliest, a pre-Pauline formula; and it boldly transfers to Jesus a great monotheistic passage from Isa. 45: 23, in which God is represented as declaring that he must have no rivals: it is now to *Kurios Iesous Christos* that every knee shall bow, and it is he whom every

[66] Baudissin, *Kyrios als Gottesname*, as in n. 52 above, ii, 12f.
[67] See the Excursus on obeisance, pp. 175f.

tongue shall confess. Professor M. Black is inclined to think that
the same passage is intended in the name of the Lord Jesus even
in Rom. 14: 11.[68] Certainly in Heb. 1: 10ff. (though this may, of
course, be later), a great, monotheistic passage in Ps. 102,
manifestly intended in the original to be addressed to God the
Creator, is boldly assumed to be addressed to Christ. I have
discussed elsewhere various proposals for explaining this apparently arbitrary assumption that anything belonging to God
belongs also to Christ;[69] but certainly the phenomenon is there,
explain it how one may. It is explicitly taken up and discussed
in Justin's *Trypho* 74, where Trypho (justifiably!) complains that
Ps. 95, which his interlocutor has just appropriated for Christ,
was spoken 'to the Father who made the heavens and the earth'.
The explanation offered in the remainder of the chapter is
entirely unsatisfactory; but it only endorses the fact of such uses
of Scripture by Christians. It is, incidentally, interesting to
speculate whether the remarkable words in 1 Thess. 4: 16 about
Christ's expected *descent* at his *parousia* may not be a reminiscence
of a passage about God in the Psalter. The two passages are as
follows:

Ps. 47 (LXX 46): 6	1 Thess. 4: 16
anebe ho theos *en alalagmō(i)*,	*autos ho* kurios *en keleusmati*,
kurios en phonē(i) salpiggos.	en phonē(i) *archaggelou kai en* salpiggi theou, *katabēsetai*...

If so, this would be in keeping with Professor M. Black's
observation[70] that the reference in Jude 14 to the coming of the
Lord, which may now be paralleled from the Aramaic Enoch, is
virtually the same as the *maranatha* which refers to Christ.

It is noteworthy that, at least in some of the instances of the
transfer to Christ of passages originally relating to God, special
care seems to be taken to safeguard, as it were, the supremacy
of God. Thus, in Phil. 2: 11, the acclamation of Christ in terms
originally intended for God is said to be 'to the glory of God the
Father'. Similarly, in Rev. 5: 9f., 12f., explicit references to God

[68] 'The Christological Use of the Old Testament in the New Testament', as in n. 29 above, 6ff.
[69] *The Birth of the New Testament* (London: A. and C. Black [2]1966), 77ff.
[70] As in n. 19 above, 189ff.

are brought in alongside of expressions of the worthiness of the Lamb. I owe to Mr P. A. Glendinning, at present researching at Cambridge, the observation that such phenomena may be an indication that the passage in question was directed to a situation in which Christians were in danger of being either misunderstood by Gentiles or attacked by Jews as polytheists, and needed to safeguard their monotheistic intentions.

What I am suggesting, then, is that the address to Christ as *maran* is, in terms of quality, not necessarily far from his description as *kurios* absolutely (let alone *ho kurios hēmōn*), nor his invocation far from his acclamation. Even when the way in which the acclamation is expressed may betoken a Gentile environment, the estimate of Jesus implied by it is not necessarily to be regarded as essentially different from the estimate implied by his invocation, as *marê'*, in early, Palestinian contexts.

If the recognition of Jesus as *kurios* is not to be regarded as a change to a completely different realm of thought from his invocation as *maran*, what is harder to conceive of as 'given' from the beginning is that which justifies and gives rise to an interpretation of his lordship as exercised over the whole of creation.[71] This cosmic lordship is certainly his in 1 Cor. 8: 6, not to mention Phil. 2: 10f., Col. 1: 16ff., etc. There are, of course, plenty of theories about how a cosmic Christology was reached. The most obvious link is that between the Wisdom of God in the universe (as in the Wisdom Literature) and Jesus as the Word and Wisdom of God.[72] W. L. Knox believed also that, when once the lordship of Christ was recognized (as in Colossians) as supreme over the world-rulers and planetary powers, the inevitable corollary was that he was Lord of the universe.[73] Thus, a cosmic Christology might be reached by identifying Jesus with figures of Old Testament and inter-testamental speculation, or by finding him supreme in the hierachy of beings. While not

[71] Perhaps an examination of the abstract noun *kuriotēs* may throw further light. See M. Werner, *The Formation of Christian Dogma: an Historical Study of its Problems* (modified Eng. trans. of *Die Entstehung des christlichen Dogmas* [2]1954, London: A. and C. Black 1957), 124.

[72] A specially interesting study of this theme in St Matthew is M. J. Suggs, *Wisdom, Christology, and Law in Matthew's Gospel* as in Introduction, n. 6.

[73] *St Paul and the Church of the Gentiles* (Cambridge: University Press 1939).

denying such possibilities, I wonder whether a more proximate cause may not have been the discovery, simply, of his absolute aliveness beyond death. The Easter experience, in itself, seems to lead to such a confession as Rom. 14: 9: 'Christ died and came to life again, to establish his lordship over dead and living.' This, to be sure, is a *kuriotēs* over human persons only; but to be Lord of the domain of dead and living is, nevertheless, a 'cosmic' position.

I am not for a moment denying that developed language about cosmic dimensions might be the fruit of long speculation and cogitation; but I am inclined to believe that a good case could be made for the ingredients for such conclusions being present immediately in the experience of the risen Christ. The question how the conception of Christ's preexistence was reached, and whether it conforms to the norm of 'legitimate development' as against 'evolution' with the addition of alien ingredients, may be more profitably discussed at a later stage in the investigation.

I have selected only four words or phrases – 'the Son of Man', 'the Son of God', 'Christ', 'Lord' – by way of demonstrating how high a degree of continuity may be detected between, on the one hand, what, so far as any reading of the evidence can probe, seems to have been implicit in the earliest impact made by Jesus himself, and, on the other hand, the usage of those periods in which the New Testament documents were taking shape. It would be possible, I believe, to extend the inquiry with similar results. For instance, Mark's Gospel is now often regarded as a deliberate corrective of false Christologies. Taking traditional pictures of Jesus as a successful and triumphant wonder-worker, Mark (so it is said) corrects this *theologia gloriae* by his emphasis on the necessity for the Son of Man to suffer: he turns it into a *theologia crucis*.[74] I believe, as who does not?, that there is, in Mark, a clear *theologia crucis*. What I am less sure about is whether the 'success story' ever did circulate entirely isolated and by itself. Is it not more likely that it was Jesus' own life and ministry that wove the two together, and is there any clear evidence that Mark received the one without the other? No doubt

---

[74] For a useful summary, see J. D. G. Dunn, *Jesus and the Spirit* as in n. 33, 69, with bibliography there.

each miracle story constituted a self-contained unit of tradition; and there may well have been catenae of such stories. But I doubt whether catenae of miracle stories, even if they can be demonstrably established as independent units of tradition,[75] can be assumed to have been used without constant reminders, provided by other parts of the traditions, of other aspects of the ministry. Were they ever presented as though that was all there was to say about Jesus?[76]

Perhaps the nearest we can get to evidence that a 'propaganda'-value was attached, on certain levels of Christian tradition, to exceptional and extraordinary manifestations of power in healing and in other activities is in the Acts. Most recently, J. D. G. Dunn has devoted attention to the distinctiveness of Acts in this respect, in contrast to other New Testament writers:

[Luke] presents the early church as another, but more powerful wonder worker than its competitors. He does not appear to recognize that there is a problem here – the problem of distinguishing the power of God from its counterfeits, the problem of weaning faith away from a diet of the miraculous. The problem is recognized and tackled by the other leading NT authors (Q–Matt. 4.1–11/Luke 4.1–13; Mark 9.38ff.; Matt. 7.22ff.; John 2.23ff.; 4.48; II Cor. 12.5–10). But in presenting his account of the early church Luke hardly seems aware of it.[77]

But this would constitute evidence of 'evolution' from a 'primitive', more nearly 'pagan', view to a more deeply religious conception only if Luke could be shown to be faithfully reproducing the outlook of a past period (as Dunn suggests is possible, *Jesus and the Spirit*, 169). It is equally possible that the picture

[75] See P. J. Achtemeier, 'Toward the Isolation of pre-Markan Miracle Catenae', *JBL* 89.3 (Sept. 1970), 265ff.; 'The Origin and Function of the Pre-Marcan Miracle Catenae', *JBL* 91.2 (June 1972), 198ff.; 'Gospel Miracle Tradition and the Divine Man', *Interp* 26.2 (April 1972), 179ff.

[76] Of course I am aware of the widespread fashion of assuming that 'aretalogies' about Jesus were in circulation in the early communities: see, e.g., J. M. Robinson and H. Koester, edd., *Trajectories through Early Christianity* (Philadelphia: 1971); and other literature cited by R. H. Gundry, 'Recent Investigations into the Literary Genre "Gospel"', in R. N. Longenecker and M. C. Tenney, edd., *New Dimensions in New Testament Study* (Grand Rapids: Zondervan 1974), 97ff.

[77] *Jesus and the Spirit* (as in n. 33 above), 168.

drawn in Acts is Luke's own more superficial interpretation of something that originally and all along had consisted of those ingredients among which profounder writers perceived the *theologia crucis*. But I do not wish to follow this matter up at present. Instead, I leave this study of select description of Jesus by phrases and titles, to inquire into the Christological significance of the evidence for the experience of his presence, especially in the Pauline epistles.

2

The corporate Christ

After stating the thesis that development more satisfactorily describes the genesis of New Testament Christology than evolution, I proceeded to test it by re-investigating the origins of four terms applied to Jesus – 'the Son of Man', 'the Son of God', 'Christ', and 'Lord'. The conclusion reached was that, so far from their evolving away from what was there at the beginning, there was, in each case, evidence to suggest that the term was dictated by what Jesus himself was (due care being taken to use that question-begging phrase carefully), and not by extraneous factors entering the stream of tradition from elsewhere. So conservative a conclusion is, in the nature of the case, suspect, because it is liable to be biassed by vested interests. I have myself viewed it with suspicion; but, in spite of this, I find myself convinced by the evidence. It is for readers to see whether they agree.

But, in any case, there are other phenomena in the New Testament which are of Christological importance besides the use of such terms as have just been examined; and it is to one of these that the remainder of this study is chiefly directed. This phenomenon is what, for lack of a better term, I call an understanding and experience of Christ as corporate. In some measure, this bypasses the use of titles in Christology and affords an independent criterion for the nature of Jesus Christ; and it has the merit of being undeniably early and well-established, for the evidence is largely in those Pauline epistles which are widely agreed to be genuine.

For that matter, even if no account were taken of an understanding of Christ as corporate, other aspects of the relation between Christ and the believer reflected in the New Testament, even apart from and besides the corporate aspect, constitute evidence of a special status. For it is not the relation simply of founder to institution, of example to imitators, or of rabbi to disciples. As J. D. G. Dunn puts it, instead of being 'simply the charismatic exemplar', Jesus

began to feature more or less from the beginning as *a source and object* of the first Christians' religious experience...religious experiences of the earliest community, including experiences like those enjoyed by Jesus himself, were seen as *dependent on him and derivative from him...* the religious experience of the Christian is *not merely experience like that of Jesus, it is experience which* at all characteristic and distinctive points *is derived from Jesus the Lord, and which only makes sense when this derivative and dependent character is recognized* [the whole of this is italicized in the original; I have italicized the phrases that are significant for the present purpose].[1]

This, in itself, testifies to an understanding of Jesus as present and alive, in a sense quite different from that in which the inspiration of some great figure of the past lives on; and it is thus Christologically significant, even if one went no further. But it is more particularly what I am calling an understanding and experience of Christ as corporate that is the subject of the inquiry that follows.

This is an extraordinary conception, as several modern thinkers have remarked. Lady Helen Oppenheimer expresses her puzzlement in these words: 'Christians have a great deal to say about the ways in which people can be related to God and to each other, and many of the things they wish to say take for granted the possibility of certain sorts of close relationships which are not on the face of it compatible with common sense'; and she goes on to quote the Johannine language of 'abiding in' persons as an example.[2] As we shall see, the Johannine language is actually less problematic, in this particular realm of thought, than the Pauline; but Lady Oppenheimer has at least put her finger on the problem of conceiving of one person's being within another.

When I read this passage in Lady Oppenheimer's book, I was reminded of a letter which I had received in June 1967 from Professor H. Cunliffe-Jones, then a Professor at the University

[1] J. D. G. Dunn, *Jesus and the Spirit* (London: SCM 1975), 194f., 342.
[2] *Incarnation and Immanence* (London: Hodder and Stoughton 1973), 17f.

of Manchester. He had been reading my small book, *The Pheno-menon of the New Testament* (London: SCM 1967), in which, among other things I had been emphasizing the striking way in which Paul's conception of Christ insists on his being an inclusive personality – one in whom believers find themselves incorporate. 'It is not', wrote Professor Cunliffe-Jones, 'that I want to challenge what you say so far as the New Testament is concerned, or that I find difficulty in the concept because I want to advocate a reduced Christology'; but he went on to say,

I find this conception of an inclusive and corporate personality extremely difficult to understand...the corporate inclusiveness of Jesus is even more difficult to me than the corporate inclusiveness of God – though I don't understand that either. On the basis of a Platonic or Neo-Platonic philosophy, I could understand the idiom. What does it mean in the intellectual context of the twentieth century?

There, in the words of two contemporary thinkers, you have expressions of perplexity about language which is undoubtedly present in the New Testament, at least in the writings of Paul, and (though with a rather different usage) in the writings of John.

From a rather different angle, another contemporary thinker, Dr A. R. Peacocke, writing as a scientist who is also a theologian, raises questions about the meaning of incorporation. He says: 'apart from the direct biological connection, it is hard to see what sort of solidarity we might have with Christ (and even more with the hypothetical Adam). Indeed the concept of solidarity seems too vacuous in any sense other than the biological, for it to be a foundation of a theory of the work of Christ...'. And, criticizing a statement of E. L. Mascall's,[3] he says that such imagery as that of incorporation in the new human nature 'fails to make clear how what he [Christ] did then is actually effective here and now to enable men to act in accord with the divine purposes'.[4] He resorts (173), instead, to a conception of the Spirit of God as all along immanent in the evolutionary processes, culminating as these do in Christ and in what the Spirit can effect through Christ in Christian men. In other words, if I understand him rightly, he is saying that little sense can be extracted from

[3] *Christian Theology and Natural Science* (London: Longmans, Green and Co. 1956), 38.
[4] *Science and the Christian Experiment* (Oxford: University Press 1971), 172.

language which speaks of us as in Christ, but more from language
which speaks of the Spirit as in us: it is more or less intelligible
to talk of the Spirit of God, immanent and operative in nature
and in men; operative in a culminating and decisive way in Christ;
and, thereafter and because of this, operating in Christian men
in a special way. But talk about men as 'in Christ' or as incorporated in the new humanity is difficult to understand.

On the other hand, the late C. H. Dodd more than once made
statements which seem, if I interpret them rightly, not only to
endorse what Lady Helen Oppenheimer and Professor Cunliffe-
Jones both allow – that this language of inclusion does appear in
the New Testament, make of it what we may – but also to suggest
that, rather than presenting obstacles, it offers important clues
to our own understanding of personal relationship. In his brilliant little book, *According to the Scriptures* (London: Nisbet, 1952),
C. H. Dodd wrote, in a passage I shall have occasion to cite again
in another connexion, of the way in which Old Testament figures
and symbols converge upon Jesus in New Testament thought:

To have brought together...the Son of Man who is the people of the
saints of the Most High, the Man of God's right hand, who is also the
vine of Israel, the Son of Man who after humiliation is crowned with
glory and honour, and the victorious priest-king at the right hand of
God, is an achievement of interpretative imagination which results in
the creation of an entirely new figure. It involves an original, and
far-reaching, resolution of the tension between the individual and the
collective aspects of several of these figures (109).

He went on to suggest (110) that this achievement was due to Jesus
Christ himself; but my immediate purpose is not to follow this
point up (it will come up for our consideration again later), but
to fasten on the phrase 'an original, and far-reaching, resolution
of the tension between the individual and the collective aspects
of several of these figures'; for, in his much larger book, published in the following year, *The Interpretation of the Fourth
Gospel* (Cambridge: University Press 1953), Dodd returned to
this theme, in a memorable paragraph to which I find myself
constantly recurring. Christ, he said,

was the true self of the human race, standing in that perfect union with
God to which others can attain only as they are incorporate in Him; the

mind, whose thought is truth absolute..., which other men think after Him; the true life of man, which other men live by sharing it with Him ...It is clear [continued Dodd] that this conception raises a new problem. It challenges the mind to discover a doctrine of personality, which will make conceivable this combination of the universal and the particular in a single person. A naïve individualism regarding man, or a naïve anthropomorphism regarding God, makes nonsense of Johannine Christology. Ancient thought, when it left the ground of such naïve conceptions, lost hold upon the concrete actuality of the person. It denied personality in man by making the human individual no more than an unreal 'imitation' of the abstract universal Man, and it denied personality in God by making Him no more than the abstract unity of being. A Christian philosophy starting from the Johannine doctrine of Jesus as Son of Man should be able to escape the *impasse* into which all ancient thought fell, and to give an account of personality in God and in ourselves (249).

I do not, as it happens, find the Johannine doctrine of Jesus as the Son of Man so significant in this respect as Dodd did. This aspect I find rather in the Synoptic Son of Man, and in the 'Man' of Pauline thinking. But one might substitute the Pauline doctrine of the corporate Christ for the Johannine Son of Man doctrine in Dodd's statement without affecting his main point, which is, I take it, that parts, at least, of the New Testament present Christ in such a way that a new insight is revealed into the relation of the individual and the corporate in the realm of the personal.

Thus, Lady Oppenheimer, Professor Cunliffe-Jones, and Dr Arthur Peacocke express puzzlement. C. H. Dodd, on the other hand, spoke of the phenomenon rather as illuminating – though (as Professor Cunliffe-Jones has observed in another letter to me) without showing precisely how it might be handled or applied. I am not going to attempt to reply to the puzzlement: I am among the puzzled myself. But I do wish to reaffirm that what causes the puzzlement is a phenomenon that undoubtedly does present itself within the New Testament, explain it how one may; and that it seems there to be a new phenomenon. Dr D. R. de Lacey, in a Cambridge Ph.D. dissertation called 'The Form of God in the Likeness of Men' (1974), throws considerable doubt on the existence of any relevant pre-Christian analogies to the idea of 'incorporative personality',[5] but finds himself driven, nevertheless, to acknowledge that Paul does use such language of Christ. 'The so-called "concept of corporate personality",' he writes,

when examined proves to be a compound of various discrete ideas, some of which may have been entertained in the distant past of the Jewish people; others of which may be evident in OT material; but many of which are irrelevant or insubstantiable. Even Adam does not appear to have been viewed as an incorporative being: evidently he has special status as the ancestor of all men, but does not seem to be viewed as involving all men in his sin. The merits, though not the sins, of pious ancestors or contemporaries could affect others, and brought blessings on them; but not in an 'incorporative' sense. The danielic vision does not appear to have given rise to a 'Son of Man' figure who incorporates Israel in himself, though he may represent the people before God or possibly have been a cypher for the people of God (as, perhaps, in 4 Ezra 12). But evidence for a more-than-individual understanding of any man is very hard to find in the OT or later Jewish development.

In contrast to this, Dr de Lacey goes on to say that Paul does *not* use incorporative language of any except Christ (except, perhaps, Adam in Rom. 5 – and here Paul seems to have to *make* his case rather than *assuming* it as already accepted).

In general we may affirm that Paul views men and appeals to men as individuals, and it is only 'in Christ' that this state of affairs might be changed.

And again:

while the language of 'corporate personality' is generally misleading and unhelpful, Paul's Jesus can only be described in supra-individual terms ...the experience of reconciliation which comes by entering Christ's death and receiving new life from him...forces Paul to develop a new understanding of the man through whom this occurred; which is then read back to Adam (folios 83f., 85f., 98).

Thus it appears to be something new that is presented by Paul, and the mere affirmation of this fact does nothing to reduce the perplexity expressed by Lady Oppenheimer and Professor

[5] He refers to G. E. Mendenhall, 'The Relation of the Individual to Political Society in Ancient Israel', in J. M. Myers, *et al.*, edd., *Biblical Studies in Memory of H. C. Alleman* (New York: Augustin 1960); J. R. Porter, 'The Legal Aspects of the Concept of "Corporate Personality" in the Old Testament', *VT* 15 (1965), 361ff.; J. W. Rogerson, 'The Hebrew Conception of Corporate Personality: a Re-examination', *JTS* n.s. 21 (1970), 1ff.

Cunliffe-Jones, or to explain to Dr Peacocke what, precisely, is meant by such language. And C. H. Dodd, who welcomed the phenomenon, only said, rather cryptically, that it might help to give an account of personality, in God and in ourselves. I am not optimistic enough to imagine that I can even give a satisfactory account of the Pauline phenomenon – let alone explain it; but I do believe that it is something that throws light, albeit perplexing light, on the meaning of Jesus for Paul, and is a Christological datum of great significance. A person who had recently been crucified, but is found to be alive, with 'absolute' life, the life of the age to come, and is found, moreover, to be an inclusive, all-embracing presence – such a person is beginning to be described in terms appropriate to nothing less than God himself.

It is a striking fact that a recent writer on Christology, whose estimate of 'the Jesus of history' is what orthodox opinion might classify as 'reductionist', and who strongly repudiates the idea of the preexistence of Christ, nevertheless finds himself, when describing the meaning of salvation through Jesus, driven to a full doctrine of what can only be called 'mystical union' between the believer and Christ.[6] So far as I understand the author, Mr David Welbourn, he believes that Jesus was, like other men, a sinner; but that, unlike other men, he *became* perfect; and that, for this reason, he is alive in an absolute sense, and is capable, as no one before or since, of becoming united with believers and empowering them. After speaking of the influence which, in a limited way, Jesus had exerted on his disciples during his ministry, he continues (78): 'From the Resurrection on, however, this influence was immeasurably more profound. Jesus now had access to the very well-springs of the disciples' personalities – a truth spoken of by St Paul and St John in terms of mystical indwelling.' As we shall see, it is slightly misleading to bracket St Paul and St John together in this respect. But, for the moment, the point is that even a writer who demands that Jesus' humanity be seen as originally sinful like our own, still finds himself explaining the Christian experience of Christ as the source of salvation in terms of some sort of spiritual *contact*, and describing Christ beyond his death in transcendental terms. He thus finds himself unable to describe the Christian experience of Christ

[6] D. Welbourn, *God-Dimensional Man* (London: Epworth Press 1972).

either as the mere looking back to a great example of the past, or as merely the experience of a community in which the memory of Christ has been developed into something new; rather it is the contact of the many with the one.

2. INCORPORATIVE PHRASES

What, then are the facts about the language in which the Pauline epistles describe contact with Christ? For a start, it may be well to consider the significant uses of the preposition *en*, 'in'. The facts though complicated, may be summarized as follows.

(i) Paul more frequently than any other New Testament writer uses the preposition *en* with some designation of Jesus Christ – *en Christō(i)*, *en Kuriō(i)*, etc.; and, although only a few of the occurrences of this formula seem to compel one to entertain the idea of 'incorporation', these few have to be reckoned with.

What I mean by this is that *en* is a most versatile preposition; and a large number of its uses with a divine name fall outside the present inquiry, because they are only instrumental or otherwise descriptive. Indeed, they seem often to mean little more than might be meant by the adjective 'Christian'. Thus – to take a random example – in 1 Cor. 3: 1 Paul says that he could not address his friends at Corinth as spiritually mature (*pneumatikoi*): he could only address them as *sarkinoi*, people in bondage to selfish instincts ('fleshly'), and as mere children *en Christō(i)*. Now this, in such a context, could not possibly mean 'children *by reason of being incorporated in Christ*'. It must mean something like 'mere novices *in the Christian life*' – children so far as things Christian are concerned. Or, again, Rom. 9: 1, 'I speak the truth *en Christō(i)*', seems unlikely to mean (though conceivably it could), 'I speak the truth *as one incorporated in Christ*'. Must it not, more vaguely, mean something like 'in Christ's presence', or 'on Christ's authority', or even simply 'as a Christian', 'in a Christian manner'? Or what of the strange phrases in 1 Cor. 9: 1f.: 'Are you not my handiwork *en Kuriō(i)*?...You are the seal of my apostleship *en Kuriō(i)*'? Presumably *en Kuriō(i)* there must mean something like 'in the Lord's service'. As examples of an almost plain instrumental usage might be quoted such phrases as 'sanctified *in* Christ Jesus' (1 Cor. 1: 2) or 'to be justified *in* Christ' (Gal. 2: 17) – though even here there is a haunting sense that there are overtones to which a mere English 'by' or 'through' hardly does justice.

At any rate, these are random examples from a wide range of uses which defy precise classification, but which can scarcely be said to demand an incorporative meaning. And the versatility or looseness with which Paul can use *en* is demonstrated by a rhetorical catalogue like that in 2 Cor. 6: 4b–7, where a translator will almost certainly have to draw upon more prepositions than one in order to render the nuances: 'in patience, in affliction, in purity, in knowledge, in the Holy Spirit' – these cannot really represent a single relationship, adequately expressible by the single preposition 'in'; and perhaps it is significant that, in that same passage, the *en*-series is followed by a trio of *dia*-phrases: 'through the weapons of righteousness, through good reputation and evil, through unpopularity and popularity', suggesting that Paul is groping round for ways of describing a succession of circumstances.

Furthermore, there are varieties of usage within the ostensibly Pauline *corpus*. In the Pastoral Epistles, scarcely once are *persons* described as *en Christō(i)*, etc. Wherever such phrases occur in 1 and 2 Timothy (they are altogether absent from Titus), it is nearly always to describe the *locus* of something impersonal: *pistis*, 1 Tim. 3: 13, 2 Tim. 3: 15; *agapē*, 2 Tim. 1: 13; *charis*, 2 Tim. 2: 1; *sōtēria*, 2 Tim. 2: 10. Only in 2 Tim. 3: 12 is there reference to persons, 'who want to live in a godly way *en Christō(i) Iēsou*'. Ephesians also exhibits a greatly reduced usage, as we shall see later.

However, all allowance made for the wide range of this preposition and the looseness of some of its uses and the curiosities of its distribution in the Pauline writings, there remains a residue of occurrences where it is difficult to escape the impression that Paul is using *en* with a name for Christ in a genuinely (though metaphorically) locative sense. Thus: Rom. 8: 1, 'There is, then, no condemnation now *tois en Christō(i) Iesou*' – 'For those who are in Christ Jesus'; Rom. 16: 7, Andronicus and Junias (says Paul) 'before me *gegonan en Christō(i)*' – 'came to be in Christ'; 1 Cor. 15: 22, 'for as in Adam all die, so also in Christ

all shall be made alive' (here the *en* might conceivably be instrumental in both instances – 'because of' or 'by means of' Adam
and Christ – but it seems more likely to mean 'because of incorporation in' or 'because of being united with'); 2 Cor. 5: 17, 'if
anyone is in Christ, he is (or there is) a new creation'; Phil. 3:
8f., where Paul declares it his ambition 'to be found in him', *hina
heurethō en autō(i)*. And, collectively, whole congregations are
similarly spoken of as in Christ (Gal. 1: 22, Phil. 1: 1, virtually,
1 Thess. 2: 14); and, with *en theō(i)*, 'in *God*', 1 Thess. 1: 1, 2 Thess.
1: 1. With this 'in *God*'[7] may be compared the strange phrase
in saying 40 of the Gospel of Thomas: '...a vine was planted
outside of the Father'.[8] (Dr E. Best, in his commentary on
the Thessalonian epistles, disallows the incorporative sense at
1 Thess. 1: 1 and 2 Thess. 1: 1, and wants to interpret it as
instrumental.[9] But this I find difficult.)

This, then, is the first point: in at least a few passages, Christ
(or the Lord) seems to be the 'place', the *locus*, where believers
are found.

(ii) The second fact about Paul's use of *en* is that references
to believers as 'in Christ' or 'in the Lord' are not (despite what
many writers affirm) balanced with a complete reciprocity by
references to Christ's indwelling in believers. In the Johannine
Gospel and Epistles, as we shall see, the *en* is completely reciprocal
and mutual; but Paul seems to evince some hesitation in this
respect. It is true that the epistles are not without some
memorable expressions of the indwelling of Christ in individual
Christians. Gal. 2: 20 springs to mind – 'Christ lives in me', *zē(i)*
...*en emoi Christos*. So, too, in Rom. 8: 10, *Christos en humin*
appears, to judge from the context, to mean 'Christ within each
of you'. But other instances of 'Christ in you' (plural), such as
2 Cor. 13: 5, Col. 1: 27, should, more probably, be understood
to mean 'Christ *among* you', which is not the same as individual

---

[7] Elsewhere in Paul, *en theō(i)* only occurs after *kauchasthai* (Rom. 2: 17, 5: 11),
    (apo)kruptein (Eph. 3: 9, Col. 3: 3), and *parrhēsiazesthai* (1 Thess. 2: 2).
[8] Convenient editions: K. Aland, *Synopsis Quattuor Evangeliorum* (Stuttgart: Würt-
    temburgische Bibelanstalt 1964), 517ff. (522); F. F. Bruce, *Jesus and Christian
    Origins outside the New Testament* (London: Hodder and Stoughton 1974), 110ff.
    (129); R. M. Grant and D. N. Freedman, edd., *The Secret Sayings of Jesus*
    (London: Fontana Books 1960), 146 (numbered 41).
[9] *The First and Second Epistles to the Thessalonians* (London: A. and C. Black 1972),
    62.

indwelling. Neither are references to Christ's *activity* within a person (speaking, 2 Cor. 13: 3 or acting, Gal. 2: 8) quite the same as references to his being or living in a man. F. J. Leenhardt has argued, it is true, that the curious phrase in Gal. 1: 16, in which Paul refers to God's good pleasure 'to reveal his Son in me', *apokalupsai ton huion autou en emoi*, means 'to reveal *that his Son was in me*'; and that the identification of Jesus with Christians in the accounts of the Damascus road encounter (Acts 9: 5, 22: 6, 26: 15) point to the indwelling of Christ in Christians, as (thinks Leenhardt) does 2 Cor. 4: 5f., with its reference to the Apostle as preaching not himself but Christ, who has 'shone in our hearts'.[10] But it is difficult to feel at all confident that these passages should be added to the few which illustrate the idea of Christ's indwelling in individuals. More impressive is the passage, also adduced by Leenhardt, in Gal. 4: 19, where Paul refers dramatically to his 'travail' (*ōdinō*) until Christ is formed (*morphōthē(i)*) in the Galatians. But even if the *humin* there is to be interpreted individually ('in each of you') and not collectively ('among you'), the 'formation of Christ' in a man sounds more like what might be called the growth of 'a Christian character' within a man than specifically the indwelling of Christ himself. We have to wait till Ephesians (with its questionably Pauline authorship) for the classic expression of Christ's indwelling: Eph. 3: 17, 'that Christ may dwell in your hearts through faith', *katoikēsai ton Christon dia tēs pisteōs en tais kardiais humōn*, where 'in your hearts' ensures that it means individual indwelling. For that matter, Ephesians it is which also has the phrase 'one God ...in all', *heis Theos...en pasin*; but that need only be a collective reference, like the quotation in 2 Cor. 6: 16 from Lev. 26: 11f. ('I will dwell and walk among them' – though there the 'dwell', *enoikēsō*, does not come in the LXX, which renders 'I will make my *abode* (*miškan*) among you' by 'I will put my *covenant* among you').

All in all, then – and this is the second point – Paul seems less freely to speak of the indwelling of Christ in Christians than of Christians in Christ. H. Conzelmann makes a shrewd comment on this phenomenon, when he says: 'It is no coincidence that the

[10] 'Abraham et la conversion de Saul de Tarse', *RHPR* 3–4 (1973), 331ff. (337–42).

concept of faith appears where Paul reverses the phrase so that it becomes "Christ in me"... The juxtaposition of "I in him" and "he in me" never makes the two participants mystically equal.'[11]

(iii) If it is characteristic of Paul to speak of believers as in Christ, but less characteristic to speak of Christ as in a believer, almost the reverse is true of Pauline phrases concerning the Spirit. *En pneumati* does occur, but in other than clearly incorporative senses. For instance, in Rom. 8: 9a, 14: 17 the phrase possibly refers to the 'realm' or 'sphere' or 'level' of the Spirit;[12] while in 1 Cor. 12: 9, Col. 1: 8 the *en* seems to be used more or less instrumentally. But phrases indicating that the Holy Spirit is in a believer are frequent enough, whether it is phrases actually with *en* (Rom. 8: 9b, 11 – the reverse of the phrase in 8: 9a just alluded to as denoting, perhaps, a 'realm' – and 1 Cor. 6: 19), or phrases such as that God 'gives' or 'supplies' the Spirit to a believer (2 Cor. 1: 22, 5: 5, Gal. 3: 5, Phil. 1: 19; cf. Eph. 1: 17, Rom. 5: 5), or that a person is filled with Spirit (Eph. 5: 18).

The third point is, thus, that, on the whole, the indwelling Agent is the Spirit. Incidentally, a curious contrast is presented by a phrase in Eusebius, *H.E.* 3. 31.3, quoting Polycrates, where one of the daughters of Philip the apostle (? a mistake for the evangelist) is spoken of as *en hagiō(i) pneumati politeusamenē*, 'who lived in the Holy Spirit' (Loeb trans.). In the New Testament it is just the contrary; and it seems unlikely that Paul could have derived his 'in Christ' formula from an 'in the Spirit' formula used by charismatic sects. This theory is discussed, but with great caution, by E. Käsemann in his commentary on the Epistle to the Romans.[13] He is less cautious in accepting that there is a reciprocity between the two phrases.

(iv) A fourth fact is that certain tendencies may be traced – though they are only tendencies, and certainly not uniform or consistent rules – in the choice between *Christos* and *Kurios* in the *en*-phrases generally, and, indeed, in other Pauline phrases also.

---

[11] *Grundriss der Theologie des Neuen Testaments* (München: Chr. Kaiser Verlag 1967), 234f.; Eng. tr. *An Outline of the Theology of the New Testament* (London: SCM 1969), 211.

[12] See (for this idea, though not in connexion with Rom. 8 or 14) E. Schweizer, article *pneuma*, *TWNT* vi, 414; and see E. Käsemann, *An die Römer* (Tübingen: J. C. B. Mohr 1973, ³1974), *in loc.*

[13] As in n. 12 above.

For, broadly speaking, Jesus tends to be spoken of as 'Christ' in the context of verbs in the indicative mood and of statements, while he tends to be spoken of as 'Lord' when it is a matter of exhortations or commands, in the subjunctive or the imperative. Roughly speaking, 'Christ' is associated with the *fait accompli* of God's saving *work*, and 'the Lord' with its implementation and its working out in human conduct. In short, if one uses the familiar Christian cliché, 'Become what you are!', then one may say that what you are is 'in Christ', and what you are to become is 'in the Lord'. To give just one example of each, one might quote 1 Cor. 4: 15 for the indicative: 'for in Christ Jesus through the gospel I begot you' (the finished work of Christ, proclaimed in the Apostle's gospel brought the Christian community into being: from that time, in Christ Jesus, they 'were', they existed). For the imperative, Phil. 4: 2, 'I beg Euodia and Syntyche to be unanimous in the Lord'.[14]

Of course there are obvious exceptions. It is difficult to persuade oneself that there is a genuine, subtle difference, when, in a single verse (Philem. 20), Paul says 'Yes, brother, let me have this benefit of you in the Lord: refresh my heart in Christ!' And what of Rom. 16, where, in a standard text, I count *en Kuriō(i)* seven times and *en Christō(i)* four times, but find it extremely difficult to tell myself why they are distributed as they are, unless it be for purely stylistic reasons and to relieve monotony?[15] And what of 2 Tim. 3: 12, which speaks of living in a godly way *in*

[14] It was M. Bouttier's book, *En Christ* (Paris: Presses Universitaires de France 1962) which first brought this home to me. On p. 55 he wrote:
'Voilà qui fixe déjà le sens de l'expression. La "nomination" [i.e. in a confession of Lordship, as in Phil. 2: 6–11, etc. (pp. 54f.)] de Jésus est intervenue à un moment donné de son ministère, par consequent *en kuriō(i)* ne saurait couvrir d'une seule et meme portée toute l'œuvre de Dieu accomplie *in Christo*, en particulier les événements rédempteurs qui précèdent l'intronisation du Seigneur. Le composante *instrumentale* de *in Christo*, qui se rattache intimement à ces événements, ne peut donc se retrouver dans *en kuriō(i)*, et lorsqu'il use de la tournure *dans le Seigneur*, l'apôtre envisage par conséquent, au premier chef, l'intervention *actuelle et souveraine* de Jésus. C'est ce que nous confirme l'examen des textes.' (The list which follows includes Rom. 16 and Philem. 20.)

[15] It is curious that, in contrast to Rom. 16, not one of the greetings in Col. 4: 10ff. carries an *en*-formula, though (verse 17) the *admonition* to Archippus does, with reference not to the admonition but to Archippus' receiving of his ministry: *blepe tēn diakonian hēn parelabes en kuriō(i) hina autēn plērois*. In the brief (and surely Pauline) letter to Philemon, the formula occurs in greeting (verse 23); *en kuriō(i)* occurs at verses 16, 20, and *en Christō(i)* at verse 20.

Christ Jesus, when one might have thought 'in the Lord' more appropriate?

It is true that M. Bouttier, who has done more than, perhaps, anyone to analyse and explain these usages, puts up a good fight to maintain a significant distinction between the two formulae even in such passages as I have named. In his valuable monograph he takes pains to meet such questions.[16] But one wonders whether he is fully convincing.

In any case, this quick review of certain facts must now be followed by acknowledgements to those who have helped to illuminate them. Long ago, J. Armitage Robinson, in his commentary on Ephesians (London: Macmillan 1903, 72), had observed the distinction between the uses of *Christos* and *Kurios*; but this and related matters have been worked out with special care by F. Büchsel,[17] M. Bouttier,[18] F. Neugebauer,[19] W. Kramer,[20] and others, and we are indebted to such scholars as these for great advances in precision. Discussions of the *en Christō(i)* formula and related formulae always go back to Deissmann's famous treatise, *Die neutestamentliche Formel 'in Christo Jesu'* (1892), but Deissmann's view is held by few today. He maintained that it was simply nonsense, and certainly not intelligible Greek, to use the preposition *en* with a personal name. One person cannot be inside another. We have already listened to Lady Helen Oppenheimer expressing difficulty over this, though she is less impatient and not ready to be so sweepingly dogmatic. Deissmann concluded that, when using the preposition in this way, Paul must have thought of Christ as a kind of impersonal *continuum*, like the atmosphere in which a man lives and which, reciprocally, is also within him like the air in a man's lungs.

It is clear that this is simply not true to Paul, whose writings reveal a vivid awareness of the personality and character of Christ. Accordingly, various other suggestions have been put forward. F. C. Porter, many years later, presented an attractive

---

[16] As in n. 14 above, 55.
[17] '"In Christus" bei Paulus', *ZNW* 42 (1949), 141ff.
[18] As in n. 14 above.
[19] *In Christus: Untersuchung zum paulinischen Glaubensverständnis* (Göttingen, Vandenhoeck und Ruprecht 1961); 'Das paulinische "in Christo"', *NTS* 4.2 (1958), 124ff. For a summary, see H. Conzelmann, *Outline* (as in n. 11 above) 208ff.
[20] *Christ, Lord, Son of God* as in Chapter 1, n. 53.

interpretation of the formula in terms of the interpenetration of two intimate friends, who may be said to be involved 'in' each other.[21] But this, which might fit the Johannine usage, will not do for Paul, for whom, as we have seen, the relationship is not symmetrically reciprocal. In discussion of these lectures the term 'sphere of influence' was offered as a possible paraphrase for the sense of the expression. Rather similarly, E. Schweizer has suggested tentatively that the phrase means living 'in an atmosphere informed by love', which is the power of Jesus.[22] A. J. M. Wedderburn strikes out on a new line by adducing the idiom in Gal. 3: 8ff., with its language about the blessing 'in Abraham' and in his 'seed' (Gen. 12: 3): Paul treats Abraham's 'seed' as the *locus* of the blessing, and finds the promise fulfilled in Christ, who is that seed.[23] J. D. G. Dunn writes:

'in Christ' (or 'in the Lord') refers not so much to the objective saving work of Christ [for which he cites Neugebauer, Kramer, and Conzelmann], not so much to the community of faith [citing Käsemann], not so much to the idea of Christ as a corporate personality [citing E. Best], or (mystically) as a sort of atmosphere in which Christians live [citing Deissmann], but rather denotes religious experience (or a particular religious experience) as experience of Christ – deriving from Christ as to both its source and its character. In all the passages noted [he has cited Rom. 12: 5, 1 Cor. 4: 15b, 2 Cor. 2: 17, 5: 17, 12: 19, Gal. 3: 26, 5: 10, Eph. 3: 12, 6: 10, 20, Phil. 1: 14, 2: 19, 24, 4: 13, Col. 2: 6, 4: 17, 1 Thess. 4: 1, 5: 12, 2 Thess. 3: 4, 12, Philem. 8], 'in Christ' or 'in the Lord' expresses not merely a rational conviction, but something more – a sense that Christ is thoroughly involved in the situation or action in question – *a consciousness of Christ*.[24]

All these, it seems to me, are either too generalizing to do justice to the peculiarity of the phrase, or too limited to do justice to its range of application. Neugebauer concludes that the phrase is an adverbial one. *En tachei* ('in speed') means 'quickly'; *en Christō(i)* means 'Christly', 'in a Christ-conditioned way'.[25] Bouttier is less ready to offer a general formulation, but he is quite explicit about the phrase's carrying in it the idea of *inclusion*:

---

[21] *The Mind of Christ in Paul* (New York: Scribners 1932).

[22] *Jesus* (Eng. trans. London: SCM 1971), 107. Cf. *ibid.* 113: 'life in the body of Christ is therefore identical with life "in Christ"'.

[23] 'The Body of Christ and Related Concepts in 1 Corinthians', *SJT* 24. 1 (Feb. 1971), 74ff.

[24] *Jesus and the Spirit* as in n. 1 above, 324.   [25] As in n. 19 above.

S'il fallait remasser maintenant en une phrase le sens de *in Christo,* nous dirions: *in Christo* évoque l'acte de Dieu par lequel, après avoir été identifiés à Jésus-Christ sur la croix et associés par grâce à sa résurrection nous sommes inclus en son corps par le Saint-Esprit, afin de participer désormais à sa vie et à son ministère et de communiquer pleinement à tout ce qui est sien, tant dans le ciel que sur la terre, tant dans le présent que dans le Royaume.[26]

Käsemann gives some countenance to a locative sense: 'Lokaler Sinn der Präposition kann weder durchweg behauptet noch geleugnet werden. Jeden Text muss daraufhin befragt werden, ob lokale, instrumentale oder modale Bedeutung vorliegt.'[27]

For my part, I still find it difficult to escape the conclusion that a (metaphorically) locative sense is involved in at least a limited number of occurrences. There is no reason why the locative category should not be adverbial: Neugebauer's requirement is not necessarily in contradiction here; but the locative sense, if locative it is, remains Christologically significant. It is Christologically significant if it is really true that Paul thought of himself and other Christians as 'included' or 'located' in Christ; for it indicates a more than individualistic conception of the person of Christ. The locative meaning of being in Christ has recently been brought into relation to the whole conception of locality in biblical thought by W. D. Davies in his remarkable book, *The Gospel and the Land.*[28] He ends his chapter on Paul with the aphorism: 'his [Paul's] geographical identity was subordinated to that of being "in Christ", in whom was neither Jew nor Greek'.

But even if it is right to find a locative sense in certain uses of *en*-phrases, much further work needs to be done, not only in elucidating and defining this strange usage, but in observing its distribution and incidence. The conspicuous change in the Pastoral Epistles has already been alluded to. Similarly, J. A. Allan has shown that Ephesians also is different from the most generally acknowledged Pauline epistles, in that it completely

[26] As in n. 14 above, 132f.
[27] *An die Römer* as in n. 12, 211; also *Leib und Leib Christi* (Tübingen: J. C. B. Mohr 1933).
[28] W. D. Davies, *The Gospel and the Land* (Berkeley/Los Angeles/London: University of California Press 1974), 164ff. (220). But n.b. W. D. Davies thinks that *in Christ* detaches Christianity from localization by the universalizing which springs from *each individual* being in Christ.

lacks such instances of *en Christō(i)* or *en Kuriō(i)* as those which, for other epistles, I am defining as 'incorporative'.[29] It is true that, more recently, R. J. Hamerton-Kelly has claimed that Eph. 1: 3, where God is spoken of as blessing Christians 'in Christ', is an example of either representation (the race being identified with the ancestor) or incorporation (in the 'macroanthropos').[30] But in Allan's analysis it is reckoned as an instance of what could, at least, be explained as an instrumental usage. This seems to be true of the very next sentence (Eph. 1: 4), where the reference is to God's election of Christians *en autō(i)*, meaning, says Allan, 'that God's electing will operates through Christ' (57). It is perhaps significant that it is Ephesians, too, which, as was remarked before, contains one of the most explicit references to the reciprocal position – the indwelling of Christ in each believer's heart (3: 17). All in all, Ephesians does seem to be distinctive in these respects, even as compared with Colossians. Even Philippians, which might be expected to stand nearer to the acknowledgedly Pauline epistles than Ephesians and Colossians together, has only one clear example of an 'incorporative' usage – 3: 9, *hina heurethō en autō(i)* – apart from the perhaps crystallized formula in 1: 1, *tois hagiois en Christō(i)* (cf. 1: 14?).[31] Otherwise, its *en*-phrases are mainly with non-personal nouns, or with ambiguous verbs. Thus, a careful plotting of the occurrence of these phrases might lead to further discoveries. But, for the present purpose, the existence of at least some clearly incorporative instances is sufficient. Before going on to relate this to other phenomena pointing in the same direction, it will be well to complete this rough sketch of the use of *en* by looking rapidly at other parts of the New Testament. By far the most conspicuous examples of *en* with a name of Jesus outside the Pauline epistles occur in the Gospel and Epistles of John; and the most noteworthy features of Johannine usage, in

[29] J. A. Allan, 'The "in Christ" Formula in Ephesians', *NTS* 5.1 (Oct. 1958), 54ff. See also R. Schnackenburg, 'Christus, Geist und Gemeinde (Eph. 4: 1–16)', in *Christ and Spirit in the New Testament* as in Chapter 1, n. 19, 279ff.

[30] R. J. Hamerton-Kelly, *Pre-existence, Wisdom and the Son of Man* (Cambridge: University Press 1973), 180f.

[31] I say 'perhaps crystallized', despite my having cited Rom. 8: 1 (above, p. 55) as a clearly incorporative instance. My reason is that in Rom. 8: 1 the phrase seems to be highly significant for Paul's argument, whereas *tois hagiois en Christō(i)*, especially in a greeting formula, must rank as less obviously conscious and deliberate.

contrast to Pauline, are that it is wholly reciprocal, and that there is much about being in *God* (in contrast to the rarity of this expression in Paul). The passages are as follows:

John 14: 10: Do you not believe that I am in the Father and the Father in me? The words which I speak to you I do not speak of myself, but the Father remaining (*menōn*) in me does his deeds.

John 14: 11: Believe me, that I [am] in the Father and the Father in me; or else, believe because of the deeds themselves.

John 15: 4: As the branch cannot bear fruit of itself unless it remains (*meinē(i)*) in the vine, so neither can you unless you remain (*menete*) in me.

John 15: 5: I am the vine, you the branches. Whoever remains (*ho menōn*) in me and I in him, he bears much fruit, for without me you can do nothing.

John 15: 7: If you remain (*meinēte*) in me and my words remain (*meinē(i)*) in you, ask what you will and it shall be done for you.

John 17: 21: . . . that they may all be one, as you, Father, [are] in me and I in you, that they too may be in us, that the world may believe that you sent me.

John 17: 22b: . . . that they may be one as we [are] one:

John 17: 23: I in them and you in me, that they may be perfected into one, that the world may know that you sent me and loved them as you loved me.

(Add 14: 23b: we [that is, the Father and the Son] will come and stay with him (*monēn par' autō(i) poiēsometha*). Cf. 1 John 3: 12.)

1 John 2: 5: Whoever observes his words (*logōn*), truly in him the love of God has been perfected. This is how we know that we are in him.

1 John 2: 6: Whoever says he remains in him ought to conduct his life just as he did.

(2: 8, *ho estin alēthes en autō(i) kai en hēmin* probably means 'as is true *in his case and in ours*'.)

1 John 2: 24: As for you, what you have heard from the beginning must remain (*menetō*) in you. If what you heard from the beginning remains (*meinē(i)*) in you, then you will remain (*meneite*) in the Son and in the Father.

1 John 2: 27: . . . remain in him (or ?in it, that is, the 'chrism').

1 John 3: 6: No one who remains (*menōn*) in him sins; . . .

1 John 3: 24: And whoever observes his commands remains (*menei*) in him and he in him. And this is how we know that he remains (*menei*) in us – it is by the Spirit which he gave us.

1 John 4: 4: . . . greater is he who [is] in you than he who [is] in the world. (But perhaps 'among you'?)

1 John 4: 12: Nobody has ever seen God: if we love one another, God remains (*menei*) in us...

1 John 4: 13: This is how we know that we remain (*menomen*) in him and he in us, by the fact that he has given us some of his Spirit.

1 John 4: 15: Whoever acknowledges that Jesus is the Son of God, God remains (*menei*) in him and he in God.

16: And we know and believe the love which God has in us (*en hēmin*).

1 John 5: 20: ...and we are in the one who is true, in his Son Jesus Christ. (Note also: 5: 19: ...the whole world lies (*keitai*) in the evil one (*en tō(i) ponērō(i)*).

In these passages the following relations are represented: (a) reciprocal indwelling between the Father and the Son; (b) reciprocal indwelling between Jesus and his disciples; (c) indwelling of disciples in Jesus; (d) indwelling of disciples in both Father and Son; (e) indwelling of Jesus in disciples, as the Father is in him; (f) indwelling of God in Christians; (g) reciprocal indwelling between Christians and God. The Johannine writings very much affect the conception of 'staying' or 'remaining' (*menein* and *monē*);[32] but the simple verb 'to be' is also used or implied, in the accounts of these relations.

It is clear enough from this survey that this group of writings, unlike the Pauline group, gives prominence to that reciprocity of mutual indwelling which is most naturally applicable to the relation of two individuals with each other. It is here that the beautiful prayer, 'that we may evermore dwell in him, and he in us' (the Prayer of Humble Access in the 1662 Order of Holy Communion), finds its roots. Paul seems more often than not to conceive of Christ as more than individual: a plurality of persons can find themselves 'in' Christ, as limbs are in a body; less often is Christ conceived of as 'in' an individual Christian. It is the Spirit that more often stands in this relation to each individual. But the Johannine emphasis is different; and the complete reciprocity between Christ and the individual is in keeping with a certain tendency throughout St John's Gospel to keep the individual in the forefront of the mind. Of course, admittedly, 1 John 4: 15 actually applies the complete reciprocity to the relation between

[32] See Peter Rhea Jones, 'A Structural Analysis of I John', *Review and Expositor* 57.4 (Fall 1970), 433ff., using the 'presiding metaphor' of 'abiding' as a key to the analysis of 1 John in relation to John 15.

the individual and *God* – and one could hardly dare to assert
that God is here conceived of as individual! The same applies
to John 14: 23. Thus, complete reciprocity cannot be claimed as
in itself a sufficient or reliable sign of an individualistic manner
of thought. But it remains true that this is the prevailing cast of
mind in these writings. Throughout the Gospel (though less so
in the First Epistle, which is more conscious of community), the
primary concern is the relation of each individual to Christ: it
is sheep to Shepherd, branch to Vine, not sheep to sheep or
branch to branch. Eternal life is for anyone who is in real contact
with Christ. Eschatology is usually the eschatology of the
individual: here and now, and on his own account, he has passed
over to life or stands condemned. Thus, it is natural that in the
indwelling relationship, complete mutuality should be as emphatic in John as it is hesitant in Paul; and the implied Christology
is correspondingly more individualistic – as we shall see is the case
also for Luke–Acts – and presents a less remarkable phenomenon
in this respect than the 'corporate' Christology of Paul. It may
be added that, in John as in Paul, the Holy Spirit is spoken of
as in Christians (John 14: 17, and cf. 7: 39). Nowhere in John are
Christians 'in' the Spirit (unless it be in 1 John 2: 27 – but this
is very far from clear).[33]

Of the other New Testament documents there is less to say,
so far as '*en Christō(i)*' phrases are concerned. 1 Peter has *en
Christō(i)* three times (3: 16; 5: 10, 14). The first characterises a
manner of life (*anastrophē*), and is comparable to the use in the
Pastoral Epistles (above, p. 55) with impersonal nouns. In Ch.
5, the first occurrence may be instrumental, while the second,
though, as I think, incorporative indeed ('those [who are] in
Christ'), might possibly be a conventional repetition of a Pauline
formula (unless 1 Peter is placed very early). There are three
occurrences, in the New Testament, of *en* followed simply by the

---

[33] For further details about individualism in John, see my 'The Individualism
of the Fourth Gospel', *Nov. Test* 5.2/3 (1962), 171ff., and 'A Neglected Factor
in the Interpretation of Johannine Eschatology', in *Studies in John presented to
J. N. Sevenster* (Leiden: Brill 1970), 155ff. But note also an observation by X.
Léon-Durfour: 'the Johannine individualism does not exclude but assumes the
more "ecclesial", presentation of the common tradition' – *Resurrection and the
Message of Easter* (London: Geoffrey Chapman 1974, from the French, Editions
du Seuil 1971), 234.

name of Jesus, without 'Christ' or 'the Lord', but only one seems to qualify even for consideration as an instance of the idea of 'inclusion' or incorporation: this is Rev. 1: 9: 'I, John, your brother and partner in the affliction and sovereignty and patience *in Jesus (en Iēsou)*...'. Dr G. R. Beasley-Murray, in his commentary on the Apocalypse,[34] says that the phrase 'reminds us of Paul's favourite expression "in Christ", and has a not dissimilar meaning' – but the meaning he offers is 'fellowship with the Lord...', which is less than inclusion. Dr G. B. Caird, in his commentary,[35] follows the NEB (in effect) in translating '...the ordeal and sovereignty and endurance which are ours in Jesus', making the phrase locative indeed (or quasi-locative), but apparently relating the events or circumstances, as much as the persons, to the position in question. In any case, it is a moot point whether this can be classed as an example of what I am claiming to be characteristic of Paul's writing. The other two instances of 'in Jesus' both seem likely to refer to events or possessions rather than to persons as being in Jesus. In Acts 4: 2, the apostles' opponents are pained that they are teaching the people and proclaiming *in Jesus (en tō(i) Iēsou)* the resurrection from among the dead (*tēn anastasin tēn ek nekrōn*). It seems highly unlikely that this means either that the apostles' proclaiming was done in virtue of their incorporation in Jesus (!) or that they were proclaiming resurrection for those who were thus incorporated. More likely it means 'in the case of Jesus' (a use of *en* illustrated by 1 Cor. 9: 15, where *en emoi* clearly means 'in my case'); and the full phrase *tēn anastasin tēn ek nekrōn*, with the repeated article, may serve to reinforce the meaning that the apostles were proclaiming that in the case of Jesus, *the* (ultimate) resurrection – the resurrection expected by Pharisaic faith at the end of history – had taken place. Finally, Eph. 4: 21 contains the baffling phrase, which, very literally, may be represented by: 'But you did not learn Christ so, if indeed you heard him and in him were taught as is truth in Jesus *(en tō(i) Iēsou)*.' It is very difficult to be sure what is meant by 'in him' and 'in Jesus' here. J. A. Allan (as in n. 29 above, 57) says: 'The two phrases here mean no more than "taught as Christians" and "Christian truth".' At any rate, none of these

---

[34] *The Book of Revelation*, New Century Bible (London: Oliphants 1974).
[35] *The Revelation of St John the Divine* (London: A. and C. Black 1966).

examples of *en* with the plain, human name Jesus seems to be directly relevant to the present quest. The Epistle of Jude (verse 20) has the phrase 'praying in Holy Spirit'; but that is likely to belong in the category of several of the Pauline instances of 'in Spirit', not as inclusive but as instrumental: 'under the influence, or in the power of the Spirit'.

Beyond the New Testament, I have already cited Euseb. *H.E.* 3. 31.3 for 'in the Holy Spirit'; and the curious phrase 'outside of the Father' from saying 40 of the Gospel of Thomas (above, pp. 58, 56). One may add saying 52: '... Twenty-four prophets spoke in Israel and all of them spoke in you.' W. Bousset[36] quotes Ignatius, *Eph.* 8: 2: 'Even the things that you do physically (*kata sarka*) are spiritual: for you do everything *in Jesus Christ*'. (Note, too, Ignatius *Rom.* 3: 3 *en patri ōn.*) K. Berger[37] quotes the following: Hermas M. 4. 1. 4, 'If anyone has a believing wife *en Kuriō(i)*' (cf. 1 Cor. 7: 39); 1 Clement 59. 1, 'Love (*agapē*) in Christ'; Philo *det. pot.* 48, 'he lives the blessed life in God' (*zē(i) de tēn en Theō(i) zōēn eudaimona*); Test. Benj. x. 11 (Joseph speaks): 'You then, my children, if you go in sanctification in the commandments of the Lord, shall dwell again in hope in me (*en emoi*; but *v.l. sun emoi*), and all Israel shall be gathered together to the Lord.' And add *Epist. apost.* 19,[38] 'all the words which were spoken by the prophets were fulfilled *in me*, for I myself was *in them*'. 'In me' here seems, again, to mean 'in my case'. This is only a haphazard collection of *en*-phenomena from a variety of documents, Christian or Jewish, over a considerable span of time. Sooner or later, a systematic study of the question needs to be carried out. As it is, these random specimens serve to show simply that *en* followed by some personal or divine designation occurs, at least occasionally, outside the New Testament range.

It is profitable to study the use of other prepositions side by side with *en*, and especially *sun*, *eis*, and *dia*. But this, though important for the question of how Christians conceive of relation with Christ, is not immediately important for the theme of

---

[36] As in Chapter 1, n. 13 above; Eng. trans., 285.

[37] 'Die königlichen Messiastraditionen des Neuen Testaments', *NTS* 20.1 (Oct. 1973), 1ff.

[38] Cited by A. A. T. Ehrhardt, 'The Disciples of Emmaus', *NTS* 10.2 (Jan. 1964), 182ff. (192).

incorporation, and must be examined on some other occasion. The same applies to the large and important question of the meaning of 'participation', in Christ and in the Holy Spirit. Any exhaustive study of the New Testament conceptions of contact with God in the period after the resurrection would have to take careful account of the use of such words as *metechein, metochoi, koinōnein, koinōnoi, koinōnia,* and J. D. G. Dunn's *Jesus and the Spirit* (see n. 1 above) goes a long way towards this. *Koinōnia* is sometimes referred to carelessly by modern writers as though it were a concrete noun meaning '(the Christian) fellowship'. But the debate over this from the time of C. A. Anderson Scott onwards[39] ought to make it clear that it is normally an abstract noun meaning 'participation', and, as such, plays an important part in the expression of the religious experience of contact with God. But this is not the place or occasion to pursue the matter further, for the immediate task is to continue the examination of Pauline terms that may reflect a more than individual understanding of Christ.

3. THE BODY[40]

If Paul's use of *en* followed by a name for Jesus seems to point to an understanding or experience of Christ as more than individual, there are other symptoms that help to bear this out; but

[39] See C. A. A. Scott, 'What happened at Pentecost', in B. H. Streeter, ed., *The Spirit* (London: Macmillan 1919), 117ff.; also *ET* 35 (1923/4), 567. Then, W. S. Wood, *The Expositor*, Ser. 8, 21 (1921), 31ff.; then J. Y. Campbell, '*KOINONIA* and its Cognates in the New Testament', *JBL* 451.4 (1932), 352ff. (reprinted in *Three New Testament Studies* (Leiden: Brill 1965), 1ff.), and H. Seesemann, *Der Begriff koinoinia im Neuen Testament* (*ZNTW* Beiheft 14, 1933).

[40] On this subject there is a great deal of literature, even in comparatively recent times. The following is only a selection: Article *sōma* in *TWNT*; H. Schlier, *Christus und die Kirche im Epheserbrief* (Tübingen: Mohr 1930); E. Käsemann, *Leib und Leib Christi* (Tübingen: Mohr 1933); E. Mersch, *Le Corps Mystique du Christ,* 2 vols. (Paris: Desclée de Brouwer/Bruxelles: L'Édition Universelle 1936), Eng. trans., *The Whole Christ* (London: Dennis Dobson 1949); *idem., The Theology of the Mystical Body* (London: Herder 1952); A. Wikenhauser, *Die Kirche als der mystische Leib Christi nach dem Apostel Paulus* (Münster: Aschendorf [2]1940); E. Percy, *Der Leib Christi (soma Christou) in den paulinischen Homologoumena und Antilegomena,* Lunds Universitets Årsskrift. N.F. Avd. 1. Bd 38. Nr 1, 1ff. (Lund: Gleerup/Leipzig: Harrassowitz 1942); T. Soiron, *Die Kirche als Leib Christi* (Düsseldorf 1951); J. A. T. Robinson, *The Body: a Study in Pauline Theology* (London: SCM 1952); E. Best, *One Body in Christ* (London: SPCK 1955); A. Cole, *The Body of Christ* (London: Hodder and Stoughton 1964); H. Ridderbos, *Paulus: Ontwerp van zijn theologie* (Kampen: Kok 1966), Eng.

a symptom of this sort is not to be found so decisively as has sometimes been claimed in the well-known collective use of *sōma*, 'body'. Nevertheless, this is such a complex phenomenon, and so much has been written on it, that it will be well to review its occurrences. Perhaps it will be useful to state, in advance, the conclusion of this review. It is that it seems to be true that Paul's use of *sōma* is not, as has sometimes been claimed, either entirely original or other than metaphorical. It appears that we are not confronted by an unprecedented usage, nor by one that has to be taken as in some strange way literal. Moreover, it is not true, in more than a very few of its occurrences, if any, that *sōma* means a transcendent and inclusive Body of Christ himself: usually, it is a metaphor simply for the community in certain of its aspects. Yet, in spite of this, the use of *sōma* still has its importance for Christology. Even if Christ is seldom or never spoken of explicitly as having a more than individual 'body' independently of the congregation or Church, the ways and the contexts in which the metaphor is used nevertheless suggest that the aliveness of Christ, existing transcendentally beyond death, is recognized as the prior necessity for the community's corporate existence, and as its source and origin. Even if he is himself not called 'the body', Christ, as a living, transcendent, inclusive, more-than-individual Person, is antecedent to the Church.

There was a time when I would have given more weight, for Christological purposes, to Paul's use of *sōma*. I would have said that his allusions to 'the body of Christ' did indeed mean that Christ himself *was* this inclusive body: not that Christ awaited the making of his body until a sufficient number of Christians had grown together to compose it, but that, antecedently, the risen Christ *was* the body, already complete; and that it was by union with this body and by incorporation in it that Christians became Christians. If Cecil Spring-Rice's verses, 'I vow to thee, my country...' contained the sentiment:

And soul by soul and silently her shining bounds increase,

that, I would have said, was far from a Pauline sentiment. For

trans., *Paul: an Outline of His Theology* (Grand Rapids: Eerdmans 1975), Ch. IX – an important study which reached me too late for consideration in this book; R. H. Gundry, '*Sōma*' *in Biblical Theology with Emphasis on Pauline Anthropology* (Cambridge: University Press 1976).

Paul, the shining bounds of the city of God are already marked out and are in no need of increase. The city will not be the larger for my entering it; it is only that I shall not be its citizen unless I enter. It is I who shall be the poorer, not that city. I depend upon the body of Christ: the body of Christ does not depend on me or my fellow Christians.

I still believe this to be essentially true. But I now doubt whether the *sōma* language, in itself, lends much support to it, if any. Perhaps the only Pauline passage which, in so many words, actually speaks of Christ as himself even like a body is 1 Cor. 12: 12: 'For just as the body [i.e. the human body in his analogy] is one and has many limbs, and all the limbs of the body, many as they are, are a single body, *so also is Christ (houtōs kai ho Christos).*' Paul does not say so also is 'the Church' or even 'the body of Christ' but simply' '(the) Christ'. The next verse, verse 13, probably continues in the same vein, though it is possible to translate it otherwise: 'For indeed in one Spirit we were all baptized into one body *(eis hen sōma).* . .' It is possible, indeed, to take this to mean that Christians were baptized *into being a single body*, and to translate it 'so as to become one body'; but, equally, it could mean 'into' (i.e. into membership in) 'one' (already existing) 'body'; and, since verse 12 has just, apparently, declared Christ to be like a body, there is certainly a case to be made for this latter interpretation, identifying as Christ himself the body into membership in which Christians are baptized.[41] One may reasonably compare Rom. 6: 3, *ebaptisthēmen eis Christon* (unless that means 'into Christ's possession'). Thus, in 1 Cor. 12: 12f., two successive sentences appear to lend some weight to the view that Paul conceived of Christ himself as a corporate entity, independently of his Church. On the other hand, the sentence later in the same chapter (verse 27), which is often triumphantly rendered 'You are the body of Christ. . .' (as though it identified the Church with what, again, might be taken to be an already

---

[41] For discussion of the exegesis see, besides the commentaries, L. Cerfaux, *La Théologie de l'Église suivant Saint Paul* (Paris: du Cerf 1947), Eng. trans., *The Church in the Theology of St Paul* (New York: Herder/Edinburgh and London: Nelson 1959), 270ff.; G. R. Beasley-Murray, *Baptism in the New Testament* (London: Macmillan 1962), 170f.; R. Schnackenburg, *Das Heilsgeschehen bei der Taufe nach dem Apostel Paulus* (München 1950), Eng. trans., *Baptism in the Thought of St Paul* (Oxford: Blackwell 1964), 26f.

existing entity, 'Christ's Body'), need only mean 'You are a body which belongs to Christ'. There is no definite article before *sōma*: so far as the words go, it is simply 'a body'; and, since the genitive is, in any case, presumably a possessive genitive ('belonging to Christ'), the body in question may as easily be the congregation he owns, as the body which is himself.[42]

Even 1 Cor. 12, then, lends only wavering support to a full doctrine of a self-existent body of Christ, such that the congregation owes its existence to incorporation in it. And it is noteworthy that the nearest parallel to the general theme of 1 Cor. 12 is in Rom. 12, and that here the words (verses 4f.) are: 'For just as in one body we have many limbs, and all the limbs have not the same function, so we, many as we are, are *one body in Christ*, and individually limbs of one another.' The meaning of 'we are one body in Christ' appears to be that Christians owe their organic unity with one another to the fact that they are 'in Christ' – incorporated in him. Thus, it is not, strictly speaking, that Christ is here identified with the body. Rather, Paul is saying that, if the congregation finds itself to be an organic unity like a well coordinated living body, this is because of its connexion with Christ. Comparable to the phrase 'we are one body in Christ' is Gal. 3: 28, *heis este en Christō(i) Iēsou*, which seems to mean, 'You constitute a single person [*heis*, masculine] by virtue of your incorporation in Christ Jesus.' (Or does it mean, rather, that each individual Christian is only *one sort of person*: he is not a man or a woman, a slave or a free man; all that he is is a person in Christ?) Similarly, in Eph. 3: 6, the Gentiles are said to be *sunsōma* ('united in a single body (with Jewish Christians)') and fellow participants of the promise *en Christō(i) Iēsou*.

In the same vein, perhaps, in 1 Cor. 10: 17, the congregation is a single body because its members participate jointly in the body and blood of Christ; and the body and blood of Christ seem, in this instance, to mean his self-giving on the cross rather than a transcendent 'body'. That is to say, Christians are, ideally at least, united with each other at the Eucharist in a single, harmonious body by virtue of their all jointly receiving, and responding to, what Christ gives because of his having given his body and blood

[42] See Cerfaux, as in n. 41, 277.

on the cross: it is a matter of their being bound together because they are all alike 'identified' with Christ's self-giving. (Possibly Rom. 7: 4, 'You have been put to death to law through the body (*dia tou sōmatos*) of Christ', is a comparable idea.) This theme is continued in 1 Cor. 11, the next chapter. When, in 1 Cor. 11: 27, 29, Paul calls Christians who 'fail to discern the body' guilty regarding the body and blood of the Lord, he does so in the context of the words of institution which he has quoted in verse 24: 'this is my body which is for you' (*touto mou estin to sōma to huper humōn*). It is true that it is not improbable that Paul is here deliberately using *sōma* with a *double entendre*, to mean not only the body of Jesus surrendered on the cross and participated in at the Eucharist, but also the 'body' which is the congregation: the selfishness and greed which he is castigating in 1 Cor. 11 constitute a failure to discern both the physical body of Christ as surrendered on the cross, and the metaphorical body of Christians gathered at the Lord's supper.[43] But in both 1 Cor. 10 and 11, the body of Christ is coupled with the blood of Christ, and both together seem to mean his individual body as 'given' for Christians. It is by participating in what is thus given that Christians become a united 'body'.

Thus far, at least, the evidence for the conception of the risen Christ as himself a corporate entity is (to say the most) not very emphatic. In 1 Cor. 6, however, there seems to be one more allusion, albeit incidental and fleeting and by implication only, to Christ as 'a body'. Paul, expostulating against fornication, says (verse 15) 'your bodies are limbs of Christ'. If whole individual bodies belong to Christ as his limbs, then he must be a more than individual body. It is true that, in the very same verse, Paul asks the indignant question: 'Shall I then take the limbs of Christ and make them limbs of a harlot?', which, if we pressed the analogy, would have to imply that a harlot too, had a more than individual body made up of a plurality of persons![44] But it is fair to assume that it is the former part of the verse that determines the usage,

[43] See my essay, 'The Judgment theme in the Sacraments', in W. D. Davies and D. Daube, edd., *The Background of the New Testament and its Eschatology*, in hon. C. H. Dodd (Cambridge: University Press 1956), 464ff. (473f.).

[44] The phrase in Eph. 4: 25 is not quite comparable: *esmen allēlōn melē*, need only mean 'we are (fellow-) limbs *with* one another (*in* a single body)'. See Meuzelaar, as in n. 46 below.

and that, having deliberately spoken of Christians as Christ's limbs, Paul only uses the outrageous phrase, 'a harlot's limbs', by a kind of false analogy, and simply to emphasize the scandal of intimate union of the same persons with both Christ and a harlot.

This exhausts the relevant uses of *sōma* in Romans and Corinthians. Notoriously, it is in the captivity epistles, Ephesians and Colossians, that there is further use of it, but then with conspicuous differences. The differences are, first, that the metaphor of the head is introduced, as well as the body; secondly, that it is the *ekklēsia* that is specified as Christ's body – and most expositors (though not all) take *ekklēsia* in these contexts to mean the universal Church, and not merely the local congregation, to which, in Romans and Corinthians, the analogy of the body (without the use of the word *ekklēsia*) seems to be applied;[45] and, thirdly – in Ephesians specially, and, to some extent, in Colossians – the body of Christ seems to be thought of as growing with the growth of adherents to the Christian Church. In other words, Cecil Spring-Rice's 'soul by soul and silently her shining bounds increase' does, after all, seem to be given some countenance by Ephesians and, possibly, by Colossians.

J. J. Meuzelaar, in an important monograph, maintains that it is a mistake to assume that, in these epistles, head and body are intended to belong in a single metaphor at all.[46] Rather, he says, Christ (or 'the Messiah', as he is careful to interpret this name, linking it with Israel-ideas) is spoken of as Head, not of the body but of the *ekklēsia* (122): 'Head' means simply 'beginning' or 'firstborn' of a family. The body-metaphor is independent of this. When, in 1 Cor. 12: 21, the head really is part of the body-metaphor, then it is not equated with the Messiah; where, in the captivity epistles, the head is the Messiah, then it is no part of the body-metaphor (121). He also urges (and here I am summarizing his position in my own words) that, in any case, there is no passage in these epistles which compels us to *identify* Christ with the 'body', that is the Church. That the Church *belongs* to him and is (likened to) a body is not necessarily the same

---

[45] P. Minear, *The Obedience of Faith* (London: SCM 1971), argues for a plurality of house-churches or congregations in Rome.

[46] *Der Leib des Messias: eine exegetische Studie über den Gedanken vom Leib Christi in den Paulusbriefen* (Assen: van Gorcum 1961).

as that Christ's own body is the Church, either in the sense that
his own body constitutes the Church or that the Church
constitutes his body. Even at Eph. 5: 30, Meuzelaar insists that
'we are limbs of his body' need only mean that we are connected
with *one another* (cf. 4: 25, *esmen allēlōn melē*) as limbs in a body,
and that this body *belongs to* the Messiah (143f.). This, though in
part it is cogently argued, does not immediately carry conviction
in its entirety. Is it, for instance, easy to believe that 'his body'
(Eph. 1: 23, 5: 30 (just cited), Col. 1: 24) only means 'the body
(of persons) that *belongs to* him'? It seems far more natural that
the phrase should mean that Christ's own 'body' is the Church.
At any rate, the passages relevant to our quest must now be
examined.

Col. 1: 18: ...he is the head of the body, the Church.

(Col. 1: 22 is expressly a reference to Christ's physical
body.)

Col. 1: 24: This is the enigmatic verse in which Paul in some
way relates his own afflictions to those of Christ. Without its being
necessary to enter into the controversies over the meaning of
this,[47] we note, for the present purpose, that it is 'on behalf of
his (i.e. Christ's) body, which is the *ekklēsia*', that the apostle
suffers.

(Col. 2: 11, once again, if it refers to Christ at all, is a reference
to his physical body.)

(Col. 2: 17, *to de sōma tou Christou*, probably means 'but the
substance, in contrast to the mere *shadow*, belongs to Christ'.)

Col. 2: 19: here is an elaborate metaphor from the growth of
a body. At first sight it certainly looks as though the head was
very much part of the metaphor. But Meuzelaar (122) points out
that here, as in Eph. 4: 16, the words 'from *whom*' (*ex hou*) are
used, not 'from *which*' (*ex hēs*), as one might expect if the feminine
noun, *kephalē*, 'head', was intended to be taken into the body
metaphor. The verse, attacking some false teacher, describes him
as 'not holding on to the head, from whom the whole body,
supplied and welded together by its joints (?) and ligaments,
grows (with) God's growth'. On Meuzelaar's showing, this means
that the false teacher is alienated from the Messiah, the one who

---

[47] See the review of the discussion by R. Yates, 'A Note on Colossians 1: 24', *EvQ*
42.2 (April–June 1970), 88ff.

is at the head of things; and that it is only from the Messiah, as leader and chief authority, that the corporate life of the community can hope to be maintained.

Col. 3: 15: this is a passing reference to the body-metaphor, and seems not necessarily to be more than an allusion to the communal life: 'let the peace of Christ be arbiter in your hearts; to this peace you were called *in one body*', which seems most naturally to mean 'inasmuch as you belong to a single organism'. It could, of course, be that that organism is *Christ's* Body; but equally it could mean simply that 'corporation' which is the local community or the universal Church. The parallel phrase in Eph. 2: 16 is discussed below.

Taking the three distinctive features that enter with the captivity epistles, one may first note the use of the head, but recognize Meuzelaar's query about its relation to the body. Secondly, in all these references in Colossians, although it seems more natural to interpret the *ekklēsia* not as merely the local community in the Lycus Valley but as the whole Church for which the Apostle suffers, yet this is not inevitable: and undeniably Col. 4: 15f. uses *ekklēsia* in the local sense. The third point – that the body is not (so to speak) already complete but is growing – is explicit in Col. 2: 19, but then it is not necessarily more than the human community that is meant.

In Ephesians, the passages are as follows:

Eph. 1: 23. This is a much-debated verse.[48] A well-supported exegesis makes it mean that Christ's (only) body is the *ekklēsia*, and it is (only) as it grows that Christ will be completed – 'the church which is his body, and which constitutes the completion ('fulness', *plērōma*) of Christ who is being progressively completed' (whatever the adverbial phrase 'all in all', *ta panta en pasin*, may mean). Others, taking the participle *plēroumenou* not as passive but as middle with an active sense, take it to refer to Christ as himself filling the whole of things (cf. Jer. 23: 24, of God, and Eph. 4: 10, of Christ), whatever exegesis may make of 'the church which is...the fulness...'. Others again, though a very small

---

[48] For a careful review, see R. Yates, 'A Re-examination of Ephesians 1²³', *ET* 83.5 (Feb. 1972), 146ff. See, further, G. Howard, 'The Head/Body Metaphors of Ephesians', *NTS* 20.3 (April 1974), 350ff. (taking *plēroumenou* as strictly middle: he fills all things in order to conform them to his sovereign will (356)).

minority, take *plērōma,* 'fulness', as in apposition not to the
Church, but to 'head' in verse 22, and construe the whole sentence to mean: '(God)...appointed (Christ) as supreme head to
the church, which is his body, *and as* the completeness of the One
(i.e. God) who fills the whole of things'. On this showing, both
'head' and 'completeness' or 'fulness' are descriptions of Christ
in God's design, and there is no question of the ecclesia being
that in which his completeness becomes realized. However, for
the present inquiry, the immediate point is that the Church is
expressly called Christ's body, and – at least possibly – is described as bringing completeness or fulfilment to Christ.

Eph. 2: 15f.: (Christ has terminated the enmity between Jew
and Gentile, abolishing what we may, for short, call 'legalism'),
'that he might create the two (Jew and Gentile) in him(self?) as
a single new man (or new humanity?), (thus) making peace, and
might reconcile both of them *in a single body (en heni sōmati)* to
God through the cross...', Does 'in a single body' refer to the
one, coherent organism which the two opposed groups become
as a result of Christ's reconciling work, so that a more idiomatic
translation might be 'that...he might reconcile them *as* a single
body...'? Or does it, rather, mean that it is because of the
incorporation of both alike in an already existing single body –
namely, Christ – that they are united? There is nothing to compel
one to the latter interpretation, and one might even argue that,
had this sense been intended, one would have expected 'in *his*
body', *en tō(i) sōmati autou,* rather than 'in *one* body'; and besides,
for what it is worth, the comparable phrase in Ignatius, *Smyrn.*
1: 2, comes down clearly on the side of the former interpretation:
'to his dedicated and faithful ones...whether among Jews or
among Gentiles, in one body of his church' (*en heni sōmati tēs
ekklēsias autou,* meaning presumably 'constituting (the) one body
which is his Church'). The parallel phrase in Col. 3: 15 has
already been considered in its own context, and seen to be most
naturally interpretable in a similar way.

3: 6: the Gentiles are fellow-heirs and members of the same
body (*sunsōma*) and joint participants (with the Jewish Christians)
in the promise *en Christō(i) Iēsou.* It has already been observed
that *sunsōma...en Christō(i) Iēsou* at least seems to present a
parallel to Rom. 12: 4 ('one body in Christ') and Gal. 3: 28 ('one

(person) in Christ Jesus'). It is possible, of course, that in Ephesians 3: 6 the *en Christō(i) Iēsou* is to be construed with 'the
promise' rather than with 'a joint body'. A decision on this will
be determined by the usage of the *en*-phrases in Ephesians
generally, and J. A. Allan's study (n. 29 above) is relevant to this
inquiry. But at least it is clear that there is no need to refer the
'body' to Christ himself: rather, it is the organism comprised
jointly by the Jewish and Gentile Christians.

4: 4: 'one body, and one Spirit...one Lord...' It is difficult
to be certain, but, on balance, the fact that 'one Lord' is separate
and subsequent lends weight to taking 'one body' as a description
of the Christian community, simply, rather than of a corporate
Christ, already existing independently.

4: 12–16. This is a complicated, not to say confused, passage.
It starts from the well-known conception of the ascended Christ
as the dispenser of gifts to men (the Scripture used is from Ps.
68: 18 in a special form),[49] and names these gifts as apostles,
prophets, evangelists, shepherds, and teachers, and describes
them as given with a view to equipping God's people (*hoi hagioi*)
for their ministry of (or, and for?) building up the body of
Christ, until they all – writer and readers alike – reach the full
stature of Christ's completeness (*metron hēlikias tou plērōmatos tou
Christou*). It appears to be this same object that is expressed
again at the end of the paragraph, in the words (verses 15f.):
'(that)...we may grow in all respects into (or, up to?) him who is
the Head, Christ, from whom the whole body, fitted and bonded
together through every joint in its equipment, grows by the
activity of each part in its due measure, thus building itself up
(*eis oikodomēn heautou*) in love'. This is a free rendering, and begs
many exegetical questions. But, for the purposes of the present
inquiry, it seems reasonably clear, details apart, that what is meant
is that the various Christian services bestowed by the risen and
ascended Christ – those of apostles, prophets, and the rest – are
intended to complete the process of creating a Christian
community, which is spoken of as Christ's body and which is to
grow progressively, by virtue of the vitality derived from Christ,

---

[49] For a discussion of the problems, see J. Dupont, 'Ascension du Christ et don
de l'Esprit d'après Actes 2: 33', in *Christ and Spirit in the New Testament*, as in
Chapter 1, n. 19, 219ff. (224ff.).

until it reaches that completeness, that full stature or height, which belongs to (or, is intended by?) Christ. It is impossible to be certain whether the idea here is that Christ himself has no 'corporate' expression except what is constituted by his Church, or whether it is that Christ already has a more than individual 'body', and that its human members need only to be attached to what is already existent, thus completing Christ's *design*, rather than (if one may be allowed to speak so) completing the corporate Christ himself. Since the actual phrase 'the *building (oikodomē)* of the body of Christ' is used, it seems more likely that what is intended is the actual bringing into existence, and ultimately the completion, of a corporate entity which does not previously exist at all.

Finally, in Ch. 5, the analogy of the relation between husband and wife is applied to that between Christ and the Church. Verse 23: 'as a man (or, a husband – *anēr?*) is head of the woman (or, of his wife?), so also is Christ head of the *ekklēsia* – himself the saviour of the body'. J. P. Sampley[50] thinks that this last, cryptic phrase is meant to distinguish the relation between Christ and the Church from that between husband and wife; on the other hand, he had already called attention to Tobit 6: 18f. (RSV 6: 17), where Raphael gives Tobias hope that he, as husband, will save Sarah if he marries her, and one wonders whether Sampley is right in rejecting this as a relevant parallel here. At any rate, the Church seems here to be spoken of (metaphorically) as Christ's 'body', though one might have expected 'wife' in this context. Later in the same passage (verse 30), 'we are limbs of his body', is reminiscent of 1 Cor. 6: 15, 'your bodies are limbs of Christ'. But it is noteworthy that in Eph. 5: 23, 30, 'body' seems definitely to refer to the human organization as saved by Christ or as belonging to him. It does not appear that to Christ himself a 'body' is attributed. Even if one presses the daring analogy suggested by verses 31f., the result is that Christ becomes *united with* the Church, as husband and wife become 'one flesh', rather than that Christians are incorporated in an already existing body. The same is true of the anticipation of the Ephesians passage in 2 Cor. 11: 2, where Paul says he joined his

---

[50] J. P. Sampley, '*And the Two Shall Become One Flesh*': a *Study of Traditions in Ephesians 5: 21–33* (Cambridge: University Press 1971), 125, 59f.

converts to one man, so as to present them to Christ as a pure virgin (*hērmosamēn gar humas heni andri parthenon hagnēn parastēsai tō(i) Christō(i)*).

In view of all this, it is intelligible when such writers as Käsemann[51] and Güttgemanns[52] incline to the view that, with the exception of Phil. 3: 21, which has yet to be considered, the New Testament attributes to Christ no body except the individual, physical body in which he died, and that 'body' which is the community of Christians; and that it is by union with that crucified body of Christ that Christians become the organized body they may become (cf. Col. 1: 22). It is, in that case, not that Christians are incorporated into an already existing more than individual Christ, but that they are identified with his self-surrender in death.

Phil. 3: 21 does, unequivocally, speak of a body belonging to Christ after his death: his 'glorious body'; and Güttgemanns believes that it comes from some other hand than Paul's. It seems to me that there is not sufficient evidence for denying it to Paul;[53] and even if there were, it would still represent an early Christian viewpoint that would need to be reckoned with in the present inquiry, when the question is 'What light does early Christian experience and understanding throw on the nature of Christ?' But it also seems to me necessary to concede that, in any case, this passage does not offer any support to the view that Paul (or any other early Christian writer) attributed to Christ an inclusive, 'corporate', more-than-individual existence independently of that 'body' which is constituted by his people, collectively; for Phil. 3: 21 seems to be expressing the Christian hope that each believer individually will, beyond death, be enabled to live in a

---

[51] See, most recently, *An die Römer*, as in n. 12, 321ff. Yet, earlier, Käsemann had written: '...er nach dem Apostel die Grenzen der Personalität in unserem Verständnis sprengt und mit seinem Leibe und in seinen Gliedern die Welt erfüllt', in *Zur Bedeutung des Todes Jesu: exegetische Beiträge* (H. Conzelmann, E. Flessemann von Leer, E. Haenchen, E. Käsemann, E. Lohse: Gütersloh 1967), 31. For an important treatment between these two dates, see Käsemann's 'The Theological Problem Presented by the Motif of the Body of Christ', in *Perspectives on Paul* (London: SCM 1971, Eng. trans. of *Paulinische Perspektiven* (Tübingen: Mohr 1969)), 102ff.

[52] E. Güttgemanns, *Der Leidende Apostel und sein Herr* (Göttingen: Vandenhoeck und Ruprecht 1966), 262, 280.

[53] Gundry (as in n. 40, 177–82) meets the case against Pauline authorship, point by point.

spiritual dimension and with a spiritual and glorious 'body' such as Paul refers to in 1 Cor. 15, and that this will be by virtue of assimilation to the glorious and spiritual body in which Jesus now exists. As such, therefore, this statement need not take us further than those more individualistic conceptions of Jesus' existence beyond death which are to be found in Luke and Acts and John (see pp. 97ff. below). Although it is not in any way incompatible with a corporate conception of Christ's mode of existence, it does not demand it; it is simply a saying of the same type as Rom. 6: 5, 8: 29, and Phil. 3 itself at verse 10, which speak of the assimilation or conformation of the believer with Christ's glorious self, by virtue of union with him.

We are thrown back, therefore, on those passages in which *sōma* is indisputably used as a metaphor for a more-than-individual organization (if not organism); and the only question is whether this invariably means simply a 'corporation' of believers, organically related to each other like limbs of a single body, or whether, at least sometimes, it means Christ himself, as a more than individual entity, independently of Christians. On balance, it seems to me that 1 Cor. 12: 12f. and 1 Cor. 6: 15 are difficult to interpret otherwise than as symptoms of a mode of thought which viewed Christ himself as an inclusive Person, a Body, to be joined to which was to become part of him. But these are, perhaps, the only such passages. All the rest appear to be speaking not of Christ but of a congregation of Christians (or, in some cases, the whole Church universal) as a corporate entity. Even Eph. 5: 30 ('we are limbs of his body'), which is so strikingly like 1 Cor. 6: 15 ('your bodies are limbs of Christ') that it might have to be interpreted in the same sense, does not necessarily mean this; for it might mean 'we are limbs of that (human) corporation that belongs to him'. Certainly, 'the ecclesia which is his body' (Eph. 1: 23, Col. 1: 24) can be interpreted to mean that Christ's only 'corporate' existence is the body constituted by his People. Thus, it is difficult to deny (unless it be in one or two exceptional cases) the contention, now powerfully supported by R. H. Gundry (n. 40 above), that *sōma*, in the relevant contexts, is a metaphor simply for the corporation of Christians.

However, it at least remains true that it is only by virtue of 'inclusion in Christ' (if this is, as I have argued, the right inter-

pretation of certain of the *en*-phrases) that the corporate existence is achieved: if a 'body' of Christians is a harmoniously
coordinated organism, this is only by virtue of belonging to
Christ. If so, the doctrine often attached to the *sōma* image is
justified, but not by the *sōma*-language in itself.[54]

Ernst Percy, in his important monograph (as in n. 40), carefully
links the *en Christō(i)* formulae with the *sōma* formulae. Summing
up, he says (p. 44, my paraphrase):

If, then, the Pauline conception that believers are in Christ means their
incorporation in Christ as their representative, who, for love of them
died for their sake on the cross and then, for their salvation, was raised
again by God, and if this incorporation is thought of as something
utterly real which relates them to that body that died on the cross, then
the Pauline description of the community as the body of Christ can, in
any case, scarcely express anything other, in the last analysis, than this
incorporation in Christ himself as the one who was crucified and raised.
The community as *sōma Christou*, accordingly, coincides ultimately with
Christ himself: only so may the words *houtōs kai ho Christos* (1 Cor. 12:
12) be rightly understood; and therefore belonging to this body coincides
with being in Christ. Therefore, this body of Christ which is identical
with the community is essentially none other than that which died on
the cross and rose again on the third day. That this is the correct
interpretation of the Pauline *sōma Christou* idea is attested both by
1 Cor. 10: 16f. (where the unity of the believers is based upon the participation in the body of Christ which was surrendered for them) and
by Eph. 2: 16 ('to reconcile both in one body to God through the
cross').

We have seen reason to entertain reservations about some of
the exegesis alluded to by Percy. Moreover, he is prepared to
reconcile Ephesians and Colossians with Romans and Corinthians more readily than some other scholars, by insisting that
the two groups are merely emphasizing different aspects of the
eschatology of one and the same experience. In this respect they
would only represent the two sides, respectively, of the familiar
paradox: 'Become what you are!' Christians *are*, already, incor-

---

[54] For a stringent criticism of such claims, see E. A. Judge, 'Demythologizing the
Church: What is the meaning of "the Body of Christ"?', *Interchange* 11 (IVF
Graduates Fellowship of Australia, Sydney 1972), 155ff. But he is not correct
in assuming that all the NEB translators alike believed that *sōma* was more than
a metaphor.

porated in Christ; yet they need to grow up into being, or becoming, his body. Whether we can agree with Percy here or not, his relating of the 'in Christ' formula to the 'body' idea seems to be sound.[55]

Turning to the background of the 'body' language, it needs to be recognized that the Pauline uses of *sōma* are not as original as has sometimes been claimed. It may be true that no secure instance earlier than the New Testament has so far been found of a society of persons being actually called, outright, 'a body', in the way in which we now speak quite naturally of 'a governing body' or 'the body politic'. Appeal has been made to an edict of Augustus discovered at Cyrene,[56] containing the words *toutous* (i.e. the inhabitants of Cyrenaica) *leitourgein ouden elason* (sic) *em* (sic) *merei tō(i) tōn Hellēnōn sōmati*, which looks like '. . . the body of the Greeks' (with 'the body' in the dative); but it has been proposed that *sōmati* should be construed separately from *tō(i)* (which then goes with *merei*), and rendered adverbially as 'in person'; so, whether this is plausible or not, it at least casts doubt on the passage as a secure instance of this use of *sōma* as 'a corporation'.

But if the application of *soma*, as a metaphor, to a collection of persons is not certainly instanced before the New Testament, it is easy to illustrate the application to social harmony of at least the analogy of the body's harmony. There is the celebrated allegory of Menenius Agrippa, defending the lazy patrician stomach among the busy plebeian limbs, recounted in Livy ii. 32, and reproduced in lively dialogue in Shakespeare's *Coriolanus*, I. i. 101–69, where the belly addresses the limbs as 'my

[55] Käsemann, however, 'Motif' (as in n. 51), 106, writes: 'It . . . seems to me idle to consider whether the notion of existence "in Christ" precedes the idea of the body of Christ. The two belong together in that they mutually interpret one another . . .' A contrary view (alluded to by Käsemann in a footnote) is in E. Brandenburger, *Fleisch und Geist* (Neukirchener Verlag 1968), 49.

[56] The data are discussed by L. Cerfaux, as in n. 41, 270ff. Following F. De Visscher, *Les Edits d'Auguste découvertes à Cyrène* (Louvain: 1940), against T. W. Manson, 'A parallel to a New Testament use of *sōma*', *JTS* 37 (1935), 385, Cerfaux disallows the parallel. See also a reply to Manson by Adolf Wilhelm in *Deutsche Literaturzeitung* 65 (1944), 31; and *TWNT* vii, 1042, n. 262; and E. Schweizer, *The Church as the Body of Christ* (Richmond, Va: John Knox Press 1964). Visscher, following a communication from P. Mazon, rendered the whole phrase in question: 'I command that they shall be no less bound, in their turn, to the *personal* liturgies of the Hellenes' (Cerfaux, *op. cit.* 273f.).

incorporate friends' (i. 136).[57] But we come even nearer to New Testament language in Seneca (4 B.C. – A.D 65).[58] In *de clem.* i.5.1 he addresses Nero in the words: 'You are the soul of the republic and it is your body' (*tu animus reipublicae es, illa corpus tuum*); in ii.2.1, Nero is the head, on whom the good health of the body, the Empire, depends; in *Ep.* xcii. 30, he says:

Why should not one think that something divine exists in it (?), which is part of god? The whole of this which contains us is a unity and is god; and we are partners and limbs of it (*quid est autem cur non existimes in eo divini aliquid existere, qui dei pars est? Totum hoc, quo continemur, et unum est et deus; et socii sumus eius et membra*);

and, in *Ep.* xcv. 52 he says: 'We are limbs of a great body' (*membra sumus corporis magni*). All this is in keeping with the Stoic idea of the cosmos as an organized body.[59]

Again, Plutarch (1. 360C = *Philopoimen* viii. 2)[60] says, referring to the aspirations of Aratus and the Achaean League, *hen sōma kai mian dunamin kataskeuasai dienoounto tēn Peloponnēson* ('they intended to make the Peloponnese into a single body and a single

[57] R. I. Hicks, 'The Body Political and the Body Ecclesiastical', *JBR* 31 (1963), 29ff. traces the idea behind the Menenius Agrippa story back to Aesop (if not earlier still). She points out that it is told not only by Livy but also by Plutarch, *Coriolanus* 6, Dionysius Halic., *Rom. Ant.* vi. 83–6, Cassius Dio, *Rom. Hist.* iv. 16, and Florus, *Epitome of Rom. Hist.* 1. 17.23. A. Ehrhardt, 'Das Corpus Christi und die Korporationen in spätrömischen Recht', *Zeitschr. der Savigny-Stiftung für Rechtsgeschichte* 70.2 (1953), 299f. and 71.2 (1954), 25ff., relating the uses of the 'Body' analogy in the period between the New Testament and Tertullian to the pressures on the Church and the need for legal definition of it, also deals in passing (70.2, p. 306) with the origins of Menenius Agrippa's ideas. For further reflexions on the subject, and for additional examples, see Dr Ehrhardt's *Politische Metaphysik von Solon bis Augustin* (Tübingen: Mohr 1959), at the points listed in the 'Literatur' idex, iii. 67, under the article quoted above. In i. 149 he quotes a striking oracle of Serapis in which the god speaks as the cosmic body; but this is from Macrobius (*Sat.* 1. 20, 17), and is thus not necessarily early enough to have influenced Paul.

[58] These passages are adduced (some or all) by W. L. Knox, 'Parallels to the NT use of *sōma*', *JTS* 39 (1938), 243f.; J. J. Meuzelaar, as in n. 46; and Wickenhauser *apud* J. Dupont, *Gnosis* (Louvain: Nauwelaerts/Paris: Gabalda 1949), 435.

[59] Sextus Empiricus, *adv. math.* 9.78, *apud* v. Arnim *Stoic. Vet. Frr.* ii. 103 p. 302, cited by W. L. Knox, as in n. 58, says that Chrysippus distinguished between *sōmata* united by a single *hexis,* and a *sōma* such as the cosmos, which was united not merely by *hexis* but by God: he denied that a body of men, such as an army, was a body of such a kind that if one member suffered all members suffered with it.

[60] Adduced by G. D. Kilpatrick, 'A Parallel to the New Testament use of *SŌMA*', *JTS* n.s. 13 (1962), 117.

force') – this, on the analogy (says § 1 of the same chapter) of the way in which, in running water, a few particles that stick firm are soon joined by others to form a fixed and solid mass. Similarly, Philo,[61] *de spec. leg.* iii. 131, says that the High Priest is the kinsman of the whole nation, who settles disputes and offers sacrifice for it, *hina pasa hēlikia kai panta merē tou ethnous hōs henos sōmatos eis mian kai tēn autēn harmozētai koinōnian* ('that every age(-group) and all the parts of the nation may be welded into one and the same fellowship as though it were a single body') (cf. *de virtut.* (*de human.*) 103). Again, Josephus, *B.J.* v. 279, says of the warring parties in Jerusalem, that 'consigning their hatred and private quarrels to oblivion', they 'become one body' (*hen sōma ginontai*).[62] Even from rabbinic writings a striking parallel is quoted to Paul's theme of the concern of members of the same body for each other in 1 Cor. 12. In *Mekilta de Rabbi Ishmael*, Ex. xix. 6, we read:

What is the nature of the lamb? If it is hurt in one limb, all its limbs feel pain. So also are the people of Israel. One of them commits a sin and all of them suffer from the punishment. But the nations of the world are not so. One of them may be killed and yet the others may rejoice at his downfall.[63]

I am inclined, therefore, to think that it is a mistake to imagine that the experience of Christ by Paul actually created the body-metaphor.[64] The parallels from Seneca and Philo, even if not from elsewhere, are so near to the Pauline use of the analogy as to invalidate any such claim.[65]

Further, as we have seen, it has to be conceded that the meaning of the figure within the Pauline or near-Pauline writings varies considerably. It may mean a local group of Christians as constituting a body by virtue of their being 'in Christ'; it may

[61] Adduced by W. L. Knox as in n. 58. Cf. *idem. St Paul and the Church of the Gentiles* (Cambridge: University Press 1939), 161.

[62] Adduced by R. H. Gundry (as in n. 40), 63.

[63] J. Z. Lauterbach, ed. (Philadelphia: the Jewish Publication Society of America, 1933), ii. 205f., alluded to by W. L. Knox as in n. 58. Cf. Sextus Empiricus, in n. 59.

[64] And E. A. Judge, as in n. 54, strongly confirms this.

[65] Very explicit is the Orphic verse from Porphyry cited by A. Ehrhardt, as in n. 57, 70.2, 307: *panta gar en Zēnos megalō(i) tade sōmati keitai*, but Porphyry himself is much later than the New Testament. Cf. n. 57 above. On Paul's position in the development of the analogy, see Ehrhardt, *Politische Metaphysik* (as in n. 57 above), ii. 11.

(possibly) mean Christ as himself the body in which they are limbs; or it may mean the Church as constituting Christ's body, with Christ as its head (or as Meuzelaar would have it, with the Messiah as its Leader).

What is distinctive about the Christian conception is, I think, not only that there is, in the Christian application of the analogy, no spiritual élite,[66] but also that the living Christ, and not just his example or his memory, is the antecedent presupposition of whatever organic unity a Christian congregation, or, ultimately, the Church throughout the world, may have. Accordingly, even at times when a Christian writer can think of the body's being progressively built up by the adherence of new members – which, logically, might imply that Christ was without a 'body' till believers adhered – the aliveness and the transcendent being of Christ still remains the necessary antecedent datum. In view of this, it seems not unfair to say, still, that a corporate, inclusive person is implied in the religious experiences reflected in the Pauline epistles.

Besides, it remains a fact that, putting the evidence at its minimum, there are at least one or two passages in the earlier epistles where it is not only that Christians form a body, but that the body is Christ's body, or *is* Christ. And it is clearly true that it is only by identification with Christ, crucified and raised – only by identification, that is, with a now living Christ – that Christians become a body; and that this identification is spoken of as 'inclusion' or incorporation. And even if the implication of certain passages in Eph. is that it would not have come amiss to that writer to speak of 'the body of Christians' (that is, the body consisting of Christians), the fact remains that we have to wait for Eusebius (*H.E.* 10. 5. 10–12) before we actually meet that phrase: *to sōma tōn Christianōn*.

In sum, parts at least of the Pauline epistles reflect an experience of Christ as a 'corporate Person', to be joined to whom is to become a part of an organic whole. It is possible to argue that such an idea is already commonplace, when a pantheist like Seneca applies it to the cosmos,[67] or, in a laudatory mood, speaks

---

[66] Ehrhardt, *Politische Metaphysik* (as in n. 57 above), ii. 76.

[67] Cf. Theophrastus, *metaph.* 16 *fin.*, adduced by Ehrhardt, *Politische Metaphysik* (as in n. 57 above), i. 217, n. 1.

of an Emperor as the head of the body politic. But it becomes a new and extraordinary phenomenon when it is not a pantheist but a theist who is speaking, and when he speaks of a known individual of recent history as an 'inclusive' or 'corporate Person'. And, in this form, it represents a religious experience which is new, and which drives us to ask, Who is this; who can be understood in much the same terms as a theist understands God himself – as personal, indeed, but more than individual? And precisely what was it in the religious experience of an early Christian that led to such a conception? Was it the Eucharist? But *eating* the body is not *being* the body. Was it rabbinic conceptions of representative figures? But representation is not inclusion; and, in any case, figures described as representative in Jewish thought were never individuals of recent times, like Jesus.[68] Even A. J. M. Wedderburn's parallel of the *en Christō(i)* with the *en Abraam* of Gal. 3: 8[69] does not take us all the way to the Pauline usage. It has sometimes been suggested that the origin of the Pauline understanding of the relation between Christ and Christians lies in such sayings as 'anything you did for one of my brothers here, however humble, you did for me' (Matt. 25: 40), and the Damascus road challenge: 'why do you persecute me?' (Acts 9: 4; cf. 22: 8; 26: 14). They are certainly entirely congruous with the Pauline conception, but could they have actually generated it? Thus, even if J. A. T. Robinson over-played his hand when he denied that *sōma* was a metaphor,[70] and has been

[68] See E. Schweizer, *Jesus Christus* (München: Siebenstern Verlag 1968), Eng. trans. *Jesus* (London: SCM 1971), 110ff., with literature there cited.

[69] As in n. 23 above, 86ff.

[70] *The Body: a Study in Pauline Theology* (London: SCM 1952); cf. *In the End, God* ... (London: James Clarke and Co. 1950), 83:
> The Resurrection of the Body is a doctrine which entered Christianity through the language of St Paul. The first essential, therefore, is to understand exactly what the Apostle meant when he used the word 'body' (*soma*). It is one of the key words of his thought. Indeed, the whole of Pauline theology might well be written round it. It is from the body of sin and death that we are redeemed; it is through the body of Christ on the cross that we are saved; it is into His Body the Church that we are incorporated; it is by His body in the Eucharist that this Fellowship is built up; it is in our bodies that the life of the Spirit has to be manifest; it is to a transforming of our body to the likeness of His glorious Body that we are destined. The subtle links between the different uses of the word *soma* provide the clue to the profound unity of Pauline thought. For none of them can really be understood independently of the other.

Cf. Käsemann, 'Motif' (as in n. 51 above), 104: 'It is not meant metaphorically

criticized in this respect by E. Best and R. H. Gundry,[71] the strangeness and novelty of the conception of inclusive personality remain.

Perhaps this is the place to observe that the strange metaphor of 'putting on' Christ is also relevant to the question how Paul conceived of contact with the risen Lord, and is not far off from incorporation.[72] In Rom. 13: 14, Paul exhorts his readers to *clothe themselves with the Lord Jesus Christ (endusasthe ton kurion...)*, just as, in verse 12, he had spoken of putting on (*endusōmetha*) the weapons of light (meaning, presumably, buckling on a breastplate or the sling carrying the quiver?). In Gal. 3: 27 he says: 'as many of you as were baptized into Christ, *put on Christ*' – apparently with an allusion to the clean garments assumed by the baptized after coming out of the water. And in Col. 3: 10 and Eph. 4: 24 there is reference to *putting on* the 'new man', with express reference, in the preceding verses, to the *discarding* of the 'old man'. It would appear that – especially in communities where baptism was administered chiefly to adult converts and by immersion (or at least by standing in water) – the discarding of clothing before baptism and the reclothing afterwards was recognized as a vividly pictorial symbol of the break with the whole realm of the past, and the *inclusion* of the baptized – the veritable wrapping of him – in a new environment. And that environment was Christ himself, the ultimate Adam. Thus, the conception of Christ as the believers' 'environment' is further evidenced by the clothing metaphor.

In the Old Testament, the converse metaphor occurs, when Jud. 6: 34 (cf. 2 Chron. 24: 20) daringly speaks of the Spirit of Yahweh clothing itself with a man (as, I suppose, a person might put on a puppet-glove). Doubtless, one must not press a metaphor prosaically: but is it significant that 'clothing oneself with Christ' and 'letting the Spirit be clothed with oneself'

when Paul says that baptism and the eucharist involve us in Jesus' death, incorporate us in Christ and allow us to participate in the divine Spirit.' (But involvement and participation are scarcely metaphors in any case.)

[71] Both as in n. 40; Best, *passim*; Gundry, *passim*, and, for the Damascus Road saying, etc., 240.

[72] J. A. T. Robinson, *The Body* (as in n. 70), 76f. interprets the 'putting on of a dwelling' in 2 Cor. 5: 2 also of baptism, and makes the 'dwelling' the *collective* abode of Christians rather than each Christian's 'resurrection body' individually. R. H. Gundry, as in n. 40, strongly opposes this.

correspond exactly to the observation made earlier that, on the whole, Paul tends to speak of Christians as in Christ but the Holy Spirit as in Christians?[73] When Christ is (so to speak) 'multiplied', it is by the spirit's entering a plurality of persons and enabling them to possess something of Christ's character. But all those individuals, conversely, are 'in Christ'.

4. THE TEMPLE

One might expect that, in addition to the analogy of the body, the figure of the temple would be relevant to the conception of Christ as the *locus* of Christian experience and the sphere in which Christian life is lived. And such an expectation might be encouraged by the fact that, in one celebrated instance, the two figures come together in a single phrase: 'he spoke of the temple of his body' (John 2: 21). But in fact the temple theme, important as it is for New Testament theology generally, is used in such a way as to throw little additional light on the conception we are examining.[74] If, at least once or twice, Christ is spoken of, as we have seen, as the body in which Christians are limbs, he is never identified with the temple in which they worship, except in the passage just referred to, John 2: 21, and in Rev. 21:22, where the seer saw no temple in the 'heavenly city, 'because the Lord God the Almighty is its temple, and the Lamb'. To be sure, these two passages are not without their importance for our quest, because they virtually claim that a locality of worship, such as is the temple, is to be superseded by Christ (or God and Christ). To that extent, indeed, Christ is here, once again, as in the body-analogy, seen as the 'area' (so to speak) of Christian experience. But elsewhere, whenever the temple theme is used, Christ, if he is mentioned at all, is neither identified with the temple, nor does he dwell in it, as the Holy Spirit does: rather, he is either its cornerstone, or, by implication, its foundation.

The passages must be reviewed.

---

[73] I owe this observation to Dr D. R. de Lacey. R. Payne Smith's (= Mrs Margoliouth's) *Syriac Dictionary* (1903), *s.v. lbš*, gives the meaning 'take possession of' (as devils of men or a king of his kingdom).

[74] See the invaluable study by R. J. McKelvey, *The New Temple: The Church in the New Testament* (Oxford: University Press 1969). See also W. D. Davies, *The Gospel and the Land* (as in n. 28 above), 185ff.

The Johannine saying is presented with a characteristically Johannine elusiveness. 'Break down this temple', Jesus says, 'and in three days I will raise it (again)' (*lusate ton naon touton kai en trisin hēmerais egerō auton*). Is this meant to sound as though Jesus was saying to his opponents that he would perform a signal miracle? They had asked him for a sign. Is his reply: 'You break down the temple, and, in no time, I will rebuild it'? But, says the evangelist, 'he was speaking of the temple which was his body'. Did the evangelist mean that when Jesus said 'Destroy this temple' he intended not Herod's temple but his own body? Or did he mean that, if and when Herod's temple was destroyed, then Christ's own 'resurrection body' would replace and supersede it? In the former case, there is a metaphor in both limbs of the saying; in the latter, only in the second limb.

At any rate, whichever way we understand its meaning in detail, this saying identifies the body of Jesus with the new *naos*. Thus, we are reminded not only of John 4: 21, 23 ('neither in Jerusalem, nor on this mountain...'), but also of Rev. 21: 22. Temples are only temporary. When, in the Christian era, the ultimate begins to be inaugurated, Christ becomes the temple; and in the ultimate consummation, God and the Lamb themselves replace the temple, transcending the temporary need for a location in which to worship God, and satisfying that need absolutely. It is like a poetical comment on Stephen's speech in Acts 7: 47f.: 'Solomon built God a house. But the Most High does not dwell in anything made by human hands...'

But this is hardly a reflexion on how Christians of the New Testament period actually experienced the risen Christ: it is rather an expression of the principle of the ultimate supersession of cultus by the reality for which the cultus stands. And in none of the uses of the temple figure to describe the present experience of Christians is Jesus Christ identified with the temple or the 'house'. Here are the remaining passages.

1 Cor. 3: 16f.: 'Do you not know that you are God's temple (*naos theou*) and the Spirit of God dwells in you (*en humin oikei*)? If anyone destroys the temple of God (*ton naon tou theou*), God will destroy him; for the temple of God is holy, and you are it (?) (*hoitines este humeis*)'.

Here, the Christians at Corinth are collectively themselves God's temple, and are dwelt in by God. But there is no reference to Christ, though, in the preceding verses 10–15, he is the foundation.

In 1 Cor. 6: 19 the metaphor is again used, but, to judge by the context, applied now to the individual body of each believer, rather than to the 'body' of believers collectively. The singular, *sōma*, with the plural possessive pronoun, *humōn*, in verses 19, 20, seems only to be rather loose writing for *to sōma hekastou humōn* ('the body of each of you'):

'Why, do you not know that your body (*to sōma humōn*) is a temple of the Holy Spirit within you (*naos tou en humin hagiou pneumatos*), which you have from God, and you are not your own (*ouk este heautōn*)?'

Here, then, the temple metaphor is applied to each individual;[75] and there is no mention of Christ. It is the Holy Spirit, received from God, who is the owner and occupant of this temple.

2 Cor. 6: 16: '...for we are a temple of the living God (*naos theou esmen zōntos*), as God said: "I will dwell among them and walk among them..."'

Here the temple is, once again, the community collectively, and, with the aid of a quotation from the Old Testament relating to God's presence among his people, God is spoken of as dwelling in it. This time it is God's temple again and it is God's presence that is in it: Christ and the Spirit are not mentioned.

Ephesians offers the most elaborate temple metaphor: Eph. 2: 20–2:

...built upon the foundation of (? = consisting of, or laid by) the apostles and prophets, Christ Jesus himself being the cornerstone (?), in whom the whole (?) building bonded together grows into a holy temple in the Lord, in whom you also are built together (?with us) into a dwelling of God in Spirit' (*epoikodomēthentes epi tō(i) themeliō(i) tōn apostolōn kai prophētōn, ontos akrogōniaiou autou Christou Iēsou, en hō(i) pasa oikodomē sunarmologoumenē auxei eis naon hagion en Kuriō(i), en hō(i) kai humeis sunoikodomeisthe eis katoikētērion tou Theou en pneumati*).

[75] Note that, in 2 Cor. 5: 1, most commentators take the *oikodomē* and the *oikia* individually; though see n. 72 above.

This, as verse 19 shows, is addressed primarily to Gentile Christians, who are being assured that they, no less than the Jewish Christians, are built on the authentic foundation, so as to become a temple for God. 'The foundation *of* the apostles and prophets' might mean 'the foundation *consisting of* the apostles and prophets' (like that of the heavenly city in Rev. 21: 14, which has a twelve-fold foundation, bearing the names of the apostles), or 'the foundation *laid by*' them. There is not much difference in the eventual meaning. In either case, the foundation is the apostles' *witness to* Christ. And that is why, by implication at least, Christ may be himself called the foundation of the temple, just as Paul says, in 1 Cor. 3: 11, that Jesus Christ is the only foundation that an evangelist can lay. But, in Eph. 2: 20, Jesus is also the 'cornerstone'. (Jeremias has argued for translating *lithos akrogō-niaios* 'coping-stone';[76] but certainly in Isa. 28: 16 the stone in question belongs to the foundation, or somewhere on ground level: '*eben bōḥan pinnaṯ yiḵraṯ mûṣāḏ mûṣṣāḏ*...(LXX *akrogō-niaion*...*eis ta themelia autēs*).) Yet, equally, it is also '*in* him' (*en kuriō(i)*...*en hō(i)*) that the whole structure is built. It is also (to add to the bewilderment) *en pneumati*.[77]

All in all, whatever we make of the details of this stately cumulus of allusive phrases, it emerges that Christ is not himself identified with the temple, as he *is* (at least on occasion) identified with the 'body'. He is the foundation, he is the most vital element in the coherence of the structure, and he is also that *in* which the whole structure coheres – he is the *locus*, so to speak, of this lesser *locus*. But he is not himself it.

Oddly enough, the building *grows* (*auxei*), as though it were a living organism – as indeed it is. The most nearly parallel passage in Col. 2: 19 keeps the metaphor single, and speaks of the growing body. A passing allusion to the building comes at Col. 2: 7, *epoikodomoumenoi en autō(i)* (the *en autō(i)* being, perhaps, like Rom. 12: 4, *hen sōma*...*en autō(i)*)). In Ephesians, however, the metaphor is a mixed one: the building is one which grows

---

[76] See *TWNT* i. 792f., but also R. J. McKelvey (as in n. 74), *s.v.*

[77] It is remarkably repetitive. It has five phrases referring to location: *epi tō(i) themeliō(i)*, *en hō(i)*, *en Kuriō(i)*, *en hō(i)* again, *en pneumati*; three referring to the Gentile Christians' condition: *epoikodomēthentes*, *sunarmologoumenē*, *sunoiko-domeisthe*; three referring to the building: *pasa oikodomē*, *naon hagion*, *katoikēt-ērion tou theou*.

like a body. In Colossians, Christ is the head (whether of the body or not, must be debated with Meuzelaar); in Ephesians he is cornerstone.

In 1 Pet. 2: 4f. the same metaphor is exploited more simply. Christians, as 'living stones', are to come to Christ, the 'living stone' and be built as a spiritual house (*oikos pneumatikos*) for (the exercise of?) a holy priesthood (*eis hierateuma hagion*).[78] Here again, Christ is the cornerstone, for he is the stone which was rejected by the builders (Ps. 118), but which turned out to be the most important stone in the building.

For completeness' sake, two further passages should be noted. In 1 Tim. 3: 15, the Church[79] seems to be spoken of as the pillar and bulwark (*stulos kai hedraiōma*) of the truth. And in Heb. 3: 6 the Christian community is Christ's 'house' or 'household'.[80] This is a striking thought, especially when God has just been named (verse 4) as the Creator of all (and therefore, by implication, of this 'house'), and when (again by implication) Jesus seems to be more or less bracketed with God in this capacity. But, whatever the implications of this passage for Christology in general, it does not, any more than the passage in 1 Tim. 3: 15, contribute significantly to the particular quest on which we are at the moment engaged.

It is now possible to summarize the difference between the ways in which the two metaphors of body and building are used in the New Testament. Christians say 'We are the temple of God', and 'We are the (or a) body of (? belonging to) Christ.' They say 'Christ is the body or the head of the body, and we are his limbs.' They say 'Christ is the foundation or the cornerstone of the temple, and we constitute other stones in the temple.' They say 'God or the Holy Spirit is in his temple.' They say 'We are in Christ.' Sometimes they say 'We are in God.' They say 'The Spirit is in us.' Occasionally they say 'Christ is in us' or 'God or Christ

---

[78] For further details, see J. H. Elliott, *The Elect and the Holy* (Leiden: Brill 1966).

[79] Unless we follow Mlle Annie Jaubert's suggestion (*Clément de Rome, Épître aux Corinthiens* (Paris: du Cerf 1971), 108 n. 1) that the phrase may refer not to *ekklesia* but to Timothy.

[80] Christ, as God's Son, presiding over the house (or household), is contrasted with Moses, as a servant in the house: Num. 12: 7. But in *Memar Marqah* 4 § 1, Moses himself is like the son set over the household. See J. Macdonald, *The Theology of the Samaritans* (London: SCM 1964), 14; and G. W. Buchanan, *To the Hebrews* (Anchor Bible, New York: Doubleday 1972), 59.

is among us.' Only rarely do they say 'Christ is the temple', and never do they say 'Christ is in the temple.' Such language as Ignatius of Antioch allows himself when he says that Christ is the altar and the Father is the temple (*Mag.* 7) does not occur in the New Testament (unless it be thought that the 'altar' of Heb. 13: 10 is Christ).

It seems to me impossible to explain with any confidence why the applications of the two metaphors differ in this subtle way. It is difficult to find a convincing clue in antecedent uses. The sectarians of Qumran had already used building metaphors to describe the nature and vocation of their community.[81] The Stoics and others had already familiarized body metaphors. But possibly it was the surrendering to death of the literal, physical body of Jesus, and the ensuing experience of him as totally alive, that led to distinctive nuances in the use by Christians of the body-metaphors as compared with the building metaphor.

When we go on to look at the implicit evidence in other writers for the more than individual experience of Jesus which, in St Paul, is explicit, we shall find that one important pointer in this direction is the fact that collective, Israel-figures are applied to Christ. Many of the Old Testament testimonia that the New Testament writers apply to Christ are collective and refer to the People of God; which seems to imply that Christian experience found in Christ not only an individual revelation of God but also the very society or corporate entity to which they belonged: they belong to true Israel because they belong to Christ. There is no need here to elaborate the Pauline instances of this phenomenon. What does need to be said, however, is that Paul, more than any other New Testament writer, develops the understanding of Christ as Adam. Paul goes beyond Israel to the scope of all humanity. He finds in Christ not only true Israel but renewed mankind. Heb. 2 exploits Ps. 8 in this direction: in Jesus, it says,

---

[81] See B. Gärtner, *The Temple and the Community in Qumran and the New Testament* (Cambridge: University Press 1965). I think that some of the passages adduced by writers on the subject are of doubtful value for this purpose. But at least the following (both based on Isa. 28) are significant: 1QS 5. 5f. 'They shall lay a foundation of truth for Israel, for the community of an eternal covenant. They shall atone for all those who devote themselves, for a sanctuary (*kwdš*) in Aaron and for a house of truth.' 1QS 8. 7f. '...It is the tried wall, the precious cornerstone' (*ḥwmṭ hbḥn pnnṭ ykr*).

and in Jesus alone, we see the realization of the glorious design which was intended by God for man, but of which man has fallen so pitifully short. Jesus, by tasting death on behalf of every man, has entered upon that glory. But this is the only passage outside Paul where the theme is pursued, whereas Paul gives it prominence both in Rom. 5: 12ff., and in 1 Cor. 15: 22. There is no need here to repeat the careful investigations of others.[82] We need only take note of Paul's Adam Christology, side by side with the phenomena we have examined in detail, as further evidence of a corporate understanding of Christ.

In the light of the phenomena that have been examined, it is possible to endorse Lady Oppenheimer's observation (p. 48 above). Christians – or, at least, St Paul – do 'take for granted the possibility of certain sorts of close relationships which are not on the face of it compatible with common sense'. Paul does seem to conceive of the living Christ as more than individual, while still knowing him vividly and distinctly as fully personal. He speaks of Christian life as lived in an area which is Christ; he speaks of Christians as incorporated in him. He thinks of the Christian community as (ideally) a harmoniously coordinated living organism like a body, and, on occasion, thinks of Christ as himself the living body of which Christians are limbs. All this is very puzzling; but one thing seems to emerge clearly from it: Paul, at least, had religious experiences in which the Jesus of Nazareth who had recently been crucified – this same person, without a shadow of doubt as to his identity – was found to be more than individual. He was found to be an 'inclusive' personality. And this means, in effect, that Paul was led to conceive of Christ as any theist conceives of God: personal, indeed, but transcending the individual category. Christ is like the omnipresent deity 'in whom we live and move and have our being' – to quote the tag from Acts 17: 28 which is generally traced to Epimenides.[83]

---

[82] See Davies, *Paul and Rabbinic Judaism* (London: SPCK [3]1970); C. K. Barrett, *From First Adam to Last* (London: A. and C. Black 1962); E. Schweizer, 'Die Kirche als Leib Christi in den paulinischen Homologoumena', *ThLz* 86.3 (März 1961), coll. 161ff.; 'Die Kirche als Leib Christi in den paulinischen Antilegomena', *ThLz* 86.4 (April 1961), coll. 241ff.

[83] Details in, e.g. F. F. Bruce, *The Acts of the Apostles* (London: Tyndale Press 1951), *in loc.*

Now, it is perfectly true, as will be seen shortly, that Paul is exceptional among the New Testament writers in articulating this understanding of Jesus Christ as more than individual. On the whole, other writers (including even the Johannine writings) tend to conceive of Jesus far more individualistically. But even they, as we shall see, conceive of him as also far more than merely an exalted individual human being: even they make it clear that they know him as uniquely close to God and (so to speak) one with the Creator in a way in which no mere created human being can be. And, more than this, these writers also assume, as universally recognized and accepted among Christians, aspects of Christian experience which require and imply, even if they do not make explicit, that more than individuality which is explicit in Paul.

Putting all these phenomena together, we shall be presented with evidence of a consistently 'high' Christology from the very earliest datable periods of the Church's life, endorsing quite independently the conclusions to which, as it seems to me, the critical study of the titles of Jesus also points.

But before drawing these conclusions, an attempt must be made to portray the conceptions of Jesus in these other writers in the New Testament.

3

Conceptions of Christ in writers
other than Paul

The preceding chapters have been concerned with Paul's understanding of Christ as more than individual, and I have maintained that this is an early and important piece of evidence about
the genesis of Christology. Quite independently of questions such
as whether a title like 'Lord' came to be applied to Jesus early
or late, in Gentile surroundings only or also in Jewish contexts,
here is undeniably early evidence, in the earliest dateable documents of the New Testament, that at least one great Christian
found himself describing his experience of Christ in what one
might call 'divine' terms. For Paul, experience of contact with
Christ takes very much the same 'shape' as the 'shape' of God
in any theist's belief: he is emphatically personal, yet more than
merely individual. The pieces of evidence for this are, no doubt,
complex and various; but out of them all, the main pieces selected
for examination were the 'inclusion' language and the body
language.

But these are largely lacking from other parts of the New
Testament. Are we to deduce from this that Paul's experience
of Christ was not typical – perhaps even that it was abnormal; and
are we correspondingly to discount his experience when
estimating the ways in which Christology was generated? Even
if Paul could be proved abnormal, his experience would still need
to be accounted for. We should still find ourseves asking, Who is
Jesus, if he thus impinges, thus early in the life of the Christian
movement, on even one – and that, an unusual – person? But
there is more to be said. In what follows, I attempt, first, to reckon
with the largely individualistic presentation of Jesus outside the
Pauline writings, but, at the same time, to draw attention to the
fact that, even so, he is almost invariably presented as more than
human. Then, two assumptions about Jesus, which are widely

held quite outside the Pauline corpus, and are found even in the most 'individualistic' Christologies, are shown to carry implications which in fact go beyond the individualism of the very writers who hold them: the assumptions, namely, that Christ died for all, and that he is the ultimate 'fulfiller' of Old Testament patterns.

The writers now to be considered all identify the risen Lord as Jesus of Nazareth, and all, or nearly all, seem to view him still as an individual, but nevertheless clearly see him as more than an exalted and glorified human being. Among the non-Pauline writers, I am not attempting to examine the Synoptic Gospels. This omission is quite deliberate. Many scholars, it is true, regard them as presenting every bit as emphatic a 'post-Easter' theology and Christology as any of the epistles. But, for my part, I am sceptical about this estimate.[1] Of course the Synoptic Gospels were all written in the post-Easter period by writers who already believed in the presence of the risen Christ; and there are at least a few passages (though I would say only a few) which seem to be virtually incompatible with the situation during the ministry of Jesus. An obvious example is Matt. 18: 20, 'Where two or three are gathered in my name, there am I among them'. But in the main the Synoptic Gospels seem to be a serious attempt (even if it was not consistently successful) to reconstruct what happened and how Jesus looked to observers *before* his death and during his ministry. And it is for this reason that I do not call them into the witness box to testify about post-Easter experience.

Confining ourselves, then, to the Acts, the non-Pauline epistles, and the Revelation, what may we say? For all of these writers the exalted Lord is the same person as the crucified man. It is himself that these writers invoke or acclaim, not his mere memory or his ideals. At no point in the New Testament, so far as I can see, is there any suggestion that Christian experience meant no more than that it was the teaching and example of a figure of the past which now enabled Christians to approach God with a new understanding and confidence, or that it was merely because of what Jesus had done and been in the past that they found the

---

[1] See C. F. D. Moule, 'The intention of the evangelists', in A. J. B. Higgins, ed., *New Testament Essays* in mem. T. W. Manson (Manchester: University Press 1959), 165ff.

Spirit of God lifting them up to new capacities and powers. On the contrary, they believed that it was because the same Jesus was alive and was himself in some way in touch with them there and then that the new relationship and the new freedom were made possible. They believed in the continued aliveness and presence, in some spiritual dimension, of the person who had been known in the past in the dimensions of hearing, sight, and touch. The transcendent, divine person of present experience was continuous and identical with the historical figure of the past.

But in what spiritual dimension was he now known? This is where the documents differ. All of them, I believe, in so far as they touch on the matter, see his existence as divine and eternal. But within this category, they conceive of him variously. The Christian Church seems always to have found it difficult to define the relation between the physical body of Jesus that was fastened to the cross and the risen Lord. Consistently affirming that the two are the same Person, Christians have described the constitution of the risen one in various different ways, from the crudest to the most sophisticated. Article IV of the Thirty-nine Articles of the Church of England contains an explicit and literal statement about Christ's mode of existence after death: 'Christ did truly rise again from death, and took again his body, with flesh, bones, and all things appertaining to the perfection of Man's nature; wherewith he ascended into Heaven, and there sitteth, until he return to judge all Men at the last day.' It is, of course, from Scripture that Article IV gets its terms. In Luke 24: 39 the risen Christ declares that 'a spirit' (that is, a ghost) has not flesh and bones as the disciples perceive that he has. And Luke and Acts it is that correspondingly present the risen Christ if not in physical, at any rate in largely individualistic terms. He is glorified and transcendent indeed; but what is indicated is uncommonly like apotheosis: it is as though a new Heracles, vindicated through his labours, had been taken up into the heavens and become a star. Jesus is transcendent, indeed, and very close to God; but still individual. He is the same Jesus of Nazareth who trod the paths of Galilee with his friends, but now glorified and exalted to heaven and to God's right hand. And in the Acts it is from heaven that he exercises his ministry, whether by sending the Holy Spirit to continue his mission, or by appearing to Paul on

the Damascus Road in a blinding flash, or by showing himself
in dreams and visions. And it is from heaven that he will come
again, just as the disciples saw him go into heaven. It is from this
conception, accompanied by the most literal ideas of physical
constitution, that a great deal of later interpretation was evidently
derived, leading up to such formulations as the one I have just
quoted. J. G. Davies, in his Bampton lectures, *He Ascended into
Heaven* (London: Lutterworth 1958), is able to quote examples
from patristic writers such as Tertullian, Hippolytus, and Methodius. They all seem to regard the One who came to us as Jesus
as having been without flesh indeed before the incarnation, but
as having thereafter taken flesh to heaven with him. Tertullian
wrote:

He keeps in His own self the deposit of the flesh which has been
committed to Him by both parties [i.e. God and man, the 'parties'
between whom he is Mediator] – the pledge and security of its entire
perfection. For as 'He has given to us the earnest of the Spirit' [2 Cor.
5: 5], so has He received from us the earnest of the flesh, and has
carried it with Him into heaven as a pledge of that complete entirety
which is one day restored to it (*de res.* 51, in Davies, 83).

Again, Hippolytus wrote: 'It is evident...that He offered Himself to the Father and before this there was no flesh in heaven.
Who then was in heaven but the Word unincarnate, who was
despatched to show that He was upon earth and was also in
heaven?' (*Contra Noetum* 4, in Davies, 87). And Methodius spoke
of 'the undefiled and blessed flesh, which the Word Himself
carried into the heavens, and presented at the right hand of God'
(*Symposium* 7.8, in Davies, 93). Origen, as one might expect, was
an exception to these tendencies, and is, indeed, the object of
Methodius' attack; and J. G. Davies is able to quote instances of
his much more sophisticated and sometimes allegorical treatment
of the theme (see 91ff.).

All those more literalistic writers, however, clearly think of
Christ, at his ascension, as taking up in advance that human
corporeity in which they hoped at the end themselves to be raised
with him to heaven. And this seems to be how the writer of Luke
and Acts sees the matter; or, if he does not insist on the
corporeity, he certainly seems to think of Jesus as an individual,

though, to be sure, glorified and exalted. Perhaps something similar has to be said also of the Epistle to the Hebrews, though the refined and subtle mind of this author certainly does not commit itself to the idea that flesh and bones belong to the risen Christ. But still, for the writer to the Hebrews Jesus is the great High Priest who has passed through the heavens so as to stand in the heavenly sanctuary making atonement on our behalf; and just as human indivuduals have to die, and then comes judgement, so, comparably, Jesus dies once and for all, and then comes judgement – though, in this case, he is not the judged but the Judge (Heb. 9: 27f.). The impression one gets from Hebrews, I think, as from Luke–Acts, is that the Jesus of the ministry – and, for Hebrews, especially the Jesus of the Temptation and Agony – has now been lifted to a transcendent state; but that, from there, he will appear at the end, still an individual, however divine and glorious. Moreover, it is, somehow, by his flesh that he has made the transition from earth to heaven, and blazed a trail for us to follow (10: 20). He is there and we are here; but he is the historical, individual person who has gone ahead of us so that he may enable us too to be there, like him. It is true that Hebrews does show some traces of a more than individual conception of Jesus, for, in chapter 2, he is identified as the one who alone has fulfilled the glorious destiny designed, according to Psalm 8, for mankind as a whole: Jesus, because of his suffering and death, is crowned with glory and honour, as mankind was designed to be. Here *in nuce* is an Adam-Christology. But it is not developed in Hebrews. Also, of course, Hebrews starts with a fully 'cosmic' Christology, in which the Son of God is associated with creation and so is preexistent. Moreover, believers are never separated from him: they are particularly close to him in worship (12: 24). But we are still left asking how the individual of the ministry and the post-resurrection glory is related to that preexistent Being.

Much the same pattern meets us in 1 Peter. Here again, rather as in Acts, Jesus is the individual who has simply been withdrawn from sight, 'whom having not seen, ye love; in whom, though now ye see him not, yet believing, ye rejoice with joy unspeakable and full of glory' (1: 8); and the same Jesus will appear ultimately as the Chief Shepherd to reward the faithful (5: 4).

Even in the Fourth Gospel, for all its elusive and sensitive spirituality, there is as much emphasis as in Luke upon the palpability of the risen Christ (he retains the stigmata), and upon his existence as an exalted individual. I say 'emphasis upon the palpability', because I am not among those who think that the encounters with Mary Magdalene and Thomas in chapter 20 are to be interpreted otherwise. Mary seems to be actually holding Jesus when he says 'Touch me not' (unless that is to overpress the implications of the present imperative, which certainly ought to mean 'Do not go on clinging to me'); and it is certainly implied that Thomas could have touched him, had he not been convinced that it was unnecessary. Thus, the Johannine message seems to be not that the risen Lord was not tangible, either for Mary or for Thomas, but that he need not be clung to and need not be evidenced by touch. And I believe that my phrase 'an exalted individual' is justified as a description of the Johannine conception because, throughout this Gospel, relations with Jesus are represented individualistically. As I have already observed (above, pp. 65f.), even when the Fourth Evangelist uses the allegory of the vine, he represents Jesus as 'in' the disciples, although no vine can literally be 'in' its branches. Vine and branches cannot be reciprocally in one another; but Jesus is in each of his friends and each of his friends in him, like that mutual coinherence which can be predicated of two closely united individuals. Admittedly, the Fourth Evangelist allows himself comparable expressions about the Spirit-Paraclete, and even about God. The parallelism between two neighbouring verses of chapter 14 illustrates this. When Judas (not the Iscariot) expresses surprise that Jesus is going to show himself not to the world at large but only to the disciples, Jesus confirms (verse 23) that each person who loves him will find his presence and the presence of the Father with him. But in verses 16f. of the same chapter, the same, virtually, is said of the Spirit of Truth who is a Paraclete – namely, that, though the world does not know him and cannot see him, he will abide permanently in and among the disciples. And, in verse 23, God himself, the Father, is spoken of as thus visiting the individual. It is scarcely conceivable that the Evangelist thought of the Father or even of the Spirit individualistically. But I think that it holds true, nevertheless, that Jesus is thought of after his resurrection as still individual. To this extent, the moving phrase in the Apocalypse, 'Behold, I stand at the door and knock' (3: 20), presents a parallel to the Gospel's conception of the Lord's personal approach as individual to individual.

For all this, even the most individualistic conceptions of the risen Christ, whether in Acts, in Hebrews, in 1 Peter, or in John, seem consistently to present him as something more and greater than what believers hoped that, by the grace of God, they themselves would become. In a word, they present him as *divine*. I said, earlier, that the more literalistic writers conceived of the risen Lord as taking up in advance that human corporeity in which they hoped, at the end, themselves to be raised with him to heaven. But it now has to be said that, however individualistically Jesus is pictured, by Luke and Acts, by Hebrews, by 1 Peter, and by the Johannine school, and even if these writers imagined Jesus as existing in some corporeal mode, he is equally kept, by all of them, in a category other than that to which the believer hoped to belong at the end. Jesus is exalted to God's right hand, he is uniquely one with the Father and close to him, and he is the origin and the active initiator of all that the believer may hope – derivately and by dependence on him – to become. This distinction between the divine, creative initiative and human response and dependence and creatureliness seems to be clear. And as soon as Christians begin to think of contact with a departed friend (and Paul is, perhaps, beginning to do so), it is not quite in the same way as they think of their contact with Christ. Rather, it is precisely because of him and by virtue of his divine initiative that they find themselves conceiving of communion with the dead in Christ.

To sum up, then: the writers we have considered conceive of the risen Christ individualistically, rather as an apotheosed individual, and perhaps even corporeally or quasi-physically: certainly as identical with the man of Nazareth. But nevertheless they attribute to him a unique closeness to God and a divine, creative initiative, which marks him off from their conception of what each believer – precisely because of him and through him – may become.

So much for this contention, that the distinction between believers and the risen Christ is clear, even when Christ is most individualistically conceived. But now I must raise, however briefly, the question of the function of the Spirit in making the contact between Christians and God through Christ; for it concerns all my contentions – the continuity between Jesus the man and the risen Lord, the variety of the conceptions of contact with him, and the essentially divine category in which he is conceived. At least for Acts and for John, it is the risen Christ who sends the Spirit. In John, of course, the Father, too, is spoken of as sending the Spirit; but it is the association of the coming of the Spirit with the glorification of Christ which is significant for our purpose, and this is underlined by John 7: 39, as well as occurring in the farewell discourses. In both Acts and John, the presence of the Spirit in a sense compensates for the absence (at least from sight) of the ascended Christ; and in both writers the presence of the Spirit continues the work of Christ. The Spirit implements in Christians the insights and the character and the activity belonging to Christ. The character of the individual Lord is, so to speak, multiplied: his presence is made manifold by the Spirit. To be filled with the Spirit is to be enabled to speak and act as a witness to and representative of Christ. To be guided by the Spirit is to be enabled to go and to act as he designs. Once, in Acts 16: 7, comes the remarkable statement that the Spirit of *Jesus* restrained the missionaries from pursuing their own intentions and sent them in a new direction. The Johannine farewell discourses speak of the Spirit as repeating the teaching and guidance of Jesus, and acting, like him, as a Paraclete or mediator between God and the disciples and as the disciples' representative in heaven. Thus, both in John and Acts, the Spirit communicates and extends the presence of Christ.[2]

And it is more accurate to say this than to say that the Spirit takes the place of Christ. The experience of the Spirit by Christians does not (and this is my point) eclipse their experience of the presence of the living Christ himself. Quite the contrary. It never seems to be equivalent merely to the sort of experience that

---

[2] For valuable light on the Spirit in Acts, see G. Stählin, ' *to pneuma Iēsou* (Apostelgeschichte 16: 7)', in *Christ and Spirit in the New Testament* as in Chapter 1, n. 19, 229ff.

is described when it is said, of some great figure of the past, that his spirit lives on among his followers. An experience of the Spirit of God that can properly be described as 'Christian' presents no analogy to an attitude or a life-style that might be described by a comparable adjective bearing the name merely of some great leader of the past – say, 'Socratic' or 'Platonic' or 'Pythagorean'. For the Christian, the divine presence is not found through the mere example or memory of Jesus, neither is it called 'the Spirit of God' without further qualification: rather, it is Jesus himself *by* the Holy Spirit. There is a German epigram which speaks of the spiritualizing of Christ and the christifying of the Spirit (*die Vergeistigung Christi und die Christifizierung des Geistes*).[3] This means, I take it, that because of the resurrection, Jesus became spiritually apprehensible and thus ubiquitized – 'let loose in all the world, Lady', as Masefield's centurion says to Pilate's wife; and, conversely, that, because of the whole event of the incarnation, death, and resurrection, the Spirit of God thenceforth comes to be experienced in the distinctively Christian way which I have been trying to describe. The Spirit is christified; Christ is spiritualized. And this only serves to underline the fact that even those New Testament writers who seem to think of Jesus as an exalted individual, think of him also as divine and eternal.

But there is more to be said than this; for I believe that the supra-individual experience which we have seen explicitly described by Paul is there by implication in other writers besides Paul. Two phenomena, at least, may be adduced in evidence – the assumption that what Christ has done is available for all, and the discovery that all the Old Testament patterns of relationship between God and his people converge upon Christ. In other words, Christ is universal Saviour and is the coping-stone of God's edifice of corporate relationship. Even the writers who work with what might be called a much more individualistic model than Paul's, take it as a matter of course that Christ's death and resurrection make life available wherever he is accepted. And even the most literalistic ideas of Old Testament prediction and its verification in Christ – as in the 'formula quotations' in Matthew – may be seen as symptoms, simply, of a much pro-

[3] See C. A. A. Scott, *Christianity According to St Paul* (Cambridge: University Press 1932), 144, n. 1.

founder conception of fulfilment – namely, the discovery that on Christ converges the whole destiny of Israel, and, through Israel, of all mankind, in its relation to God. Christ is found to be the stone, rejected by the builders but essential to the building; the despised martyr who turns out to be a redeemer of others; the Son of Man of Daniel 7, who faces the Panzer armaments of the horned and clawed monsters with nothing but his naked fidelity, and is vindicated in the court of heaven; the royal Son of God, who implements his Father's will and realizes his sovereignty; Adam, crowned with glory and honour because of his suffering of death. All this, which is by no means confined to Paul, carries the same inclusive and more than individual implications about Christ which are explicit in the Pauline writings.

Thus, it is Paul, mainly, who is explicit about a conception of Jesus which may be called (if the rough description may be permitted) God-like, in the sense that Jesus is found to be, as a theist finds God to be, personal but more than individual. The other writers whom we have considered mainly reflect a conception that might rather be called angelic or apotheosed: Jesus is seen by them as an exalted individual being – as it were, an apotheosis of a man. And yet that description does not do justice to the facts, because Jesus is consistently presented as one with God in a way in which neither man nor angel is; and as the divine initiator of man's salvation as no created person can be. If one were to import anachronous terms, one might say (as a friend of mine observes) that, essentially, these writers are affirming Christ to be *homoousios* with God, whereas man is only *homoiousios* with Christ or with God – even if, paradoxically, Christ is *homoousios* with man. Besides, even the non-Pauline writers imply a good deal more than they state: as I have said, their conceptions of atonement through Christ and of his fulfilment of Old Testament patterns are instances of such implicit Christology.

It is these two pointers that must now be examined in greater detail.

4

The scope of the death of Christ

There are aspects of the religious experience reflected in the Pauline epistles which make it difficult to avoid the conclusion that Paul thought of the risen Christ in much the same way as a theist thinks of God – as personal but supra-individual. This, as we have seen, is what seems to emerge from an examination of Paul's incorporative language. By contrast, we have just seen that, for most of the other writers in the New Testament, Jesus, though transcendent and uniquely close to God, is conceived of in much more individualistic ways. And yet – and this is the point of this chapter and the next – there are certain assumptions, made in common by Paul and the non-Pauline writers alike, which, by implication, point to precisely that supra-individual aspect of Christ which the non-Pauline writers do not make explicit. In other words, my thesis is that Paul's 'corporate Christ' alone 'makes sense' of the experience reflected even by the writers who do not explicitly acknowledge it: their assumptions go further than their expressions.

It is two such assumptions that will now be considered. The first, in this chapter, is the assumption that the results of the death of Christ are available universally. The second, in the next chapter, is the assumption that Christ fulfils Scripture.

How do New Testament writers handle the theme of the death of Christ? Among the statements made about Jesus, one at least falls within the strictly historical field and, at any rate in principle, could have been objectively verified; and it is almost universally believed – the statement that he died. There have always been those, of course, who do not believe that he ever lived. But these are few and eccentric. There have been more who distinguish between the mortal being who died and a transcendental being who was unscathed: these are the docetists, alike in Christianity and in Islam. There have also been those who hold that Jesus did not die but only swooned: the resuscitation theorists. But the great majority, if they agree on nothing else, will allow that Jesus of Nazareth lived and truly died. It was a death, and it took place when Pontius Pilate was prefect of Judaea. So much may be established as a historical event, as objectively as the death of Julius Caesar.

But how is that death to be interpreted and estimated? There are at least three ways of estimating the death of Christ, and all three have to be reckoned with. One is what we may call the external story – essentially the ancient historian's story. The second concerns the attitude of Jesus himself, as the early Christians discerned it. The third concerns the relation of the total event on all its levels to those who refer to it.

The external story has been told in a number of different ways, and it is important to distinguish between them. There are, for instance, the 'self-surrender' theories (as we may call them), which interpret Jesus' final journey to Jerusalem as (in one way or another) a deliberate self-immolation. Jesus went up to Jerusalem – we are sometimes told – in order to die. He knew that he had to sacrifice himself, so he went deliberately to fulfil prophecy and to lay his life on the altar. A less honourable form of that theory is the extraordinary fantasy that Jesus contrived an elaborate scheme by which he was to achieve the messianic sufferings which are conceived to have been required by popular expectation, but to survive them. I do not know which I find the more repulsive – the artificiality of a self-immolation in order to fulfil prophecy or the crafty scheme to have your cake and eat it. But, in any case, it is not one's subjective reactions that matter, but the evidence; and neither the uncritical use of bits and pieces of the Gospels nor the more literalistic, prophecy-fulfilment motive, seems to me really to reckon with the evidence. Unsuccessful also are the attempts of the late Paul Winter and the late Professor S. G. F. Brandon to make Jesus a would-be revolutionary whose coup failed, or at least a sympathizer with the advocates of violence.[1] This requires cavalier treatment of the

[1] S. G. F. Brandon, *Jesus and the Zealots* (Manchester: University Press 1967); P. Winter, *On the Trial of Jesus* (Berlin: de Gruyter 1961). For a reply see M. Hengel's review of Brandon in *JSS* 14 (1969), 231ff., and his *Was Jesus a Revolutionist?* as in Chapter 1, n. 40.

evidence. It means that one has to lean heavily on the supposition that, whereas Jesus was a messianic pretender, Mark's Gospel is a tendentious attempt to conceal the fact, and to persuade the reader, instead, to incriminate the Jews; it means that one has to make far-reaching deductions from the fact that one of the Twelve was called Simon the Zealot, and correspondingly ignore the fact that equally a member of the Twelve was Matthew the tax collector; and that one has to minimize the clashes between Jesus and the religious authorities that appear essential to the very structure of Jesus' teaching and way of life.

Instead of any of these interpretations of the death of Jesus, it seems to me that such evidence as we have suggests that Jesus (if we confine ourselves for the moment to the external story, the historian's view) did not seek death; he did not go up to Jerusalem *in order* to die; but he did pursue, with inflexible devotion, a way of truth that inevitably led him to death, and he did not seek to escape. It seems that he went up to Jerusalem on that last, fatal journey, partly to keep the Passover, like any good Palestinian Jew; and partly, like the passionate prophet that he was, to present his nation with one last challenge – to make a final bid to save them from their disastrous course of religious and political blindness.[2] But he knew he was, in fact, bound to die, and he made no attempt either to escape or to defend himself. In that sense, he was the victim of his own loyalty to his vocation.

This is by no means a view unanimously held by scholars. Dr J. C. O'Neill has suggested[3] that there are only four possible reasons for that journey to Jerusalem: either it was because Jesus was a psychotic (a view denied by Albert Schweitzer's early psychiatric study), or it was a political effort of some sort, or it was with an apocalyptic expectation, or in order to enable Jesus to sacrifice himself. Schweitzer himself, in a way, combined the last two. 'The Son of Man' had not come, as Jesus had hoped he would. So Jesus went to take upon himself the suffering which had to be borne before God would bring in the Kingdom, and

---

[2] J. Downing, 'Jesus and Martyrdom', *JTS* n.s. 14.2 (Oct. 1963), 279ff., suggests that Jesus may have begun his ministry seeing himself as a prophet-martyr witnessing *against* his people, but came to see himself as a prophet-martyr suffering *for* his people.

[3] In a lecture at Cambridge, 9 February 1974.

thus to make the wheel of destiny to turn. It did turn – and crushed him. And it was by this heroic self-immolation that Jesus as it were transcended himself. By thus dramatically destroying the apocalyptic illusion in his person, he made it possible for subsequent generations to understand God's design in a quite different way. Thus, he lives for others only in the sense that his death has inspired others to similar heroism, though in a different cause.[4]

But I hope that, on the purely historical level, the account that I have given of Jesus' last journey to Jerusalem adds a fifth possibility, and a plausible one. In any case, whatever account may be given on the first 'level' – the level of the 'external' story – there is a second level. The early Christians believed that Jesus met the inevitable with sovereign freedom. They represent Jesus as always in control of the situation. 'Externally' speaking, his death may have been inevitable (though, for the New Testament writers, the inevitability is that of God's purposes, not of human circumstances). But not for a moment does Jesus treat it merely as something to be endured. Always, he exercises a sovereign mastery over it. Just as he had told his disciples that 'if a man will let himself be lost for my sake and the Gospel, that man is safe' (Mark 8: 35), so for himself he says, 'No one has robbed me of [my life]; I am laying it down of my own free will' (John 10: 18); or 'the Son of Man is to endure great sufferings' (Mark 10: 12, etc.); or 'Abba, Father...not what I will but what thou wilt' (Mark 14: 36). All this is in no spirit of mere resignation. It bespeaks a most positive and affirmative attitude. Thus, the external necessity is, in the inward life of the will, turned into an act of sovereign, creative power, as is the case whenever the surrender of life rises to the heights of martyrdom.

But there is a third way of estimating the death. If, viewed externally, it is intelligible as the society's revenge on a figure too disturbing and too revolutionary to be tolerable; if, viewed internally, it is the affirmative, creative acceptance of the situation

---

[4] A. Schweitzer, *Von Reimarus zu Wrede* (original edition 1906), Eng. trans. *The Quest of the Historical Jesus* (London: A. and C. Black [3]1954). On the psychiatric question, *idem. Die psychiatrische Beurteilung Jesu* (Tübingen 1913), Eng. trans. in *The Expositor*, Ser. viii. 6 (1913), 328ff., 439ff., 554ff., and C. R. Joy, *The Psychiatric Study of Jesus* (Boston: Beacon Press 1948).

in the name of God; how, thirdly, is it described from the point of view of one who finds himself benefiting from that creative act? The death of Jesus is constantly described as 'on behalf of others'. What does this mean, and what does it imply?

I

We need to ask, first, what meanings attach to the statement that somebody died 'for another'. And we ask it outside any reference to Jesus, and, in the first instance, outside even any specifically religious frame of reference. If this section is illustrated by biblical phrases, this is only a matter of convenience: it does not, at this point, involve religious presuppositions. On this 'secular' level, it is possible, first, to apply such a statement to two individuals with purely external and physical connotations. To say that a good shepherd lays down his life for the sheep need mean no more than that the good shepherd dies – or is ready to die – in fighting the wolf to defend the sheep. He dies quite literally *instead of* the other: the shepherd dies that the sheep may live. The preposition in Greek could appropriately be *anti*, 'in the place of', though in fact New Testament Greek sometimes uses the vaguer and more general preposition, *huper*, even when the sense is that the action is strictly vicarious. In John 13: 37 (cf. verse 38), Peter boasts to Jesus that he will lay down his life for him (*huper sou*). Perhaps it is in no deeper a sense than this that, in John 15: 13, the greatest possible love is said to be exhibited when a man lays down his life for his friends (*huper tōn philōn autou*). In Rom. 5: 7, the possibility is recognized that a man may die for a good person (*huper tou agathou*); and in Rom. 16: 4, Aquila and Priscilla are said to have risked their necks for Paul's life (*huper tēs psuchēs mou*).

It is equally possible, of course, to speak in such terms when the death is not successfully vicarious. The shepherd may be said to die for the sheep even if he fails to save its life. When the wolf has killed the shepherd, it may itself be unhurt and may go on to demolish the sheep, or the entire flock. A parent may fling herself in front of her child, but the gunman may still shoot them both. But one can still say, 'That shepherd gave his life for the sheep'; 'That woman died for her child'. But this is not strictly *anti*, 'instead of': it is *huper*, 'for the sake of', in an attempt to protect or help.

In either case, here are simple examples of lives surrendered with a view to the physical benefit – the preservation of the lives – of others. And it is evident that, in such cases, a single person is sometimes successful in rescuing many individuals. One shepherd might save the whole flock by killing the wolf at the risk of his own life. When, in 1 Macc. 6: 44, Eleazar Avaran stabbed an elephant from beneath and suffered the inevitable fate, 'he gave himself', says the narrator, 'to save his people and to win himself an eternal name'.

In other ways, too, one person may, by a self-sacrificing act, contribute to the physical wellbeing of many, not only of his contemporaries, but of all generations to come. A friend of mine died young of a disease contracted in the course of pathological research. What he discovered by his dangerous experiments was, perhaps, not a spectacular breakthrough: but it must have contributed at least something to the conquest of disease for future generations. In that sense, this one man died on behalf of many. And if, as I suspect, he knew the risk, he gave his life consciously that others might live.

It is also possible, of course, for a life given unwillingly to save others. Millions of animals used in medical research die each year that men may live: but they die without willing it or knowing what it is for. Those who believe that the execution of a criminal has a deterrent effect, might claim that the criminal dies, in a sense, for others; but his life, like that of animals used in vivisection, is taken forcibly, not willingly given. It is in this sense that Caiaphas, in John 11: 50 (cf. 18: 14), is represented as saying that it is expedient for one man to die rather than that the whole nation should perish. It is the evangelist who interprets the saying on a very different level.

But now, still not going beyond the secular ambit, there are other ways besides the purely material and physical, in which men may be benefited by the surrender of a life; for it is appropriate to say that one dies for others when the death in question exercises some spiritual or moral influence for good. The death of Socrates set up in history a monument to integrity and courage which will never be forgotten as long as the story is told, and

which will go on for an indefinite length of time having its effect
on the hearts and minds and ideals of all who hear it. So, again,
those who die in battle for what they genuinely believe to be a
noble cause leave behind them an incentive to do likewise.

And here an important fact emerges. Whereas on the material
and physical level one dies that others may live, when it comes
to the spiritual or moral level, the level of ideals and of honour,
the death of the one may carry the others with it through the
same experience, rescuing them not from death but from
cowardly escaping death. Socrates dies not instead of others, but
in such a way that others, like him, may dare to die in the cause
of truth. His life may be said to be given 'for' them (*huper*), but
not strictly 'instead of' them (*anti*). The Vietnamese and
Czechoslovak self-immolations of our day, as extremist demon-
strations against tyranny, constitute a special case of this sort of
moral influence.

Thus far, nothing has been said which goes beyond the bounds
of the secular and could not be accepted by a humanist. We have
either kept within the limits of material and physical benefits, or,
when these have been transcended, it has been in terms of moral
uplift and influence, exercised by one on another by the direct,
rational means of holding up an example. And it is noteworthy
that, when such influence is analysed, it seems to work by an
individualistic relationship: it is a matter of each person's being
individually influenced. The story of Socrates has to be heard by
each individual on whom his death is to exert its influence –
unless, indeed, one is prepared to argue that, by an act of
courageous devotion to truth and duty, a whole society is so lifted
to new ideas, that any member of it, whether or not the story
is heard, is placed in a more advantageous context. Even if one
did allow this – and it would be difficult to establish – this change
or reform in society would still only take place when each member
of it was able to convince his neighbour that the new moral level
was right and good: it would still be a rational process of mutual
instruction and influence and interaction.

II

But, now, supposing a religious factor is introduced: supposing God is brought into the reckoning, or a mystical notion of man, what then? On the crudest level imaginable, when God is brought into the reckoning, the theory will be that it is possible for man to bribe God; and the most impressive bribe conceivable will be a human life offered up to God. When Mesha King of Moab sacrifices his own eldest son on a wall to his god (2 Kings 3: 27), he believes that he is surrendering a very precious possession in order to propitiate the god and secure his favour for his army; and the Hebrew narrator seems to have thought that it worked. Similarly, Abraham's readiness to go to the same lengths, although he was excused from the actual deed, brought blessing, not only to Abraham but to his posterity (Gen. 22: 18, as frequently, if wrongly, interpreted).

On an immensely higher but still essentially mercenary level, it is possible for a religious mind to interpret the heroic act of martyrdom as a deliberate self-immolation to persuade God to be propitious. In 2 Macc. 7: 37f. the martyr hopes that he and his fellow-martyrs may have stayed the wrath of God: *en emoi de kai tois adelphois mou stēnai tēn pantokratoros orgēn*. So in 4 Macc. 17: 21ff. the obedience of Eleazar and others in the extreme degree of martyrdom is treated as a propitiatory sacrifice: *hōsper antipsuchon gegonotas tēs tou ethnous hamartias*. This curious phrase is taken by Dalman (*apud* S-B ii. 279) to mean that Eleazar's obedience is offered in *exchange* for the *sin*-stained *soul* of the people. It seems to me more natural not to attach the '*-psuchon*' part of the compound word to the nation, but rather to the martyrs, and to interpret *antipsuchon* as meaning, perhaps, a 'life given in exchange', as a compensation to God for the despite done him by the nation's sin. But in any case, the generally compensatory (indeed, propitiatory) sense is clear; and the next verse reinforces it: *kai dia tou haimatos tōn eusebōn ekeinōn kai tou hilastēriou tou thanatou autōn, hē theia pronoia ton Israēl prokakōthenta diesōsen*.

The same sort of thing may be said of any signal act of dedication and obedience to God's will, even when not expressed in actual death or in physical suffering at all. Thus, in the Qumran

Manual of Discipline, the inner group of twelve 'laymen' and
three priests are, by their devotion, *to atone* for sin (*l*ᵉ*raṣṣōṭ ʿâwôn*,
1QS 8. 3). So, in Sirach 44: 17, *Noe heurethē teleios dikaios, en
kairō(i) orgēs egeneto antallagma*...And, much later perhaps, there
is the well-known saying about the vicarious suffering of two
rabbis, Judah and Eleazar ben Simon. It was said that for the
duration of their sufferings (which included toothache!), no one
died prematurely, there were no miscarriages, and there was no
shortage of rain.[5] Going back to canonical Scripture, there is the
noble passage in Exod. 32: 32, where Moses asks to be expunged
from God's book of life if that could save his people. And, most
famous of all, there is the Suffering Servant of Isa. 53, whose
suffering is described in terms of compensation, and through
whose bruises healing comes to others. Whether the 'compensation' here is intended as a cultic metaphor or simply as a legal
or quantitative one is a debatable point, though the NEB comes
down on the cultic side, translating *'âšâm* by 'a sacrifice for sin'.
But in any case it is to God, presumably, that the compensation,
whether cultic or legal, is thought of as paid. (It is strange,
incidentally, that the Maccabaean stories never apply Isa. 53 to
the martyrs.)[6]

These allusions, from the lowest and most barbaric up to the
most noble and sophisticated – from Mesha of Moab to the
Servant of II-Isa. and the heroic martyrs under Antiochus Epiphanes – are all illustrative of an interpretation of the effect of
the death or sufferings of the one on the many in terms of a
corporate structure of relationship. It is not a matter of material
gain – a person giving his life so that others may live – nor *only*
even of spiritual or cultural uplift reaching other individuals
directly from the sufferer's example. It is a matter, rather, of the
sufferer's offering to God that which God will accept for the
benefit of the rest. Essentially the same structure of corporate
relationship is implied also by the rabbinic doctrine of the merits
of the fathers. This religious (or at least *mystical*) interpretation

[5] Mishnah, Baba Meṣiʿa 85a: see S-B ii. 281, and E. Lohse, *Märtyrer und Gottes-
knecht* (Göttingen: Vandenhoeck und Ruprecht 1955), 32, n. 3.
[6] See Lohse as in n. 5, 72 n. 6; cf. 105, 110; and F. Hahn, *The Titles of Jesus in
Christology* as in *Introduction*, n. 12, 55; it is possible that baptism for the dead,
in 1 Cor. 15: 29, means the offering of total self-dedication by the living in
baptism on behalf of the unbaptized dead.

of the *huper*-idea, this interpretation of 'on behalf of', differs from interpretations which may be confined within a humanist (or rational) frame of reference, in its assumption that it is through God, or at least by way of some 'mystical' interconnectedness of men with one another if not also with God, that the many may be affected by the one. Whereas those other interpretations of 'he died for us' – the interpretations which are not necessarily more than rational – operate in terms of essentially individual and horizontal relationship, the 'mystical' interpretations postulate a corporate inter-connexion, and the religious interpretations place this within the ambience of God's presence.

And this will hold good, even when ideas of propitiation and sacrifice are left behind. If one who believes in this mysterious relationship with God says 'such and such a person died for us', he means that the self-surrender of that person in obedience to the will of God constituted something that God could (as it were) use and 'relay' for the benefit of his whole family. And although to put it so, even if it obviates the crudity of propitiation, may still suggest a very crude 'model', as though heaven were a kind of clearing-house or telephone exchange, yet it need not be so. If one ponders on the structure of personal relationships, even in the limited degree to which any one of us understands it (say, within the organism of a family), vistas of immeasurable suggestiveness open up, in which the relation of one to another is part, ultimately, of the relation of all to God. It throws a new light on the sense in which one may be conceived of as giving his life for others. The analogy of the living body suggests itself – which means that we have arrived, by a different route, at the point where we left St Paul. He, as we saw, borrowed the analogy of the body. In its already established uses, in Stoic and other circles, it had served as an analogy for a corporation of persons in harmonious cooperation. The remarkable innovation in Paul was that he brought it into close relationship with the risen Christ, thereby reflecting, as I have argued, an understanding of Christ as more than individual and describing experience of Christ in terms such as theists use of God. But even leaving Christ out of account, and even in pre-Christian contexts, conceptions of the transmission of the benefits accruing from some good life, or from the noble surrender of life in the cause of loyalty to God, seem to imply an organic understanding of human society within the providence of God. A religious use of *huper*, unlike a secular use, goes beyond the rationalization of it in terms of the inspiring effect of a fine example or a noble ideal: it operates with an organic 'model' of society, and relates it to God. Thus, each limb or organ of the living organism of the community is conceived of as having its measure of influence on the entire 'body'; of acting 'on behalf of' all, not merely by the direct and rationally intelligible means of stirring the imagination or arousing idealism, but more subtly and mystically, inasmuch as the entire organism is seen as a living unity. It is in such a context of thought that the functioning of intercessory prayer may begin to become more readily conceivable.

So much, then, for conceptions of the sense of a phrase like 'he died for us' in a generally and broadly theistic context of thought.

III

Now, when Christians recite the death of Jesus as an article of their belief, they add (if they are using the Nicene Creed) that it was 'for us' that he was crucified: *staurōthenta te huper hēmōn*. This interpretation of that death goes back at least as far as the middle of the first century A.D. Not all the New Testament writers express it. Acts, on the whole, associates the death with the vindication of Christ and of God's design, rather than with the redemption of others. But St Paul, reciting in 1 Cor. 15 information about Jesus which he had received by tradition, adds that it was 'for our sins' that he died (an example, incidentally, of the comparatively rare use of *huper* with the sins expiated rather than the persons redeemed); and in other passages Paul says similar things, as do certain other New Testament writers, each in his own way. Here is a list of passages in which the death of Christ is related to others by a simple prepositional phrase, mostly with *huper*, together with a few examples of other ways of expressing the same idea. Prefixed is a summary note on the use of prepositions in this connexion.

A summary note on prepositions

Huper c. gen. occurs only twice (according to Hatch and Redpath's concordance) in the LXX of the Pentateuch (Deut. 24: 16 (*'al*) and, in a purely literal sense, 28: 23); but outside the Pentateuch Judges 6: 31 (B, Hebrew *le*), 9: 17 (A, Hebrew *'al*) are good examples of its meaning 'on behalf of'. *Peri* is usual in the LXX after *exhilaskesthai* (*kpr*), governing both 'sins' etc. and the persons atoned for. The Ep. to the Hebrews (with reference to the Levitical system) reproduces this double usage in 5: 3 (*peri tou laou...heautou...hamartiōn*), though it also uses *huper* doubly (5: 1, *huper anthrōpōn...hamartiōn*; so 9: 7, cf. 10: 12). The New Testament uses *huper* mostly with persons. Departures from *huper* with persons and *peri* with sins etc. are asterisked in the following list of significant New Testament passages.

Mark 10: 45 (*anti* pollōn*).

Mark 14: 24 (*huper pollōn*); Matt. 26: 28 (*peri* pollōn*); Luke 22: 19f. (*huper humōn*); 1 Cor. 11: 24 (*huper humōn*).

John 6: 51 (*huper tēs tou kosmou zōēs* – hardly to be asterisked).

John 11: 51f. (*huper tou ethnous...ouch huper tou ethnous monon...*).

Rom. 5: 6, 8 (*huper asebōn...huper hēmōn*).

Rom. 8: 32 (*huper pantōn*).

1 Cor. 15: 3 (*huper* tōn hamartiōn hēmōn*).

2 Cor. 5: 14 (*heis huper pantōn*).

2 Cor. 5: 21 (*huper hēmōn*).

Gal. 1: 4 (*huper* tōn hamartiōn hēmōn*).

Gal. 2: 20 (*huper emou*).

Gal. 3: 13 (*huper hēmōn katara*).

Eph. 5: 2 (*huper hēmōn*).

Eph. 5: 25 (*huper autēs, sc. tēs ekklēsias*).

1 Thess. 5: 9f. (*peri* hēmōn*).

1 Tim. 2: 6 (*antilutron huper pantōn*).

Tit. 2: 14 (*huper hēmōn*).

Heb. 2: 9 (*huper pantos*). Note also 5: 1, and cf. 5: 3; 9: 7; 10: 12.

1 Pet. 2: 21 (*huper hēmōn*).

1 Pet. 3: 18 (*dikaios huper adikōn*).

1 John 3: 16 (*huper hēmōn*).

Cf. Heb. 5: 9 (*aitios sotērias aiōniou*); 9: 12 (*aiōnian lutrōsin heuramenos*); 9: 24 (*nun emphanisthēnai tō(i) prosōpō(i) tou theou huper hēmōn*); 9: 28 (*eis to pollōn anenegkein hamartias*); 1 Pet. 2: 24 (*hou tō(i) mōlōpi iathēte*); 1 John 1: 7 (*to haima Iēsou . . . katharizei hēmas apo pasēs hamartias*).

1 Cor. 1: 13 (*mē Paulos estaurōthē huper humōn;*).

Yet, Col. 1: 24; Eph. 3: 1, 13; Rom. 9: 3; 2 Cor. 12: 10; Phil. 1: 29.

If, now, with this list before us, we ask what, if anything, marks these Christian uses of the 'on behalf of' formulae as distinctive, one feature, at least, is impressively persistent. This is the universality – or, at least, potential universality – assumed for the effects of the death of Christ. It could not be maintained that this, in itself, is absolutely distinctive; but it is perhaps distinctive in its pervasiveness.

It is true, admittedly, that one particularly famous saying, with echoes elsewhere, speaks of Christ's death as 'for many', which might seem to suggest that it was not 'for all'. Mark 10: 45 (Matt. 20: 28) speaks of the Son of Man giving his life as a ransom for many. So, too, the Marcan and Matthean words of institution (Mark 14: 24, Matt. 26: 28), and the phrase in Heb. 9: 28. Many scholars insist that this represents a Semitic idiom which uses 'many' for 'all'.[7] For my part, I am sceptical of this claim. But I believe that, in all these sayings, the point is in the contrast between the *one* and the many: it is the plurality of results achieved by the one deed (exactly as in Rom. 5: 12ff.). If so, it follows that the 'many' is not intended in the least to suggest a limitation to only some rather than all, but to emphasize the remarkable fruitfulness of the one act of self-surrender.

In practically all the other phrases on the list, either the word 'all' occurs or some equivalent (such as 'the life of the world'), or the reference includes persons who were not of Jesus' own circle or even generation, but are alluded to simply because they happen to be persons reached by the gospel, however alienated from or oblivious of Jesus Christ they may have been before. The same phenomenon could be illustrated also from other statements in the Pauline epistles which happen not to contain the

---

[7] See. e.g., J. Jeremias, *Die Abendmahlsworte Jesu* (Göttingen: Vandenhoeck und Ruprecht [4]1967), 171.

huper-formula, such as Col. 1: 21f., where Christ is said by his
death to have reconciled those who were formerly estranged; and
the same is true of some of the passages collected at the foot of
the list already given, on p. 119. *Potentially*, the death of Jesus is
'for' all who will accept him.

The claim of a potentially universal applicability is very persistent in our documents, and this, as I have suggested, is one
distinctive feature in the Christian application of the 'on behalf
of' formula to Christ. However, it is impossible to deny that any
such claim is ever made, outside Christianity, for the effects of
one person's death on others. Others besides Jesus are conceived
of as *voluntarily* suffering for the benefit of a plurality of persons;
have we not already seen that there are certainly passages in
Hebrew-Jewish literature before the NT, such as Isa. 53 and the
Maccabaean stories, where such a conception is expressed? It is
true that they are not numerous. In the Old Testament, Exod.
32: 32 and Isa. 53 are practically alone. In Judaism, 2 Macc. is
perhaps the earliest example. But still, they *are* to be found. Of
an Eleazar (or, for that matter, of a Socrates) it may be intelligibly
said that his death brought, and continues to bring, benefit to
an unlimited number of others, whether because of the example
he set, or because of the blow he struck for truth or, more
'mystically', because of the obedience he, as it were, injected into
the total organism of mankind – and this (a theist would add) in
its relation to God.

Interestingly enough, one can compile from Paul himself, a
catena of allusions to his own sufferings as in some way beneficial
to others. He declares in Col. 1: 24 that his own sufferings are
on behalf of Christ's body, the Church; and there is something
comparable in Eph. 3: 1, 13. Again, he says in Rom. 9: 3 that he
would gladly become an accursed thing, cursed by Christ or
banished from his presence (*anathema apo tou Christou*),[8] if that
could benefit his Jewish brothers (*huper tōn adelphōn mou*) – an
idea strongly reminiscent of Exod. 32: 32 once more.

Incidentally and in parenthesis, there is even the passage in
Phil. 1: 29 where Paul speaks of *Christians'* suffering on behalf

[8] For a recent discussion of this, see W. C. van Unnik, 'Jesus: Anathema or
Kyrios (1 Cor. 12: 2)', in *Christ and Spirit in the New Testament* as in Chapter 1,
n. 19, 113ff. (119).

of *Christ* – but that evidently means suffering *in loyalty* to him, not (as it were) so as to benefit him(!). It is comparable to the phrase 'to suffer for the name' (Acts 5: 41). It is a significant fact that nowhere in the New Testament are Christians really placed on a level with Christ in this respect. Contrast the following sentiment from an Indian lyric by Subba Rao: [addressing Christ] 'It is enough, if, like you, I don't die for myself, better still to become God like you by dying for others...'[9] It is significant that Paul, expostulating with his readers (or hearers) for attaching themselves to his own name in a partizan way, cries out in indignation (1 Cor. 1: 13): 'Was *Paul* crucified for you?' (*mē Paulos estaurōthē huper humōn;*) – as much as to say, there is one, and one only, of whom it can properly be said that he died for you.

Why this indignation? Where lies the distinctiveness that is so intensely claimed by New Testament writers for the death of Christ? Whence is it derived, and what does it signify? To the remarkable and persistent, but not absolutely unexampled, claim to a wide and even, perhaps, universal scope for the death of Christ,[10] must be added a further factor. This is the claim that it is a *fait accompli* and one whose results are still actively present. It is its achievedness, its 'doneness'; and, in addition, the strange fact that it is constantly accessible, always and everywhere. The death of Christ is a past achievement, often spoken of in the aorist tense; and yet, it is available and accessible now, in a special sense: it may be appropriated by all, anywhere and at any time.

In Mahayana Buddhism there is a noble universality and comprehensiveness of ideal: but it is as yet unfulfilled; it is a future aspiration. We hear of 'the man who truly knows the truth... dedicated to the universalizing of enlightenment and willing to postpone his own final release from birth and death until the goal is achieved'.[11] Here, indeed, is a purpose with a universal scope: the redemptive intention of one on behalf of

[9] Quoted by S. J. Samartha, *The Hindu Response to the Unbound Christ* (Christian Literature Society of Madras 1974), 125.
[10] See F. Young, 'New Wine in Old Wineskins: XIV Sacrifice', *ET* 86.10 (July 1975), 305ff.; and *Sacrifice and the Death of Christ* (London: SPCK 1975). In the above article, she writes: 'The new dynamic is to be found... in the startling way in which the death of Jesus Christ becomes the focus of all sacrificial thinking' *ET* 86.10, 308a.
[11] D. Fox, *The Vagrant Lotus: an Introduction to Buddhist Philosophy* (Philadelphia: Westminster 1973), 197.

the many. But the Christian claim is distinctive, in that it is not only for the potential universality of the redemptive power of the death of Christ, but also for its being a fact already achieved. A past tense is attached to it: it is *there*, it is done. But also it is *here* and is now active, in a much fuller, more dynamic sense than the sense merely that a fine example is there for all time and is permanently effective. It is not a mere incentive, like the example set by a Bodhisattva or a great hero. It is not an ideal, realizable only in theory, but an achieved fact, extending into a present reality, which Christian faith may actually lay hold of. The Christian hope is an anchor as well as a goal (Heb. 6: 19 as well as 12: 1).

In a word, it is incarnation and resurrection that lends distinctiveness to the Christian phrase 'Christ died for us'. It is the *fait accompli* of the cross, *plus* the constant accessibility of the risen Christ, and the universal scope of God's action in Christ. What Christ is, all others are potentially involved in becoming: 'one man died for all and therefore all mankind has died' (2 Cor. 5: 15); but also, 'as in Adam all men die, so in Christ all will be brought to life' (1 Cor. 15: 22). How natural it is for a Christian to find Christ's death all-inclusive is illustrated – though it might have been illustrated in countless other ways – by the following meditation. A young man lost his life in a road accident abroad. Somehow, in some unaccountable way, this led to illumination for his bereaved sister. Here is a friend's meditation on these events. (The jibe against the Pharisees is not essential to the meaning: the author is well aware of the criticisms levelled against Christian writers for their treatment of the Pharisees, and knows that any considered account of the circumstances of the death of Christ would need to reckon carefully with their actual status and outlook. What he intended to suggest was that physical and even mental reactions are a luxury, and that in moments of real significance there is neither time nor need for feeling. In this context, 'Pharisees' meant, at least partly, those who enjoy religious feeling, including the pleasure of acknowledging sin, more than the reality.)

> A sudden death, they say, has no Gethsemane;
> but perhaps in the moment of this other death
> our time lost meaning, and the swerving car

was filled with a rhythm stronger than the world could bear.
For when He died, a sudden clarity
gave death a content. Through the clouds of emptiness
(for pain and feeling now had fled
to titillate the well-fed Pharisees)
a cry of 'Finished' saw life's end, and poured
blood and water from his side
upon the twisted metal and marks of scorching tyres.

And as the mountain blossomed as a plain,
its dews baptised the awakened eyes of a girl
which shone with love to undo that death
by which, although we gaze uncomprehending
at the silhouette of memory, she lives.

David Dunford, April 1968

If I have correctly located the distinctiveness of the Christian claim, it still remains to ask how Christians were led to recognize and express it. It seems to me that the only answer that can be given is in the actual experience of the earliest Christians: they found that Jesus was alive and (in this strange sense) somehow inclusive. Paul may be the only writer in the New Testament who formulates the idea of inclusion in Christ and membership in his body. But – and this is the point of this chapter and the next – there are certain assumptions held by other writers in common with Paul, which, when analysed, point to just this same conclusion. One such assumption is precisely that the results of Christ's death are (at least potentially) all-embracing. Other Christians besides St Paul may not say 'We are in Christ', or 'He is the body and we its limbs and organs'; but they freely say 'He died for us; in his death is our life'. And that implies an 'Adam-Christology', even when this is not formulated.

Dr Morna Hooker, in a notable article on 'Interchange in Christ',[12] stresses the representative and inclusive character of Christ, as against an exclusive vicariousness, and (rightly, as I believe) traces the basis of this not to his death alone but to his entire ministry and person – in a word, to the incarnation: he was made under law, that he might ransom those who are under the

----

[12] *JTS* n.s. 22.2 (Oct. 1971), 349ff.; cf., independently, J. D. G. Dunn, 'Paul's Understanding of the Death of Jesus', in R. J. Banks, ed., *Reconciliation and Hope* (for L. L. Morris) (Exeter: Paternoster 1974), 125ff. (130).

law (Gal. 4: 4f.); he became sin (?) for us that, in him, we might become God's righteousness (2 Cor. 5: 21). And Father Gerald O'Collins has warned us against tracing our salvation exclusively to the incarnation and not also to the death, or to either or both of these and not also the 'posterior mysteries', as he calls them, of the exaltation, Pentecost, the birth of the Church and the *parousia*.[13] I take his point; and to find salvation in the whole of this 'Christ-event' is the same thing, I suspect, as finding the unique quality of the death of Christ in the potentially total inclusiveness of the life thereby made available.

And if humanity as a whole may be spoken of as having caused the death of Christ, all those who accept his Lordship will voluntarily admit this and identify themselves with his death, accepting his obedience as their own. Thus it comes about that, in the Pauline or near-Pauline epistles, words compounded with *sun-* ('together with') are used to describe this identification of any Christian and of all Christians with Christ's death: to share its form (Phil. 3: 10), to become fused or united with it (Rom. 6: 5), to die with him (2 Tim. 2: 11), to be buried with him (Rom. 6: 4; Col. 2: 12), to suffer with him (Rom. 8: 17), to be crucified with him (Rom. 6: 6; Gal. 2: 19). It is often pointed out that, whereas such verbs, denoting suffering and death, are found in a past tense in Romans and Galatians as well as elsewhere, verbs denoting sharing Christ's risen life are found in a past tense exclusively in the captivity epistles: to be raised with Christ, Eph. 2: 6; Col. 2: 12; 3: 1, and to sit with him in the heavenlies, Eph. 2: 6. However, G. M. Styler has pointed out that in Rom. 6: 11, 13, Paul bids his readers reckon themselves, or present themselves as, alive to God, which shows that Paul does not relegate this aliveness exclusively to the future; and, from other phrases also, it is clear that Paul reckons that Christians enjoy here and now a new sort of life (Rom. 6: 4; 2 Cor. 5: 17).[14]

Thus, to gather up the features that seem to make Christ's death 'for us' distinctive, we may say that we have found that any man who has the courage and devotion to go, or be willing

---

[13] *The Easter Jesus* (Darton, Longman and Todd 1973), Ch. 10.
[14] 'The Basis of Obligation in Paul's Christology and Ethics', in *Christ and Spirit in the New Testament* as in Chapter 1, n. 19, 175ff. (181ff.). See also R. H. Gundry, as in Chapter 2, n. 40, 57.

to go, to death in his loyalty to God and to truth, brings benefit
to others – in some cases, material benefit, but in all cases
spiritual; and that he may therefore rightly be said to have
endured 'for' others – for certain others, if not for all others. Isa.
53, for instance, may be read as denoting universal atonement.[15]
But it is of Christ alone that Christians found themselves saying:
This one 'died for us, that whether we "wake" or "sleep"
[? survive to the *parousia* or die first] we might live together
with him' (1 Thess. 5: 10); or, again (with reference to any
Christian whatever), 'You have been purchased at a price' – that
is, at the price of his death (1 Cor. 6: 20); or (with reference to
any and every Christian 'brother'), he is one 'for whom Christ
died' (Rom. 14: 15); or, 'he laid down his life for us' (1 John 3:
16); or, 'one died for all, therefore all have died' (2 Cor. 5: 14);
or, perhaps most remarkable of all, 'for this purpose Christ died
and lived again, that he might be Lord of dead and living' (Rom.
14: 9).

It is this universal scope, assumed by Christians as a matter of
course, that seems distinctive about their estimate of the meaning
of Christ's death; and it is dependent on his experienced aliveness
and his universal inclusiveness.[16] And those in every generation
from then to now who know him alive are able to turn A. E.
Housman's bitterly ironical 'Easter Hymn' into a genuine
invocation:

> If in that Syrian garden, ages slain,
> You sleep, and know not you are dead in vain,
> Nor even in dreams behold how dark and bright
> Ascends in smoke and fire by day and night
> The hate you died to quench and could but fan,
> Sleep well and see no morning, son of man.
>
> But if, the grave rent and the stone rolled by,
> At the right hand of majesty on high

[15] F. Hahn, *The Titles of Jesus in Christology* as in Introduction n. 12, 348.
[16] For remarks about the distinctiveness of Christian claims for Jesus, see Jürgen
Roloff, *NTS* 19.1 (Oct. 1972), 38ff., suggesting that they go back to the *diakonein*
of the eucharistic tradition. Cf. Robert A. Traina, *The Atonement, History, and
Kerygma: a Study in Protestant Theology* (Drew University 1966: University
Microfilms, inc., Ann Arbor, Michigan), 187: 'he accomplished something in
his coming and in his life unto death on behalf of men which was necessary
for atonement and which men could not have done for themselves, though
their free response still remains indispensable to make complete at-one-ment.'

You sit, and sitting so remember yet
Your tears, your agony and bloody sweat,
Your cross and passion and the life you gave,
Bow hither out of heaven and see and save.[17]

If we ask what are the doctrinal implications of this understanding of Christ as making himself available, through his death,
to all men, the answer is that they constitute one more factor in
a Christology which finds in Christ not just an example but the
Mediator between God and man. It means, if it is justified by the
evidence, more than that Jesus Christ *indicates* how a man may
become rightly related to other men in an ideal society.[18] It means
that Jesus Christ, crucified and raised from among the dead,
actually *is*, or *constitutes* that ideal society: he is the ultimate Adam,
to be incorporated in whom is to belong in the renewed society.
But this will need to be further discussed in the light of the
summing up of our findings. Meanwhile, it will be appropriate
to look at the second of the assumptions which point to a corporate Christ even in writers who do not explicitly acknowledge
it: this is the fulfilment theme.

[17] A. E. Housman, *More Poems* (London: Jonathan Cape 1936), 15.
[18] A. R. Peacocke, *Science and the Christian Experiment*, as in Chapter 2, n. 4, and
'The Nature and Purpose of Man in Science and Christian Theology', *Zygon*
8. 3–4 (Sept.–Dec. 1973), 373ff.

5

The fulfilment theme in the New Testament[1]

In Matthew's Gospel, Ch. 2, in connexion with the beautiful story of the Wise Men from the East, and the horror story of the massacre of the innocents, comes the story of the flight of the holy family to Egypt. When, ultimately, they returned from Egypt, this (says the Evangelist) took place '...that what was spoken by the Lord through the prophet might be fulfilled, when he said "Out of Egypt I called my son"'.

He is quoting Hos. 11: 1, 'I called my son out of Egypt'. But that was not a *prophecy* at all – not a *prediction*, that is. It was simply a statement about the past (a 'postdiction', if you like). So how could it have been *fulfilled?* When Hosea 11: 1 says, 'I called my son out of Egypt', the reference is, of course, to the exodus. It is 'Israel', according to Exod. 4: 22, who is God's son, his firstborn; and Hosea is making a poetic reference to the celebrated beginnings of Israel as a nation in covenant with Yahweh.

Is there any sense, then, in which the Evangelist can properly appeal to Hosea 11: 1 as a prediction *fulfilled* in the story of Jesus? Even if the flight into Egypt actually took place and is not legend, how could it be said to have *fulfilled* what was spoken by the Lord through the prophet when the prophet is himself describing something which was already in the past?

I have started from one instance – taken almost at random – of a use of the Hebrew Scriptures by the New Testament at which most readers today will feel discomfort and dissatisfaction because it seems to ignore the original meaning of the words and takes them out of their context. Matthew is doing here something

[1] I owe thanks to the editors of *The Journal of Theology for Southern Africa* for permission to reprint here part of a lecture published in that journal (No 14 (March 1976), 6ff.) under this title.

that the men of Qumran did also.[2] That Jewish sect which has come to be well known to scholars in our day through the discovery of the Dead Sea Scrolls at wadi Qumran, practised just the same techniques in their use – or one might say their *ab*use – of Scripture. They took the book of Habakkuk, for instance, and read off current events from it (or, rather, read current events *into* it). What the prophet had written originally, perhaps, with reference to the Chaldaeans of his day, six centuries earlier, is now annexed, so to speak, quite arbitrarily by the Dead Sea sectarians, and declared to concern the Seleucid Greeks or even the Romans of their own day, shortly before the Christian era.

Most of Matthew's so-called 'formula quotations' (that is, his quotations from Scripture which are introduced by some such formula as 'that it might be fulfilled...') seem to be doing much the same. Ignoring the original context and doing violence to the original meaning, the Evangelist fits the ancient words by force into a contemporary, Christian meaning: 'The virgin shall be with child...', 'You, Bethlehem, are not the least...', 'Rachel weeping for her children...', 'He shall be called a Nazarene...'. What are we to make of this use of Scripture which seems to treat it as a two-dimensional plane surface, from any part of which texts may be arbitrarily culled? Does not such a use of Scripture evacuate Scripture itself of any authority it might have, and depend, instead, on antecedent convictions altogether unrelated to that Scripture? The men of Qumran interpreted Habakkuk in the way they did, not because Habakkuk contained that meaning, but because they believed themselves to be living in the last, climactic days, and because they held that Scripture's function was to point to those last days. Do Matthew's 'formula quotations' prove more than that Christians, in their turn, were convinced, on other grounds, that Christ was the supreme Fulfiller, and were simply using Scripture as a vehicle for this independent conviction?

I believe that this is undeniably true. But I also believe that there is another and a much profounder sense in which Jesus Christ is the fulfilment of Scripture; and the thesis of this chapter

---

[2] O. Betz, *Offenbarung und Schriftforschung in den Qumransekte* (Tübingen 1960); F. F. Bruce, *Biblical Exegesis in the Qumran Texts* (London: Tyndale Press 1960).

is that what I have ventured to call the arbitrary use of Scripture (causing discomfort and dissatisfaction to most readers today) is a symptom of a deep reality which can be seen as a true and organically connected part of the meaning of Scripture. Or, to put my thesis in a nutshell, I shall argue that what I am calling the 'vehicular' use of Scripture by Christians – the arbitrary use of words, that is, as a vehicle, simply, for something that is derived from elsewhere – is a symptom of the discovery that, in a deeply organic way, Jesus was indeed the fulfiller of something which is basic in the whole of Scripture. In the case of Jesus – in contrast (I think it has to be said) to the Qumran sect's leader – there was found to be fulfilment in a far profounder, and a deeply religious sense. Although a writer like this Evangelist does not seem to discriminate between the more superficial and the more profound, I believe that there is significance in the very fact that he wanted to find those more superficial and more arbitrary coincidences and relate them, not like the Qumran sectarians, just to current affairs, but to *Jesus*: it is only to be explained by recognizing that already the Evangelist and his fellow-Christians had discovered in Jesus an overall fulfilment, on the deepest level, of what Scripture as a whole reflected.

My point, then, is that, although many of the New Testament's claims about Jesus as fulfilling prophecy are, to our critical eyes, manifestly forced and artificial and unconvincing, yet the very fact that those claims were made at all points to an underlying motive. The incentive and impetus behind this search for *testimonia* turns out, I believe, to be a profound fact of relationship. Jesus had, in the experience of his followers, actually been found to embody, to represent, and to enable them to share an ideal relationship with God; a relationship which their 'Old Testament' Scriptures (as Christians call them) had adumbrated, but of which God's People had constantly fallen short, or against which they had even rebelled. Moreover, this seemed to be true of Jesus in a collective as well as in an individual sense. Jesus, in an extraordinary way, turned out to be occupying the position that, according to the Scriptures, had always been intended for Israel, and, through Israel, for all mankind. In this profound and organic sense Jesus was indeed the fulfilment of Scripture because he was the fulfilment of man-in-relation-to-God; and the

ingenious discovery or invention of abstruse details of alleged
fulfilment of alleged prediction is only a symptom of a deep
conviction based on a truly personal and organic religious event.

The people of Qumran believed that they were living in the
final days before the wind-up of God's work of rescue for Israel.
So they went to their Scriptures, and, with the impetus of this
initial conviction, they attached to words of Scripture – the words
of Habakkuk, for instance – a significance that did not originally
belong to them. If one asks the question, 'Why did they do it?
What led them to believe that their days were so crucial and so
decisive?', the answer, I suppose, is that they saw the Jewish
establishment tottering, that they believed themselves called to
be the heroic, suffering nucleus of a renewed and reformed
Israel, and that they had – or had had – a notable leader in 'the
Teacher of Righteousness' (or 'the Authentic Teacher'). Their
circumstances and their believed vocation led them to see God's
hand at work in a climactic way in their day and through their
community, and in their leader. Incidentally, this leader appears
himself to have claimed to have been given a special endowment
of ability to interpret Scripture (see 1QH 12. 13ff., 1QpHab 7.
4f.). Martin Hengel vividly reconstructs some of the features of
this remarkable leader and of the crisis to which he was responding, in his *Judaism and Hellenism*.[3] Now, in a similar way, Christians believed themselves to be the true Israel, living in the last
days, charged to be the growing-point of the new age. But the
most conspicuous difference distinguishing the Christian 'sectarians', if we may so style them, from the sectarians of Qumran
was twofold. First, Christians found themselves an outgoing,
world-affirming, missionary movement, unlike Qumran's reclu-
sive, monastic sect. And, secondly, they had for their leader not
a mere instructor or teacher, whom they followed during his
lifetime and to whom they looked back after his death, but one
whom they recognized as a present, living person who himself
embodied true Israel, and, indeed, true Adam, as well as representing God himself in their experience of new life in him. In
himself Jesus represented, somehow, the right relationship to

---

[3] Eng. trans. (London: SCM 1974), i. 224ff., from *Judentum und Hellenismus,
Studien zu ihrer Begegnung unter besonderer Berücksichtigung Palästinas bis zur Mitte
des 2 Jh.s v. Chr.*, *WUNT* 10 (Tübingen: Mohr ²1973).

God, both of each human individual, and, collectively, of God's representative, suffering, missionary people; and, beyond them again, of mankind inclusively. In him they found a new life, individually and socially; incorporated in him, they entered a renewed humanity; and upon him, therefore, they recognized as converging all the strands of right relationship: he was the coping-stone of the whole edifice of God's relations with his People. That is why Paul can describe a distinctively Christian experience of God's Spirit as the experience of the Spirit of God's Son, or, of 'the Spirit of adoption' – that is the Spirit that causes us to be adopted as God's sons, the Spirit that enables us to cry, 'Abba, dear Father, your will be done' (Rom. 8: 15, Gal. 4: 6). The formula-quotation from Matthew from which we began applies to Jesus, arbitrarily enough, a phrase from Hosea which happened to speak of a calling from Egypt, and which described Israel, collectively, as God's Son; but independently of the ingenuity of any midrashic school in the fanciful use of Scripture, a widely shared and recognized experience had found in Christ that corporate sonship, that true Israel, indeed that Adam or renewed mankind, by belonging to which Christians found a right relation both to God and to one another as fellow-members of the People of God.

It is on Jesus, as on no other figure in Jewish myth or history, that his followers found converging all the ideal qualities of a collective body of persons in a right relation with God; and if Paul speaks of the Church as the Body of Christ (or as a body because incorporated in Christ),[4] that is partly because he has found in Christ all that the People of God were designed to be.

Christian interpreters of those days may have thought of Scripture as a two-dimensional field from any part of which a suitable word or phrase might be culled to reinforce their estimate of Jesus; but in fact the Old Testament is very much three-dimensional: it contains a great deal of historical depth and perspective; it reflects generations of dialogue between God and man, of trial and error, of response and failure; and it therefore contains paradigms and patterns of relationship. And it is the relational patterns that Jesus can be seen to have fulfilled,

---

[4] See the discussion in Chapter 2 above.

whether or not those other alleged correspondences in the 'formula-quotations' are valid.

Accordingly, I find myself distinguishing two uses of Scripture as respectively 'vehicular' and 'relational'. By a vehicular use, I mean (as I have already said) the use of Scriptural words simply as a vehicle. In themselves, such words do not authenticate what they bear: they merely convey it. 'Out of Egypt have I called my son' is a phrase which had no authority of its own to lend to Jesus; it is merely a vehicle of words to carry a particular understanding of one whose authority is derived from elsewhere. But when words describing some actual structure of relationship are applied to Jesus, then it is because Jesus turns out to be their real fulfilment – the realization or climax or epitome or embodiment of the relationship in question; and such a '*relational*' use of Scripture represents a profound religious insight. If the Old Testament is the story of how God achieves his design for man through the suffering minority who minister to others, through the rejected few whose faithfulness is their ultimate vindication, through those who obey even when they know it leads to extinction, and even if they cannot see the ultimate creative event beyond extinction, and who are ready to trust God as their Father even in the darkness of annihilation, then, to find that Jesus of Nazareth fulfils these patterns is to discover a new depth in fulfilment.

Illustrations of what I mean are ready to hand, but need not be elaborated, because this has been done elsewhere. The best illustrations are, perhaps, 'the Son of Man', if my interpretation of this phrase is correct, and 'the Son of God'; and both of these have already been discussed (pp. 11–31 above). Other figures in the complex network of Old Testament testimonia used in the New Testament are elucidated in the late C. H. Dodd's brilliant little study, *According to the Scriptures,* in which he ventured to attribute the creation of this remarkable 'sub-structure of New Testament theology', as he called it, to the mind of Jesus himself. In a passage from which I have already had occasion to quote, he wrote:

To have brought together...the Son of Man who is the people of the saints of the Most High, the Man of God's right hand, who is also the vine of Israel, the Son of Man who after humiliation is crowned with glory and honour, and the victorious priest-King at the right hand of God, is an achievement of interpretative imagination which results in the creation of an entirely new figure. It involves an original, and far-reaching, resolution of the tension between the individual and the collective aspects of several of these figures...This is a piece of genuinely creative thinking. Who was responsible for it?...to account for the beginning of this most original and fruitful process of re-thinking the Old Testament we found need to postulate a creative mind. The Gospels offer us one. Are we compelled to reject the offer? (109, 110).

It is true, as I have said, that New Testament thought was sometimes on a very different and much more superficial level. Acts 17: 2f. well summarizes the purely 'verbal' sort of apologetic that evidently went on in the early Church, when it describes Paul as discoursing from the Scriptures and presenting his hearers with the position that the Christ had to suffer and rise from among the dead, and that this Jesus, 'whom I declare to you', is the Christ. But I am suggesting that the application to Jesus of the more superficial sort of fulfilment, in which Scripture is merely 'vehicular', is explicable only by the discovery of the deeply 'relational' and organic sort of fulfilment, in which Jesus is seen as the Fulfiller in a supreme sense. And my reason for calling attention to the motif of fulfilment is that it seems to me to constitute an important example, that takes us well beyond the limits of merely Pauline thought, of an understanding of Jesus which makes no sense unless we allow that he must be in some way more than individual. To find him to be the coping-stone of the whole edifice of God's relations with man is, ultimately, to recognize him as the one who fills the cosmos and fulfils God's design for all creation.

That is the purpose of adducing the fulfilment theme in this sequence of investigations. Before leaving this theme, here is a purely linguistic observation which may or may not be significant. The word *pleroun* bursts into proliferation in the New Testament. It is used indiscriminately, both of Jesus' verification of alleged predictions and of his fulfilling the Law and the Prophets in a deeper sense. In a study of it (suggested to me by a hint in a book by Professor Richard Longenecker)[5] I asked whether this sudden

---

[5] See my 'Fulfilment-Words in the New Testament: Use and Abuse', *NTS* 14.3 (April 1968), 293ff.

efflorescence of its use might not have been touched off by some usage of Jesus' own; and I showed, at least, that an impetus was given to it by the sort of insights on the part of the early Church that I have been describing. Certainly, for whatever reason, it is a striking linguistic phenomenon.

After the New Testament the idea of fulfilment runs riot, and the Epistle of Barnabas, as well as Justin's *Trypho*, shows what can happen when ingenuity gets to work on an arbitrary selection of texts. 'Who is this', says Justin Martyr triumphantly to Trypho (126),

who was once called 'Angel of great counsel' [the allusion is to Isa. 9], and, through Ezekiel, was called 'man', and 'what seemed a son of man' through Daniel, and 'servant' through Isaiah, and 'Messiah' and 'God to whom obeisance is done' through David, and 'Messiah' and 'Stone' through many, and 'Wisdom' through Solomon, and 'Joseph' and 'Judah' and 'Star' through Moses, and 'branch' ['sprout'] (*anatolē*) through Zechariah, and 'the suffering one' and 'Jacob' and 'Israel' again through Isaiah, and who was called 'rod' and 'flower' and 'corner stone' and 'Son of God'...?

In that welter of allusion you can see just the same mingling of far-fetched fancy with a profound perception of Christ as the ultimate pattern of man's right relationship with God, the epitome of all that Adam and Israel meant. Thus, the deeper insights are not forgotten and the work of revelation in Jesus Christ himself is not undone. Whatever the misguided ingenuity of a Christian midrash may do, it cannot conceal the profound roles of suffering service and obedient sonship which Jesus Christ embodies and makes possible for those who become embodied in him. Matthew and Justin both present us with the question, 'Who is this?'

6

Retrospect

It is time to look back over this inquiry into the roots of Christology and to collect up the findings; and then an attempt will be
made to draw some conclusions.

The contention has been that development is a better analogy
than evolution for the genesis of New Testament Christology.
That is to say, it is not that new conceptions of Jesus were
generated in an evolutionary succession of new species by the
creative imagination of the Christian communities as they drew
upon the resources of other religions and cults. Rather, communities and individuals gained new insights into the meaning
of what was there all along – 'from the beginning' as the writer
of 1 John would say. To say this is to maintain that New Testament conceptions of Jesus are all, in their different degrees, 'true'
to the Person, Jesus himself, even if some are more profound
than others.

This, admittedly, looks like a rash and question-begging claim.
As was recognized at the beginning of this study, it might be
argued that it either means more than is warranted by the
evidence, or that it means nothing because it is a circular statement. It would, indeed, be a totally circular statement if 'true
to Jesus' simply meant true to the Jesus whom New Testament
writers believed themselves to have found. But that is not the
meaning intended throughout this study. The meaning intended
is, rather, that there is a continuous identity between the Christ
of the ministry and the Christ of the first believers after Easter;
and that the characterizations of Christ in the new Testament are
better accounted for as springing from contact with Jesus himself
than as springing from contact with extraneous sources. In other
words, there is a reply to the charge that, if one includes 'Jesus
after his resurrection', then one opens the door to any and every

understanding of this exalted Being, and one might as well capitulate to an 'evolutionary' scheme after all, since 'Jesus after his resurrection' could well mean Jesus as imagined by those who, in fact, were drawing upon pagan Saviour-cults for their conceptions. The reply is in the continuity which the preceding study claims to find between the undoubtedly historical Jesus and the New Testament experiences of him; and this constitutes also the reply to the objection that this claim goes beyond the evidence.

This claim to continuity is not based mainly on the words of Jesus. Any case for a 'high' Christology that depended on the authenticity of the alleged claims of Jesus about himself, especially in the Fourth Gospel, would indeed be precarious. This claim to continuity rests, rather, on the evidence that, from very early days, Jesus was being interpreted as an inclusive, Israel-wide – indeed, Adam-wide – person: one who, as no merely human individual, included persons and communities within him, and upon whom Christians found converging all the patterns of relationship between God and man with which they were familiar from their Scriptures. It is contributory evidence, pointing in the same direction, if 'the Son of Man' is best understood as Jesus' own symbol for his destiny, if 'the Son of God' represents a relationship that actually emerges from authentic traditions about Jesus, if 'Messiah' is a title that seems to have been attached to Jesus because of his own very original interpretation of his role, and if the title *Kurios* is better explained as continuous with Semitic titles than as first derived from pagan cults. Thus, such evidence as has been examined in this study does appear to converge upon the conclusion that it is the Person himself, both immanent and transcendent, who is the source of these remarkable estimates.

But does this apply to all of the various Christological views of the New Testament? What about the virginal conception? What about preexistence? If it comes to that, what about the designation 'God', applied within the New Testament to Jesus? Are all these understandings of Jesus to be claimed as 'true to the original'? For my part, I hold no doctrine of the inerrancy of the New Testament, no brief for the view that every estimate of Christ within it is to be accepted uncritically, simply because it is within the canon. But my belief is that it is the more individualistic Christologies, such as that of Luke–Acts, that are less adequate and less close to the original than the more inclusive Christology of Paul; and it seems to me that, with the latter (and with many of the implications even of those more individualistic Christologies), go the very highest Christologies that are to be found in the New Testament.

It is open to doubt whether Jesus was called 'God' outright as early as Paul himself. It is true that B. M. Metzger has made a remarkably cogent case for so understanding the crucial verse, Rom. 9: 5, for he shows that, quite apart from anything that may be gathered by minute considerations of early punctuation, it is syntactically odd, in that particular complex of words, to understand the phrase 'God blessed for evermore' otherwise than as applied to Christ.[1] Yet, there is something in me that agrees with C. H. Dodd's instinctive reluctance to allow that a Jew of Paul's upbringing could have used *theos* in quite that way. But, whether by Paul or not, Jesus is certainly called 'God' within the New Testament (John 20: 28 and probably Tit. 2: 13). Is this not a deviation from 'what was from the beginning'; is it not a new species, evolved in the transit from Palestine across the Levant? If Metzger, and others who hold his view, are right about Rom. 9: 5, it would be difficult (in that particular context) to maintain that it was a non-Jewish borrowing from pagan ideas. But even if it is found only in the Fourth Gospel and the Pastoral Epistles, it is far from clear that this designation is alien to the *implications* of what is demonstrably 'there' at an early date or that it is incompatible with authentic evidence about what Jesus was. Part of the strength of *The Riddle of the New Testament*,[2] by the late Sir Edwyn Hoskyns and the late Noel Davey, was that, whatever reservations one might have about much of its argument, it showed the impossibility of analysing out gospel traditions that made any sense at all, without the divine factor attaching to them. 'To dissect' is, in this case at any rate, 'to murder'. The divine is inseparably there all along.

[1] B. M. Metzger, 'The Punctuation of Rom. 9: 5', in *Christ and Spirit in the New Testament* as in Chapter 1, n. 19, 95ff. (103ff.).

[2] First published in 1931 by Faber and Faber, London; many subsequent reprints and translations.

As for preexistence, this is an elusive idea. It is not easy to conceive of a genuinely human person being conscious of his own preexistence, and it would not be right to build upon John 17: 5 as though this, in itself, constituted evidence of Jesus' *ipsissima vox*. But it is arguable that when Paul (Col. 1: 15ff.) and John articulate the belief in the preexistence of Christ, they are only drawing out the implications of their experience of him as transcending the temporal.

I have already argued that Paul's understanding of Jesus is like a theist's understanding of God – that he is personal but more than individual. I have also argued that, even in those parts of the New Testament where Christ is conceived of much more individualistically, he is nevertheless conceived of as definitely transcendent and divine; and that, in fact, conceptions of him as the convergence-point of all the Old Testament patterns of relationship between God and his people, and as the universal Saviour, carry more than individual implications even for those writers who are not explicit about this.

In the light, then, of all this evidence about how Christ was understood and experienced by Christians after his death, it is possible to approach the question: What does this mean regarding preexistence? Mr J. L. Houlden has recently asked, once again, what led Christians to attribute preexistence to Christ, and, as a tentative answer, suggests that it was the new life which they found through Jesus: '...must we not say' (he writes) 'that the understanding of Jesus as the pre-existent agent in creation was rooted in an experience, as a result of him, of freshness in relation to *everything*?'[3] I agree with that, except that I want to be more specific about the person of Jesus himself. I want to say not only that, 'as a result of him', they experienced a new world; but that they experienced Jesus himself as in a dimension transcending the human and the temporal. It is not just that, owing (somehow) to Jesus, they found new life; it is that they discovered in Jesus himself, alive and present, a divine dimension such that he must always and eternally have existed in it. If, subsequently to his death, he is conceived of as an eternally living being, personal but more than individual, one with God and the

---

[3] 'The Place of Jesus', in M. Hooker and C. Hickling, edd., *What about the New Testament? Essays in honour of Christopher Evans* (London: SCM 1975), 103ff. (110).

source of salvation, and if he is still firmly identified with Jesus of Nazareth, then what of his preexistence? I am well aware of the vast difficulties presented, especially to modern thought, by the notion of the personal preexistence of the One whom we know as Jesus. No doubt John 17 and Col. 1 imply it, but the question is, Can we think like that ourselves? and Is it true to 'the original Jesus'? I am well aware that the majority, probably, of modern Christologies have abandoned such a notion altogether; and that the *religionsgeschichtliche Schule* of New Testament research will regard it as something evolved away from the original. But I am bound to say that the examination of the reflexions, in the New Testament, of what may be called his post-existence, makes me hesitate to dismiss the idea. It is easy enough, of course, to say that only the Logos was preexistent, and that the Logos did not become identified with the person whom we know as Jesus until Jesus was conceived and born. 'A Christology from below', as we have learnt to call it, is content to say that when Jesus came, he fitted perfectly with God's design and thus coincided (as it were) with the preexistent Logos. This is rationally intelligible and attractive, and it leaves room for Jesus to be himself a product of biological evolution and a man from among mankind. But then what becomes of the sequel? If this Jesus of history turns out, in subsequent Christian experience, to be eternal and more than individual but still personally identical with the One who was known as Jesus, how are we to deny him a personal preexistence comparable to this? We are bound indeed to agree with ancient writers that there was no question of flesh and bones until 'the incarnation' as we call it. Equally, we shall probably all find ourselves bound to part company from those same writers when they aver that Jesus retained his flesh and bones in his 'post-existence' (as I am calling it). But is it not another matter when we come to consider not his physical constitution but his *personal identity*? This somehow is retained after his death – in terms, we might possibly think, of the 'spiritual body' of 1 Cor. 15, though, if so, in a more than merely human category, and, for Paul at least, in a more than merely individual way. The same person, Jesus, is now known as transcendental and in the categories – personal but not merely individual – in which theists think of God.

But if the identity of Jesus of Nazareth is thus retained after his death, in a different dimension and in one to which it is difficult to deny the epithet 'eternal', what are we to say of him before his birth and conception? Can 'eternal' personality existing after the incarnation be denied existence before it? Must we, conceivably, entertain some such idea as that he had (or was?) a 'body' in the Pauline sense, though not of flesh and blood, before as well as after the incarnation? Surely, I tell myself, this is an impossibly crude question! Besides, what does it do to the doctrine of creation? And yet, and yet...: possibly it is a question worth asking, in the light of undoubted New Testament experience; and, I also ask myself, if we reject it as a stupid or an improper question, then what are we doing to the doctrine of the Trinity?

Thus, a case is, perhaps, to be made even for the idea of Christ's preexistence being a legitimate way of describing an aspect of 'what was there from the beginning'.[4]

Whether I have overstated my case or overplayed my hand, it will be for my critics to judge. It is certainly true, as I said at the beginning, that the edges of the 'development' model and of the 'evolution' model will be found to be blurred, and that it is unrealistic to draw too sharp a distinction between them. But I am convinced that they represent a real difference at least in tendency, and I shall be satisfied if I have made a case for reconsidering the basic appropriateness of the 'development' model. The virginal conception I do not propose to discuss here. It has been very widely discussed even in recent years.[5] But, even putting it at its most reduced level and assuming it to be a myth,

---

[4] I do not think that I am plagiarizing, for this essay represents my own thinking; but before writing it I had read Lady Helen Oppenheimer's striking book, *Incarnation and Immanence* (as in Chapter 2, n. 2), and there are parts of it that seem to me to be not far from the position I am adopting. If I have unconsciously borrowed ideas, let this be my acknowledgement. If my own ideas are really alien to Lady Oppenheimer's intention, let this be my apology for implicating her.

I owe thanks to the University of Aberdeen for an invitation to lecture on 1 May 1975, when some of this material and some of that in Chapter 3 was first presented; and to the University of South Africa for welcoming me with lavish generosity on a visit in July–August of the same year, when I presented it again. This lecture has appeared in *Theologia Evangelica* (Pretoria) 8.3 (Sept. 1975), 137ff.

[5] See Introduction, n. 7.

one might still maintain that it was an expression of that transcendental quality which, from the very beginning, seems to have attached to Christ; and, incidentally, it seems that one would not have to go outside Judaism for the material of the story.

It remains to ask what are the wider implications of this view.

7

Prospect: the 'ultimacy' of Christ

The New Testament specialist cannot be content to stay within his own field for ever. Sooner or later, he is bound to ask himself what his findings mean for Christian doctrine in its larger setting, in religion today, in human society, and, indeed, in relation to the whole universe. Accordingly I find myself asking questions which I am aware of being incompetent even to formulate correctly, let alone to answer. But I ask them unashamedly, because every Christian, whether expert or not, has to ask them; and I include them in this study as a bridge to that which lies beyond it. What bearing do the findings of a limited inquiry into New Testament Christology have upon what is often called the 'finality' of Christ? 'Finality' is a question-begging word: 'ultimacy' is possibly a less unsatisfactory one – though it is questionable whether *finis* really means anything essentially different from *ultimum*. But, in any case, the question is whether God's continuing revelation of himself in man's constantly widening experiences may still be meaningfully described as 'in Christ'. Can it be reasonably maintained (on the analogy of the position that has been maintained for the New Testament period in this book) that, in progressively learning more about man and his psychology, about his personality and his mutual relations, about society and the corporate character of human life, and about the universe, we are only finding a 'developing' insight into what, all along, has been given in Christ? Is the understanding of Jesus as more than individual, as transcendent and eternal and all comprehensive, which already emerges in the New Testament, valid for all time? Does the Christ of the New Testament keep pace, so to speak, with new discoveries? It seems to me that modern psychological and sociological research does often confirm insights already gained through Christ; and, conversely, that New Testament insights into the meaning of human life and of community do often illuminate modern investigation into psychology and sociology. But can one generalize and say that this is always so, and will always be so? The study of Christology needs must take account of modern insights into personality and society; but will the result be only a developing insight into what was, from the beginning, implicit in Christ, or will Christ be left behind and Christology cease to be a relevant term? That is at least part of what is meant by asking about the ultimacy of Christ.

There is also the question of Christ's relation to the whole universe. Is it reasonable to claim 'cosmic' ultimacy for Christ today, or were the cosmic Christologies of Colossians, Hebrews, and John meaningful only so long as cosmology was itself anthropocentric? Now that the planet Earth has been cut down to its relatively infinitesimal size, does cosmic Christology lose all credibility? The answer depends, presumably, on how far a Logos-Christology may be pressed and on what value is allowed to human personality. Despite its microscopic bulk, it is conceivable that, in terms of the quality of relationship, the human race still represents the apex of God's creation. But even if not, it is also conceivable that the same utterance or Logos of God whom men know anthropomorphically in God's incarnation in flesh and blood, may be knowable elsewhere in some quite different form – allomorphically, if you like. It has been argued in these chapters that the one who was identifiable as Jesus of Nazareth came to be known and experienced in the way in which God is known and experienced – as personal, indeed, but more than individual. But if Jesus Christ is thus found to be like God and one with God, it follows that he must be able to communicate himself, as we may conceive of the Creator communicating himself, to any beings in any part of the universe, in whatever is the most appropriate form.

> With this ambiguous earth
> His dealings have been told us. These abide:
> The signal to the maid, the human birth,
> the lesson, and the young Man crucified.
>
> But not a star of all
> The innumerable host of stars has heard

How He administered this terrestrial ball.
Our race have kept their Lord's entrusted Word.

Of His earth-visiting feet
None knows the secret – cherished, perilous;
The terrible, shamefast, frightened, whispered, sweet,
Heart-shattering secret of His way with us.

No planet knows that this
Our wayside planet, carrying land and wave,
Love and life multiplied, and pain and bliss,
Bears as chief treasure one forsaken grave.

Nor, in our little day,
May His devices with the heavens be guessed;
His pilgrimage to thread the Milky Way,
Or His bestowals there, be manifest.

But in the eternities
Doubtless we shall compare together, hear
A million alien gospels, in what guise
He trod the Pleiades, the Lyre, the Bear.

Oh be prepared, my soul,
To read the inconceivable, to scan
The infinite forms of God those stars unroll
When, in our turn, we show to them a Man.

Alice Meynell.

But even when thought is limited to earth, Christological speculation still has to face the question, What if Man evolves on earth into a new species? Will the incarnation then cease to be the fullest expression of God for that new race? Presumably, some form of Logos-Christology, again, will have to be invoked. If the Logos can be conceived of as expressed in non-human ways elsewhere in the universe, this would presumably hold good also for a post-human species on earth. Indeed, why should not this already hold good for non-human or pre-human existence? Is it possible, perhaps, that the Creator expresses his 'Word' as fully as possible at some point in the history of each level of existence, from the most basic form of matter to the most complex level of inanimate existence, and then (if this is not already an arbitrary division) from the most primitive living cell up to the threshold of the human? Or was this whole process (one wonders reverently) recapitulated in perfection in the conception and birth of Jesus? If Jesus was perfect man, was he made up of physically perfect parts? Or is this merely to beg the question of what perfection means anyway?

Returning, however, to the question about the post-human, it may be that this sort of speculation is misconceived; for it seems possible that man as an individual has already reached the peak of that line of evolution, and that future evolution will be not in the emergence of a new, post-human species, but rather in the direction of new ranges of essentially human social life and culture and interrelatedness: the 'new man' will, on this showing, be not a post-anthropic species but rather a better developed human society.[1] When science fiction attempts to picture superman, it often ends up with only a more intensely human form of life, where individuals are better and more sensitively related to one another in a better integrated society, perhaps by some highly developed extra-sensory perception which enables them to be instantly *en rapport* with one another. This may be merely because humans cannot stand outside human ways of thought; but it might be because that, in fact, will be the direction of actual progress. At any rate, the immediate question is whether Christ will be found to be constantly the ultimate for every age of human existence, or whether he is, even within human existence, only relative and liable to be superseded. This, as I have said, is strictly outside a purely phenomenological report on the religious experience of the New Testament period, which is what constitutes the bulk of this book. But it is an obvious question arising from it which no concerned Christian can leave untouched.

In a lecture delivered at the annual meeting of the Society for the Study of Theology at Lancaster in April 1973, I argued that, just as, in the New Testament period, Christ was recognized, indeed, in terms of various familiar categories and yet each time proved to be too big for that category and burst out of it in startling ways, so one might deduce, by extrapolation from this, that he would continue to confront each generation in the same way – familiar yet startling, recognizable yet always transcending recognition, always ahead, as well as abreast: the ultimate from

[1] See, once again, A. R. Peacocke, *Science and the Christian Experiment* as in Chapter 2, n. 4.

whom each generation is equidistant. The lecture was printed in
Theology 76. 641 (November 1973), 562ff., together with a comment by Dr Haddon Willmer of the University of Leeds (*ibid.*
573ff.). To this I replied, and Dr Willmer responded, in *Theology*
77. 650 (August 1974), 404ff. My lecture repeats in summary form
some of the material given more fully in earlier parts of this book,
but it seems best to leave it as it stands, since otherwise the
balance might be destroyed. The whole dialogue is here reprinted, by kind permission of the Editor of *Theology*, with only
very small adjustments, and I offer, at the end, some brief
concluding remarks.

I. THE DISTINCTIVENESS OF CHRIST

It is not easy to decide precisely what questions are implied by
this title, or which of them ought to be considered under it. I
am going to assume, for the purposes of this paper, that they
include, among others, the two questions, (i) What were the most
distinctive of the claims made about Christ? and (ii) Is there any
way of ascertaining how far such claims were historically
justified? And I shall confine myself to some reflexions on these
two questions, and that without going further afield than the New
Testament period. Naturally, the title could, and sooner or later
must, include also the doctrinal question of Christianity *vis à vis*
other faiths today. But, as a start, I prefer to stick to my last, except
in a sentence or two at the very end.

Even within this limited field, I shall not attempt to be exhaustive. I hope it will be sufficient to start a discussion if I take
certain well-known claims for early Christianity and consider
their validity.

I

When Christ was proclaimed by the early missionaries, or borne
witness to by the early believers in incidental conversation, how
far would he have seemed, to the hearers, to belong to recognizable categories already familiar to them, and how far distinctively different?

a. It has been fashionable for some to say that, at least in the

Hellenistic world, he would have been at once placed in the category of *theioi andres*, that is, of thaumaturges regarded as semi-divine or at least as possessed of divine powers. One popular view of St Mark's Gospel, for instance, is that it is taking traditions of Jesus as a triumphantly successful *theios anēr* and transforming them instead into a picture of the suffering, hidden Son of God: in other words, that Mark converts an earlier thaumaturgic *theologia gloriae* into a secret epiphany, a *theologia crucis*. There is value, I believe, in some of the ideas behind this view, but it requires a good deal of qualification.

In the first place, it is far from evident that the term, *theios anēr*, represented an immediately recognizable category at all. Most assertions about it go back to a single monograph by L. Bieler,[2] which, when examined, is not altogether conclusive for the existence of a single, recognizable type under this name. Secondly, it is impossible to be sure what Mark may have done to his sources, for the simple reason that unless the still usual assumption of Marcan priority is abandoned we have no direct evidence as to what they looked like before he used them. All that we can say for certain is that in Mark's Gospel Jesus is portrayed as one who does spectacular deeds indeed, but seldom, if ever, does them merely for the sake of displaying his power, but, normally at least, in order to help somebody, and usually in response to faith on the part of the person in need, and as unobtrusively as possible. Whether this portrait is the result of a deliberate modification of traditions by the Evangelist, or whether these two ingredients – exceptional power and self-effacing service of others – were already combined in the traditions (or, indeed, in Jesus himself) it is harder to establish. But there is no cogent evidence that Jesus was ever proclaimed merely as a wonder-worker, and the burden of proof lies upon those who say that

[2] L. Bieler, *Theios Aner, Das Bild des 'gottlichen Menschen' in Spätantike und Frühchristentum* (Wien: Höfels, i, 1935, ii, 1936). A valuable critique of Bieler's views is to be found in D. L. Tiede, *The Charismatic Figure as Miracle Worker*, SBL Dissertations Series 1 (Montana 1972). On the context of the idea, see Morton Smith, 'Prolegomena to a Discussion of Aretalogies, Divine Men, the Gospels and Jesus', *JBL* 90.2 (June 1971), 174ff. And, for recent studies on various theories about Mark's method and purpose, see P. J. Achtemeier, 'The Origin and Function of the Pre-Marcan Miracle Catenae', *JBL* 91.2 (June 1972), 198ff., and R. P. Martin, *Mark – Evangelist and Theologian* (Exeter: Paternoster 1972).

he was. Is it not more reasonable, in the absence of evidence to the contrary, to assume, rather, that Mark's surprising portrait of Jesus was not a new and alien construction due to the religious genius of the Evangelist, but was derived from an impression actually made by Jesus? If so, we have already stumbled on what seems to have been among the distinctive claims made for Christ within the New Testament, namely, that, while his ministry was signalized by startling events, the motive behind them was strikingly different from what was expected in a successful wonder-worker. The wonders themselves were, for the most part, not wholly unfamiliar to the imagination, or even the experience, of the hearers. Thaumaturgy was a familiar idea, and, to some extent, an actually known phenomenon. But here, it was claimed, was a thaumaturge completely free from exhibitionism and concerned only with God's Kingship and its impact on persons: a thaumaturge who, so far from trying to authenticate himself by his wonders, appealed to them as evidential only rarely, if at all, and for the most part tried to conceal them. Even the very sympathetic and attractive picture of Apollonius of Tyana by G. Petzke does not offer any true parallel here.[3] Here, then, was something new, which the hearer would find it difficult, if not impossible, to fit precisely into an already known category.

b. But the claims for Jesus seem to have been equally distinctive when measured by another category of Gentile thought, namely, the title *kurios*. Since Bousset,[4] it has been customary to say that, while Jesus may have been *invoked* (merely) as *mar* ('Master') on Palestinian soil and in other Semitic contexts (*marana tha*), his full *acclamation* as *kurios* belonged to a later stage and to Gentile contexts, and was derived from the Hellenistic Saviour-cults (*kurios* Serapis, etc.). But this now requires to be modified.

In the first place, it is clearer than it used to be (owing, partly, to the Genesis Apocryphon of Qumran)[5] that the Semitic word

---

[3] G. Petzke, *Die Traditionen über Apollonius von Tyana und das Neue Testament, Studia ad Corpus Hellenisticum Novi Testamenti* (Leiden: Brill 1970).

[4] As in Chapter 1, n. 13; see also F. Hahn as in Introduction, n. 12.

[5] 1Q Gen. apoc. 20. 14, 16; 22. 16, etc. See also, M. Black, 'The Christological Use of the Old Testament in the New Testament', *NTS* 18.1 (Oct. 1971), 1ff., adducing also the use in targums, in Jewish liturgy, Daniel, the Elephantine Papyri, and the Aramaic Enoch.

mar (*maran*, etc.) was applied to God or to gods, as well as simply to a human Master or Rabbi. Conversely, whatever the Greek word *kurios* might suggest in a world of cult deities, Greek-speaking monotheistic Jews could use it for God, and freely applied *kurios*-passages about God from the Greek Old Testament to Jesus. It is true that, since surviving exemplars of the complete Septuagint are all of Christian provenance, and since genuinely Jewish fragments show other ways of representing the tetragrammaton, it has been questioned[6] whether *kurios* had universally been associated with the name of Yahweh from the earliest days. But such writers as Philo and Josephus can use *kurios* for God;[7] and the New Testament *kurios*-quotations themselves are evidence of this Septuagint usage at a date too early for a wholesale rewriting for Christian purposes to be plausibly postulated. It seems reasonable, therefore, to assume that *kurios* was already closely associated with God in Greek-speaking Judaism when Christians began to apply it to Jesus.

Accordingly, it appears that the use of *kurios* for Jesus has behind it both Semitic and Greek associations of considerable significance. *Mar* could, indeed, be used for a mere man; and possibly the vocative is most 'human' of all (just as, undoubtedly, *kurie* normally means no more than 'Sir!', whereas *kurios* is a title of much more distinction). But, all the same, you do not call upon a dead Rabbi to 'come' (*marana tha*); and, since it is demonstrably possible for *mar* to signify also a divine or transcendent being, it appears that in this context it must have done so. Conversely, *kurios*, too, could be applied to men. Let alone the very ordinary vocative use, even in other cases it was, at certain periods, used, for instance, of the Emperor. But it carried transcendental associations in cultic contexts; and, in the Greek-speaking Jewish Christianity from which Gentile circles must have received their earliest instruction, it was closely associated with God himself. Thus it may be misleading to think of the use of *kurios* for Jesus as a comparatively late phenomenon of a Gentile phase of Christology, to be sharply distinguished from earlier Jewish and

---

[6] See S. Schulz, as in Chapter 1, n. 60, and summary in H. Conzelmann, *Outline*, as in Chapter 2, n. 11, 83f.

[7] K. Berger, as in Chapter 2, n. 37, 414, n. 3, e.g., cites Josephus *Ant.* v.12; Philo, *mut. nom.* 111, 11f.

Palestinian phases and traced to the influence of Hellenistic cults. It may be more realistic to conceive of it as the result of linguistic and liturgical developments growing continuously from the earliest experiences of Jewish Christianity; and, if so *Kurios Iēsous* must be seen as occupying a position in religious thought distinctly different from that merely of one more cult deity recently added to the pantheon.

A closely related and overlapping phenomenon is presented by the position occupied by Jesus in relation to God in many of the opening formulae of the New Testament letters. These are nothing short of astounding, when one considers that they are written by monotheistic Jews with reference to a figure of recently past history.

c. But, returning now to Jewish circles, in them a familiar idea, evidently, was that of one or another of the figures who were to herald or implement God's completion of Israel's destiny. I use this cumbersome phrase deliberately, so as not to confine these expectations to messianism alone, but to include all or any of such figures as the Elijah of 'Malachi's' hopes or the prophet like Moses, as well as an anointed one. It is a mistake to imagine that Israel's hopes were monolithic and invariably messianic. A messiah was only one of the figures of the expectation, and a messiah (an anointed one) might be a prophet or a priest just as well as a Davidic King. There was a great fluidity in the speculations concerning God's way of salvation, and it is misleading to apply the adjective 'messianic' to all Israel's hopes promiscuously.[8]

Given, then, a background of such varied and wide-ranging expectations, was Jesus presented by the early Christians as fitting any of them, or was he completely distinctive?

Once again, the answer is, Yes, he did recall recognizable categories – but in a highly distinctive and startlingly new manner. In the first place, when he was presented as an anointed one – 'Messiah' or 'Christ' – it was in an almost unrecognizably paradoxical guise. Who had ever before heard of a crucified

---

[8] See, for instance, M. de Jonge, 'The Role of Intermediaries in God's Final Intervention in the Future According to the Qumran Scrolls', in O. Michel *et al.*, edd., *Studies in the Jewish Background of the New Testament* (Assen 1969), 44ff., and article *chriō, christos*, etc., in *TWNT* ix. 482ff.

Messiah? Some pre-Christian Jews, it appears, had daringly thought of a suffering Messiah – even a martyred Messiah;[9] but never one martyred with this degree of ignominy. And, secondly, the other most remarkable feature of the Christians' presentation was that not only was Jesus claimed to be an anointed one, but also a whole welter of other figures converged upon him – figures both for individual saviours and also for the realization of the true destiny of Israel as a whole. As far as I know, this is unparalleled in the whole of ancient Jewish literature. One individual and another was claimed as Messiah, shortly after Jesus, if not before his coming; and the Qumran literature contains *florilegia* of expectations, combining a certain number of different expectations in a single anthology.[10] But I know of no individual of the ancient world in whom so much that was relevant to the ideals of the Old Testament People of God was claimed to have been realized.

And here we meet a remarkable phenomenon. The idea of the mere verification of predictions is a familiar idea in the ancient world, and many writers, Jewish, Christian and pagan, set much store by a god whose prophets could predict correctly and whose great figures could be shown to be verifying the predictions. The modern Christian mind will be disposed to attach little, if any, religious value to such phenomena, even if they can be shown to be better than arbitrarily claimed. But in the New Testament, prediction-verification (which undeniably interests many of these writers, for instance the writer of Matthew's Gospel) is found to be – often unconsciously – deepened into the fulfilment of patterns of personal relationship.

Let me try to expand and justify this statement. Christians of the New Testament found themselves describing Jesus and his ministry in terms of the vocation of Israel. What Israel was meant to be in relation to God, Israel had failed to be; but Jesus had succeeded. Faithful at every point in the wilderness temptations; utterly one with the Father's will, as his own Son, his first born; obedient even to the length of death, like Daniel's human figure, and vindicated in God's heavenly court over the bestial, sub-human, persecuting powers; the means of the rescue of others

---

[9] See J. Jeremias in article *pais theou* in *TWNT* v. 653ff. (685ff.).
[10] 4Q patr., 4Q test., 4Q flor.

through his ministry as the suffering servant of God – all these figures, and many others besides, originally intended to portray ideal Israel or Israel's ideal vocation, are found converging on Jesus. In comparison with this tremendous discovery, mere messianism is comparatively unimportant. To say that Jesus is Christ, the anointed leader of Israel, is only one more of such convergences – and by no means the most profound (however surprising a crucified Messiah may be). In other words, in the New Testament we are witnessing something very much more organic than alleged prediction-verifications, something of profound religious significance, and an important clue in any inquiry about the distinctiveness of Christ: at Jesus all the lines of God's relations with men and men's with God are found to be meeting. And I say 'men' not 'Israel', for, after all, Israel in the thought of the Old Testament and Judaism is only representative man, the High Priest, as it were, of the whole of humanity; and the vocation and functions of ideal Israel epitomize Adam's relation to God on the one side and to the rest of creation on the other. Israel represents the position intended, in the Genesis creation-stories and in Psalm 8, for Adam: mankind, obedient to God and supreme over Nature. St Paul was the one who saw this most clearly and acted upon it at great cost to himself. What had been found in the Christian experience of Jesus Christ far transcended the parochialism of Israel: it was the fulfilment of man. Christ was ultimate Adam, and it was the acceptance of this radical finality that cost St Paul his life through the animosity of the more parochially minded of his former collagues in Pharisaism.

I am not aware of any other instance of the claim being made for a single individual that he gathered into himself the destiny of all Israel and so of all mankind. It does not happen in the Old Testament, nor in the related documents of Judaism. The Dead Sea Scrolls and the closely related Damascus Document discovered fifty years earlier reflect great reverence for the leader and hero of the sect, 'the Authentic Teacher' or 'the Teacher of Righteousness'. But he is not identified as the convergence-point, the focus, of the whole story of God's dealings with Israel and so with man. The Qumran *florilegia* of expectations are not applied to him. It is extraordinary enough, to be sure, as I have said, that a crucified leader should ever have been called Messiah;

but even the recognition of a crucified figure as God's royal representative is less extraordinary than the recognition of an individual as the focal point of Man.[11]

d. But most distinctive of all was the Easter-belief. The idea of the return to life of great men of the past – Elijah or one of the prophets (Mark 8: 28) or John the Baptist (Mark 6: 16) – is no parallel. Such an idea might have meant a return to the old mortal life (so as to die once again), or some kind of a reincarnation or re-embodiment, or (less 'miraculously') simply the re-enactment of the former person's ministry. But it is clear that the Easter-belief represents none of these. The Easter-belief was not that Jesus had returned to the old mortal life (as the disciples may have believed those raised from death by Jesus himself to have done). Nor was it a belief merely in the persistence of his 'spirit', or the representation of it in some successor. It was the belief that Jesus himself, identical with his former self, had gone beyond death into life absolute, life eternal. And it is not true that Pharisaism had already provided this sort of expectation. Pharisaism had provided a framework of thought in which a transcendental life was conceived of as coming to God's People, the righteous, collectively, at the end of history. But there is no precedent (as far as I know) for the conviction that one individual had already entered, before the wind-up of history, upon that eternal life which the various forms of Pharisaic hope looked for at the end of history and for the righteous collectively. No doubt it can be urged that, in the earliest days, the Christians jumped to the conclusion that the wind-up of history must have taken place and that they must all be collectively entering, there and then, upon the life of the age to come. To formulate early Christian belief so is to make it coincide with the pattern of Pharisaic expectation. But even if this were a true reading of the earliest Christian convictions (which is questionable), it was still only the one man Jesus who had given rise to these convictions: there is no evidence that anything else in the disciples' circumstances suggested any such situation; and it could not have taken long for them to discover that those circumstances were, indeed, otherwise unchanged, and that what Paul calls 'this present evil

---

[11] For details, see Chapters 2 and 5.

age' was still very much with them. Yet, the Easter conviction about Jesus persists undimmed, and imparts to practically the entire texture of New Testament thought the distinctive and characteristic tension which the jargon of scholars knows as the 'eschatological' tension of 'the already and the not yet', and which issues in the distinctively Christian form of the ethical imperative, namely, 'Become what you are!'

   e. Hand in hand with the attribution to Jesus of the life and the glory of the age to come and the distinctive results seen in the 'tension' of the authentic Christian message, goes a tendency to associate Jesus also with the primordial. If he is Lord of the End, is he not Lord of the Beginning also? Once he is recognized as God's agent in the consummation, it is not a big step to find in him the Mediator of God's initial creation also. But precisely when this type of Christological affirmation first emerged, and whether it followed patterns already laid down in pre-Christian cults of the divine Wisdom is debated. With special reference to the terms of reference of this paper, concerned as they are with what is distinctive, two observations may be made. First, there is (so far as I know) no direct evidence for what can strictly be called a religious cultus of the divine Wisdom before the beginnings of Christianity. That Wisdom is personified and praised – even that 'aretalogies' are written about her – is undeniable. But is this the same thing as treating Wisdom as the Mediator of *worship*? I am sceptical about postulating the existence of conventicles of Wisdom-devotees before Christianity.[12] Secondly, even if it could be established that the cult of Wisdom already existed, it would still be a new thing that a man of recent history, who had been crucified the other day, should come to occupy the position of this divine Wisdom. The Wisdom language was ready-made: the vocabulary of mediation was ready at hand. But I suspect it was something new to find it adapted to genuinely *liturgical* uses; and it was certainly dramatically new to find the man Jesus occupying the position of the divine Mediator between God and creation. When *Logos* and *Sophia* are applied to Jesus of Nazareth, this is an unprecedented distinctiveness.

[12] See J. T. Sanders, *The New Testament Christological Hymns: their Historical Religious Background* (Cambridge: University Press 1971), with my review in *JTS* n.s. 23.1 (April 1972), 212ff.

In passing, it may be added that the virtual non-attribution of the term spirit to Jesus is almost as startling. Whereas the Wisdom literature had used *logos* and *sophia* and *pneuma*, if not as interchangeable terms, at least in the closest conjunction, the New Testament almost consistently reserves *pneuma* for the activity of God among Christians *through* Christ rather than applying it to Christ himself; and, by the same token, *pneuma* has virtually no cosmic or creative function in the New Testament (and, indeed, *ruach* has not much of such association in the Old Testament either). The appropriation of *logos* and *sophia* but rejection of *pneuma* for Jesus seems (for whatever reason) to be something decidedly distinctive of the Christian response to events.

II

If the claims of the New Testament writers and the antecedent traditions emerge as distinctive in a variety of ways, is it possible to go on, by a critical reconstruction of the Jesus of history, to check these claims for their plausibility or otherwise? Notoriously, the trend in current New Testament scholarship is emphatically against the view that Jesus' own consciousness can be retrieved; and many scholars would say that it is a waste of labour to attempt any strictly historical reconstruction even of his activities. The most that the majority of scholars will allow (beyond the acknowledgement of his life and death) is that, by a rigorously critical sifting, a certain amount of his original teaching may be recovered with some degree of confidence. The techniques by which this is achieved are dominated (for the most part) by two principles. First, that reports of the words and deeds of Jesus were repeated and altered in the course of transmission, and that, therefore, if they can be retrieved in their original shape at all, it will only be by making allowance for all the shifts in circumstances and application between the lifetime of Jesus and the setting within the post-Easter Church. Secondly, that the only sayings which may, with even a measure of confidence, be accepted as dominical are those which are demonstrably not influenced by the outlook of Judaism before, or of the Church after, Jesus.

However, several writers have pointed out that, whatever may be the purely theoretical validity of both these canons, our hopes of actually applying them satisfactorily are limited.[13] For the first, the data are not plentiful. It is impossible, for instance, to find criteria by which a later and modified form of a tradition can be infallibly recognized or an earlier form infallibly restored. Of the second it has to be confessed that no historian in his right mind would try to construct a portrait of a figure of the past solely from views, sayings or characteristics which he shared neither with his predecessors nor with his successors. Just as Jesus obviously used much of his Jewish heritage, so, too, his disciples must have accepted and assimilated much of their Master's most original teaching; and that which was new in the outlook and practices of Jesus, but which was also never accepted by his followers (even if we possessed means of discovering it with any confidence), is a slender and lop-sided basis for understanding him.

A more satisfactory approach, perhaps, is to rely on the total impression gained, cumulatively, by putting side by side the various portraits that are presented by the traditions of Jesus in his various activities: teaching, healing, disputing, training his disciples, and so forth. Without attempting any more than a rough-and-ready sifting, leading to the rejection of only the most obviously late accretions in each category, the general effect of these several more or less impressionistic portraits is to convey a total conception of a personality striking, original, baffling, yet illuminating. And it may be argued that it is difficult to account for this except by postulating an actual person of such a character. The very fact that the total impression is made up of several different strands of tradition, originating (one may reasonably presume) in different circles, compensates in some degree for the absence of any rigorous test by which the authentic and original has been isolated within any one strand of tradition. If all of them, for all their diversity, combine to create a coherent and challenging impression, this is significant. And if, as has recently been suggested, there is reason to believe (despite form-critical assumptions) that oral tradition did not suffer any very radical changes until the Evangelists themselves shaped and placed their

---

[13] See, among others, E. P. Sanders, *The Tendencies of the Synoptic Tradition* (Cambridge: University Press 1969); and M. D. Hooker, 'On Using the Wrong Tool', *Theology* 76. 629 (Nov. 1972), 570ff.

pieces in position, then the case for believing in the authenticity of this total impression is the stronger. Professor E. Trocmé sums up his own conclusions, after following such lines of approach, as follows:

Thus the 'mystery of Jesus' is not a more or less artificial creation by later generations. It is rooted in the behaviour of Jesus himself, completely devoted to his humble task, but convinced that for this mission he possessed an exceptional authority from God; involved in several simultaneous dialogues and not trying to draw them into a unity; too great to be wholly understood by any of his interlocutors, but grasped in part by many of them. This mystery already necessitated the groping efforts of the evangelists and theologians of the first century. It has never been finally eliminated, either by historians or by theologians. It never will be.[14]

This, if it is a justified conclusion, certainly presents us with a figure of supreme distinctiveness. Of course, if one believed that the Evangelists made no attempt to embody early traditions but were simply presenting, in quasi-narrative form, the credal convictions of the post-Easter churches to which they belonged, their evidence would have no independent value whatever, and the second part of this paper would amount to no more than the retelling of the conclusions of the first part from one, limited, section out of all the New Testament documents already laid under contribution in that part. But if there is reason to believe that the Evangelists have preserved a certain amount of early tradition, then the impression won from them separately may without impropriety be used as evidence against which to test the validity of the estimates expressed in the New Testament as a whole. On this showing, the distinctiveness here uncovered in this second section is significant and confirmatory. I would, myself, add that there is a strong case to be made for Jesus having used the human figure of Daniel 7, to which he made allusion as 'the Son of Man', as a symbol for the vocation to which he believed true Israel (on behalf of mankind) to be called, and of which he saw his own vocation as the very heart.[15] If so, then that distinctive

[14] E. Trocmé, *Jésus de Nazareth vu par les témoins de sa vie* (Neuchâtel: Delachaux et Niestlé 1971), 141f.; Eng. trans., *Jesus and his Contemporaries* (London: SCM 1973), 125.

[15] See M. D. Hooker, *The Son of Man in Mark* (London: SPCK 1967); and my 'Neglected Features', as in Chapter 1, n. 5. Whether or not this position is

claim, made so forcibly by Paul, that Jesus was 'ultimate Adam' may, in essence, go back to something recognized by Jesus himself, and receive independent confirmation from the gospel traditions.

If there is anything in all this, it certainly does not point to any exclusive claims for Christianity, in the sense of excluding all other ways to God as invalid. Rather, the distinctiveness of earliest Christianity is found in a Person whose achievement includes the hopes and expectations of the Judaism and paganism of his day, but does so in paradoxical and distinctive ways, so as greatly to transcend them. And this pattern, *mutatis mutandis*, seems to me to be applicable also in what I have deliberately omitted from this paper, namely the relation of Christianity to other faiths today. If Christianity claims to be not merely one religion among others, but uniquely all-inclusive, its origins certainly do not belie the claim. It arose in a Middle East compound of Greek and Jew, but its derivation seems to be not wholly explicable either in terms of Jew or of Greek, but only in terms of an event inclusive, but without parallel. In reply to the time-honoured question, 'But does not such a claim imply the denial that there is "salvation" in any other?' one may say that, on the contrary, it is precisely because God is revealed by Christ as a God who became incarnate that he is able to save those who sought or who seek him in other ways, whether before the incarnation or beyond the range of its acknowledgement. But, equally, this implies no slackening of the 'missionary' motives; for if God is, indeed, the God of all because he is the God and Father of our Lord Jesus Christ, then it follows that those who know him by his incarnate name must long for and be committed to the bringing of all men, so far as in them lies, to the fullest possible understanding of him in this way.

deemed eccentric, one thing is undeniable, that the Christian and post-Christian usage is highly distinctive in the almost invariable use of the definite article in the phrase, as contrasted with the almost invariably anarthrous form in pre-Christian usage. A high proportion of the scholars who write about it seem not even to notice this, and use 'Son of Man' and 'the Son of Man' indiscriminately.

2. *A COMMENT* BY HADDON WILLMER

Professor Moule, in my view, faces the real difficulty of the distinctiveness of Christ, because he wishes at once to take the history of Jesus seriously, to maintain the missionary character of Christianity and to beware of the offence of exclusiveness. The problem evaporates if any one of these elements is omitted. To meet the question Professor Moule suggests that when we see the distinctiveness of earliest Christianity in a Person whose achievement included (fulfilled) the hopes of Judaism and paganism, yet so as greatly to transcend them, we have a pattern which would be applicable to the relation of Christianity to other faiths today.

What exactly is this pattern? My difficulty here is that Christianity seems to be portrayed in language which suggests a self-contained religion, over against others, possessing an *achieved transcendence* in relation to its context, which is part of its self-awareness as a religion. That there is an element of truth in this view I do not doubt, but its limits must not be overlooked, since they also serve to define the distinctiveness of Christianity. One limit is that the description of Christianity as achieved transcendence is only made possible by a withdrawal from the historical to the ideal. Professor Moule is explicitly concerned with the *claims* made by earliest Christianity, claims which could be stated only as a result of a selective treatment of source material, by a process of idealization or withdrawal from the openness of history. The conceptual chain, Jesus – Israel – Man, is dependent on history, at least in that it was in historical Israel that it became possible for 'Israel' to be read as 'Man', and yet it also involves a break from historical Israel, since Judaism from the first would not allow that Jesus was true Israel. This is not to deny outright the Christian claim which depends on the link; but it is to emphasize its precariousness, and to counterbalance the easily given impression of achieved transcendence. From the first, the claim was highly dubitable; and it cannot be made less so by the historical justification for the early Church's claims about Jesus which Professor Moule seeks, since that, on the whole, is only a demonstration that the early Church's claims were anticipated by explicit or virtual *claims* made by Jesus or by others during his life. Can we expect history to do more? It can show us where the claim originated but it cannot prove the truth of the claim, especially since in the last analysis the claim concerns the relation of God to Jesus. It is not clear to me that because in its origins Christianity was culturally and religiously eclectic, it is 'uniquely all-inclusive'. Eclecticism is a necessary characteristic of all historical novelties, most of which are obviously far from being unique or all-inclusive.

The claim that Jesus is true Israel becomes, in a way, more convincing when there is not a Jew at hand to dispute it. But only if the claim is made in close living relation with Judaism can it be plausibly a fulfilment of Judaism. In what sense can a Christianity which lives at a distance from Judaism (perhaps even so far away as to be anti-Semitic) justifiably claim to *include* the *hopes* of Judaism? This is an extreme example of the fact that if the hopes are too far or too paradoxically transcended, it is hard to say that they are fulfilled. A Christianity, however, which lives close to Judaism – the condition of fulfilling it – is in danger of never transcending it, and never being distinct from it.

Jesus and the early Church both made distinctive claims and lived so closely with their context that their claims never seemed obvious, or easy to accept. This means we must not only say that there was achieved transcendence but also that the existence of early Christianity was a process of ever renewed transcending. 'Disputing' is one of the activities of Jesus mentioned by Professor Moule which deserves more attention here, since it may be the key to the relation of Christianity to other faiths. Disputing is the outward form or the activity in which fulfilling and transcending can at once be realized, and the precariousness and assurance of the claim can together be recognized. Was there anything distinctive about the fact that Jesus was a disputer, or about the manner and intention of his disputing? What, for instance, is the significance of the parabolic method of teaching for the interrelation of Christianity and other faiths?

I think reflexion on Jesus the disputer must lead to some criticism of the way we conceptualize the problem of the relation of religions. We class Jesus as the founder of Christianity, and so tend to attribute to him all the distinctness which Christianity has acquired culturally and historically. This tendency is not inhibited by concentrating on him as a Person ('striking, original...'), for this also tends to abstract him as an individual from the setting and the way in which he was actually historical. Instead we should perhaps think of Jesus as a Jew in dispute with Judaism, i.e., in a position where he could carry out the risky process of both fulfilling and transcending. And early Christianity, too, for a while shared this relation. Neither Jesus nor the Church can be defined apart from that with which they are in hopeful but deep dispute.

Much of the contemporary discussion of the relations between religions seems concerned simply to avoid disputes, and to promote the undeniable blessings of toleration and mutual understanding. We are not in a position to talk of fulfilment and transcendence – at least not in the form that it occurred in Jesus – because we see the religions so much as self-contained culturally bound traditions, entities to be treated in egalitarian fashion. But Jesus was not a man of a distinct religion asking merely for liberty to practise it; he was ready for death as part of a religious dispute, a man between religions, transcending Judaism only as he was sacrificially involved with it. Christians may seem to possess him as the founder of their religion; but perhaps he is involved with Christianity in another way, disputing with it, ever and again transcending it and only so calling it to fulfilment.

Christians can speak of the achieved transcendence of Jesus Christ only because they are continually being transcended by him. At the same time, they may in relation with him be the means by which that part of the world with which they are involved – not only 'other faiths' – is fulfilled and transcended; or perhaps it is so transcended that it cannot recognize its fulfilment.

I do not think that I am necessarily contradicting Professor Moule in these comments, but I should like to entice – or goad – him into saying more.

3. *THE DISTINCTIVENESS OF CHRIST*: FURTHER COMMENT
BY C. F. D. MOULE AND HADDON WILLMER

PROFESSOR MOULE WRITES:
I am grateful to Dr Haddon Willmer for his courteous and generous but demanding comment on my paper about the dis-

tinctiveness of Christ (*Theology* (November 1973), 573). He says that he would like to entice or goad me into saying more. Certainly his observations deserve a reply, so I must try.

His main points, if I rightly understand him, are these. First, he makes the negative comment, that, if there is an element of truth at all in seeing Christianity as a self-contained religion 'possessing an *achieved transcendence* in relation to its context', then the limits of such an estimate need to be clearly recognized. These limits are constituted, he says, by the fact that such an estimate is made possible only by a withdrawal from the historical to the ideal, for the claims made by earliest Christianity 'could be stated only as a result of a selective treatment of source material, by a process of idealization or withdrawal from the openness of history'. This is not to say that the claims may not have been correct; but their justification, he holds, rests on precarious foundations – witness their rejection by Judaism, and witness the fact that one can do no more than refer the claims of earliest Christianity back to still earlier claims – those made by Jesus himself or by others during his lifetime; and to do this is only to support claims by claims, not by any solid facts; it gives no ground for seeing Christianity as uniquely all-inclusive. Furthermore, the claim only goes unchallenged when there is no Jew at hand to challenge it; yet, it is only as Christianity remains close to Judaism that any meaning can be given to the idea of its fulfilling Judaism.

It may be that I have failed properly to grasp it; but I feel at present inclined to dispute this criticism at more points than one. First, I question the statement that the claims of earliest Christianity were the result of a selective treatment of source material and a withdrawal from the openness of history. As I understand it, the earliest Christians did not select what evidence seemed to them convenient, but, on the contrary, were driven to their conclusions by the force of what was happening to them. They had an intimate knowledge of various attitudes and positions in Judaism, and I know of no reason for thinking that they left out of account any explanation of their own circumstances which might have been suggested by these; but nothing, apparently, seemed to fit their circumstances and to make sense of the course of events except those estimates of Jesus which we know now as Christian estimates. Certainly Judaism challenged these; certainly not all men believed; but does that necessarily mean that the Christian claims were no better than mere opinion, reached by an arbitrary selection of evidence and by withdrawing from history? Secondly, I do not, in any case, hold that the claims of Christianity have nothing more solid to appeal back to than certain antecedent claims made by or for Jesus. It is notoriously questionable whether Jesus made any explicit claims for himself. The claims of earliest Christianity were based not, primarily at least, on claims explicitly made by Jesus, but rather on the implications of his life, his actions, his teaching, his death, and, most notably, its extraordinary sequel. And if it was all these factors that led to the Christian estimate of Jesus, then I submit that it is not just a chain of spoken and unverifiable claims that lies behind the claims of earliest Christianity, but historical events demanding evaluation, if not explanation.

Certainly there is idealization, if by this is meant the interpretation of historical events in terms of what transcends history and therefore cannot be historically verified, and is not accepted by all alike. The conceptual chain, 'Jesus – Israel – Man', is certainly not accepted by all, and is not self-evident. But it was reached, none the less, not by arbitrary theologizing, but by observing, in Jesus, all that is implied in a right relation to God, and finding this clinched by the absolute and irreversible aliveness which (as his disciples believed) belonged to him.

Then, further, I do not fully understand why the claim that Jesus is the fulfilment of Judaism can plausibly be made only in close relation to Judaism. Certainly Jesus himself had to live inside Judaism and in painful dialogue with it, to be what he was and do what he did. But, as far as I can see, the expulsion of Christians from the synagogue and their alienation from Judaism does nothing to invalidate the claim that Jesus fulfils and transcends Judaism. If that claim is true, it remains true, whether Judaism is physically near or far.

Dr Willmer's positive point is that perhaps Jesus is essentially in dispute, as, in his lifetime with Judaism, so still, both with Judaism and with Christianity. This I welcome as a deep insight. Jesus, like God in the Old Testament, is constantly disputing with his people. And this is what condemns us all, every time we settle down complacently with an organization instead of a movement. Jesus is always greater than his people; and if we try to contain him within our own system and tidily exhibit him as bringing an achieved transcendence to *us*, of course he will judge us. But it seems to me still that history, both at the origins of Christianity and ever since, refuses to let the historian, if he is honest, evade or bypass this Figure who fulfils while he transcends and redeems while he judges.

DR WILLMER REPLIES:

Many thanks for your response to my comments. I am glad you think it worth pursuing the question further, for it seems to me that confusion or evasion here saps the will to work at *Christian* theology today, because it leaves it without an adequate basis for a distinctive existence. And perhaps Christian *believing* is at stake also, which is more serious.

I am afraid I can only be a blundering partner in the discussion. Certainly, I haven't so far made my line of thought as clear as I would like; consequently, it is not your fault that you tend too much to separate my positive point, which you like, from my negative points, which you reject. For me the two points hang together, and only then are they a criticism of parts of the argument and a defence of its substance.

My original comment was really meant to put two questions to you. 1. If you say, as I think rightly, that the justification for the claims made for Jesus Christ must come out of the pressure of the history of Jesus Christ, have you not to take the whole history of Jesus Christ more into account than in fact you do? 2. If you say, as I am glad you do, that it is not impossible that we can still get through to the history of Jesus and so be under its pressure, can you not show more concretely how our life and thought (in this case, in relation to other religions) are (to be) shaped by that pressure? Let me try to show why I feel you have only begun to deal with these questions and why they may call for revision of parts of your argument.

I am not sure that when you talk of the 'force of what was happening to (the earliest disciples)' you have a basis for a presentation of Jesus which in principle is universal or distinctively inclusive. On your account, they were convinced of something about Jesus from their historical experience of him and expressed that conviction more or less adequately in language available to them in their cultural context, with the result that in various ways universality and finality were claimed for Jesus. Now the question that concerns me here is not the one you thought I was driving at: I am not asking whether the claims of the disciples involved arbitrary, indefensible historical selection. That is a problem, indeed, but I would try to answer it in much the same way as you do in your comment. My positive point cannot begin to be developed if we have to conclude that since all claims for Jesus are disputed, all is arbitrary, and only scepticism is honest. One might also ask here whether the convincing 'something' in Jesus either is or involves that universal nuance of some of the language the disciples used about him, or whether the development of such claims depends not on what Jesus actually was but on the accident of the language in which he was described. But I am not immediately concerned with that. What I want to ask is rather what these claims mean in the light of the history after the convincing of the first disciples, for this history also grows out of, or is a manifestation of, the pressure of what happened to them in Jesus. The impact of Jesus cannot be limited to the bringing of the first disciples to Easter faith. We can say at once, that, helped by other factors, world mission and a world religion grow from this pressure, and that means that a movement with some kind of universality and inclusiveness is here. But we cannot overlook the fact that we also have here a history of division, of absences or denials of universality, which may be essential for the manifestation of claims of distinctiveness.

To simplify, but not dangerously, what is the implication for the truth of these claims of the fact that by them mankind is split into believers and unbelievers? I don't see how we can hold on to the presence of this inclusiveness in history when history turns out as it has done. At least, I think it more of a problem than it appears to be for you, when in your comment you tend to dismiss Jewish and other kinds of unbelief as irrelevant to the question of the universality of Christ. Perhaps I misunderstand you. Would you not agree that Romans 9–11 shows how important for Paul was this obvious non-inclusiveness of Christ at the beginning of the history of Christianity and also what a desperate

problem it is? Paul here can only speak in hope, faith and love
against history and in the end he falls back on the mysteries of
divine predestination and eschatology – he cannot find an answer
in history.

I wonder whether you are not in a similar position and that
in the end you too really give up even the history of Jesus as the
basis of inclusiveness. The doubt lurks, for example, in the final
paragraph of your article, where you speak of inclusiveness not
in Jesus Christ but in the God revealed in Jesus Christ. The
expression is ambiguous, and I do not know how you would
develop it. One direction in which it might be pushed is to put
the emphasis on the *God* revealed in Jesus, as though we can know
him apart from Jesus Christ. Then we can make statements like
'God is love' and use them apart from and even against much
of this history of Jesus and the history from Jesus. The impressive
history of Christian liberalism and enlightenment rests on this
possibility. In his paper, John Hick provided a persuasive example of this approach:[16] because we are able, apart from Jesus
Christ, to talk about the '*same* infinite divine reality' lying behind
the religions of the world, we must see Trinitarianism as religious
(and dispensable?) mythology, for, if it is treated as a 'theological
hypothesis', it is meaningless and involves an unacceptable ex-
clusivism. Now there are many important differences between
your approach and Hick's – not least that the early history of
Christianity is taken more seriously in principle and practice by
you, as it ought to be in any *Christian* theology of other religions
– but here I see the possibility of a striking similarity. And if in
fact you are calling upon the universality of God to save the lack
of universality of Jesus Christ, are you not giving up the basic
historical approach?

Alternatively, we may interpret the phrase 'God revealed in
Jesus Christ' in such a way that Jesus Christ is the event of that
revelation and the decisive criterion of what 'God' means and
so also of what the inclusiveness of God means. It may of course
simply be obstinate and insensitive traditionalism – nothing to be
pleased about – that makes me feel that if a Christian theology
of other religions is worth developing at all it is because there

[16] John Hick, 'Towards a Christian Theology of other Religions', in *God and the
Universe of Faiths* (London: Macmillan 1973).

is truth in this interpretation, for all its dangers and difficulties.

In the end, the first interpretation rests on an idea or experience of God such that the non-universality of the history of Jesus need not worry us. The second approach assumes or looks for distinctive-inclusiveness in Jesus Christ and so is vulnerable to the way things turn out.

I think that basically you adhere to this second approach. You want to look at the history of Jesus Christ to find out about God and his relation to the divided religious history of mankind. But then there is the danger that you escape from history in the way I have already suggested. This comes to light not only in the wording of your final paragraph but also in the body of your historical argument. You escape from history, paradoxically, precisely because of the attention you give it and the confidence you have that it has a force leading to faith and to specific theological judgements, for example, about Jesus Christ. Because of this, you are committed to the study of the history of Jesus up to and including the resurrection, but is it fair to say that this history relieves you from worrying too much – theologically, I mean! – about what happens in the history after the resurrection? The truth of Christianity is established in the resurrection; the absolute and irreversible aliveness of Jesus here revealed is the one thing that matters, let the Church be never so dead or erring.

I would not want to deny this outright; a Jesus Christ distinguishable from the Church is essential for any healthy understanding of the Church. But if we approach theology and Christology in this way we end up with a Christ who is simply an idea. Even if we have an historical Jesus who revealed God in his life, it may still turn out to be no more than an idea unless the action of God in Jesus Christ is continued after the resurrection into the present. An historical memory is as much an idea as a metaphysical abstraction. Especially if an historical event is God's final or inclusive act, one cannot ignore what happens after it. If Jesus is alive, then we should be able to interpret our history as having him as an actor – at least in principle. While we may pay attention to the resurrection as a single event, with revelatory or apologetic significance, we must most of all think of the Risen One. Then the resurrection cannot be used to bracket off the history of Jesus from the history of the Church or of subsequent events generally. This later history must somehow affect our understanding of what was done in Jesus Christ by God. In your approach, this does not happen, and that is why I made the criticism that the openness to history is limited.

That there was in Jesus Christ an all-inclusive act of God is difficult to believe in the light of subsequent developments. Yet some Christians do believe it and I think it is superficial to write off this history of division simply as a denial of inclusiveness. It may be that in this history, despite appearances, there is an inclusiveness at work. Only inspection and interpretation of the history can enable us to say whether that is so or not. It is not a matter of saving the history of Christianity; it is also a question whether we can see in Jesus an inclusiveness at work, for there too it can only be despite appearances.

Christians believe this, partly because like Paul in Romans 9–11 they do not think that history is yet finished. But that of itself is an escape from history, and we take history too seriously to be satisfied with that route alone. Can we say more? Perhaps. A condition for an authentic belief in the universality-inclusiveness of Jesus is that those who so believe are involved in a process, a history of reconcilation. Because this process is necessitated by a broken situation – it is genuinely historical – it goes on paradoxically, sharing the brokenness and so often not looking like reconciliation. And because the goal is eschatological, in God, it remains true that the process does not always mean the immediate end of all disputes, though this is never to be a ground for justifying or glorifying conflict. To the moment of Paul's thinking in Romans 9–11, we must here add 2 Corinthians 5: 16ff., interpreting the ministry of reconciliation in the light of Paul's self-description in Chapter 6, which may have been seen as a concretization of Romans 9: 1–3. Here Paul is involved in a disputatious life; the dispute comes from his assurance of reconciliation and yet appears to call it into question.

It is important to reflect on what disputing means. I don't believe it implies that everything is consigned to mere opinion, and that the Christian's claim must be judged as arbitrary. It shows rather how in Christian faith assurance of truth and openness to question go together, as indeed they must in any persuasive, inclusive or reconciling process. I am reminded here of your analysis of the way cartoons work as a model for understanding the purpose of the parables of Jesus.[17]

The inclusiveness of God's action in Christ is not necessarily invalidated by a history of disputes; it is only invalidated by the kind of disputes which do not go, as it were, from reconciliation to reconciliation. The cross is the centre of God's dispute with men, men's dispute with God and with each other. Yet Christian faith goes on seeing this as the event of reconciliation, for which it seeks understanding. Of course, the danger of disputing is that it can so easily deny reconciliation, but there is no evading it. In peace negotiations, the representatives of the warring sides cannot simply say 'Peace'. There must be disputing as a process by which the demands of both sides, pitched high in the bitterness of war, are scaled down with some fairness. These disputes can be really hard, very long affairs; it is always possible that they are what they appear to be, a prolongation of war under the guise of negotiation; but they may also be genuinely reconciliatory.

So, I want to say that disputing may be a mode of inclusiveness, and that in view of the actual history of Jesus and from Jesus, this is the only basis on which we can talk of inclusiveness in it. Now, I think it follows that we must have the proximity of the disputing parties – not simply physical proximity but spiritual, intellectual and actual proximity (1 Cor. 9: 9ff.). And looking at the historical development of Christianity, it seems to me that it has lost this proximity with Judaism, in dispute with which it originated, and that, as a result, the categories and language in which we tackle the problem of Christianity and other religions embody and perpetuate a failure of inclusiveness. Only by revision here can we be true to the gospel and in the process follow more the way of *Jesus*, which is what I would like you, as a New Testament theologian *and* historian, to speak of in more detail.

Proximity to the Jew means, I think, that we cannot but be shaken when he disputes with us and says: 'The Old Testament,

[17] C. F. D. Moule, 'Mark 4: 1–2 Yet Once More', in E. E. Ellis and M. Wilcox, edd., *Neotestamentica et Semitica, Studies in honour of Matthew Black* (Edinburgh: T. and T. Clark 1969), 95ff.

as you call it, is my Book, and the correct conceptual chain is Man
– Israel – Man, not Man – Israel – Jesus – Man.' But you do not
seem as worried by this as I am, perhaps because of the way you
understand Christianity as the fulfilment of Judaism. In your
view, Judaism appears to be a religion that developed up to the
time of Christ and is now available to us as ideas – that is,
through historical means, we see it as a fund of religious concepts
which can be applied to Jesus, though they do not exactly correspond to his history, and this application enables us to say that
they were transcended as well as fulfilled. By contrast, I believe
we ought to think of Judaism as relating to an actual people. Here
is not a fund of concepts but a people upon whose claim to be
the people of God the claim of Christ and of Christianity must
rest, *if it is to be historically founded*. And this people is still with
us, though greatly changed through the centuries. Paul saw it in
this way; that is why his Christian universalism is not a spiritual-
intellectual ecclesiology which sees no more significance in the
Jew-Gentile distinction. He has, rather, a universalism which is
served by and played out between this distinction. So it says to
the Jew, *not* 'Your ancient privileges now mean nothing for you
as a people; they are concepts, disengaged from their historical
matrix, which we may now take over allegorically for the Church',
but 'In this Christ, you as a people inherit the promise and as
such are a blessing to all nations.' This necessarily requires an
analysis both of the promises and of Jesus and the movement
stemming from him to show this is the case. Such a universalism
preserves the element of dispute – the difference between Jew
and Gentile – within the realization of reconciliation.

From early times, the Church was also working with a much
simpler and so more manageable and popular concept of universality, according to which Judaism is a fund of ideas which
can be detached from the Jewish people. By the third century
this was dominant in Christian thinking and was a sign of Christian dominance over and lack of openness towards Jews. The
development was a breaking off of genuine dispute, and it opened
the way for the language of achieved transcendence to become
the total framework of Christian thinking. Especially the metaphysical element in the language of traditional orthodoxy gives
this impression. The human Jesus is not denied but he is related

to God metaphysically, that is, directly and simply, without the history of Jesus being allowed to appear in all its concrete and bemusing detail. Despite the fact that what you say is derived from the New Testament and is not in its content and method deduced from this kind of dogma, may it not be that the tone and structure of your argument is remotely indebted to this dogmatic style?

I conclude that it is only safe for the Church to believe in the universality of God in Jesus Christ when it speaks of it in the midst of the nations, where they can really hear and really dispute. There is an achieved transcendence in Jesus Christ, but I doubt whether it is right or safe for us or appropriate to Jesus Christ to seek to isolate it or to speak of it apart from its context in the way of Jesus, for which 'dispute' and 'proximity' seem to me to be good terms. So, the relation between Jesus and the Church (disciple, missionary, theologian, Christianity and Christianity's relation with other religions) is not only: 1, Jesus as achieved transcendence: to be *proclaimed* by those who have not achieved transcendence (unlikeness of Jesus and disciple); but also 2, Jesus as the process of transcendence, both as actor and recipient: so not only the Truth, but the Way and the Life to be shared by the disciple (likeness of Jesus and disciple). Thus, we do not need to ignore the later history in order to talk of inclusiveness in him; his inclusiveness was always only of the disputing kind. We can never approach a Christian theology of other religions as though there is anywhere a possibility of getting beyond dispute: there is only the way of disputing creatively and recreatively rather than destructively.

There are many loose ends in all this; for example, I have said nothing about the really important matter of describing in detail the difference between good and bad disputing – the attempt to do so might bring my whole way of thinking to breaking point. At the moment, though, all I want to do is to argue for a basic description of the problem of the distinctiveness of Christ which requires such an analysis of disputing, in place of one which can do without it.

Thus far Dr Willmer. An adequate reply is beyond my ability, for it would require expertise well beyond any competence I may have. But I can at least welcome Dr Willmer's conviction that, while criticizing parts of my argument, he is defending its substance; and I am sincerely grateful for his sensitive and perceptive insights into the heart of the problem. I offer my reflexions on what he has written for what they may be worth.

He has, I think, two main points. The first is the dilemma with which he poses me: if I trust history enough to find, in the genesis of the Easter-belief, its verdict on the aliveness of Christ, then I cannot, without inconsistency, refuse to trust history enough to allow subsequent events to reverse or modify that verdict. To trust a certain bit of history and turn a blind eye to the rest is tantamount to escaping from history or appealing to something beyond it: it invalidates the historical basis of my argument.

To this I am inclined to reply that I am not sure whether there is a dilemma quite like that. In the first place, as Dr Willmer himself recognizes, history is not yet complete. Paul's position in Rom. 9–11 seems to depend in part on this fact also. He seems to expect the universality of Christ to become evident before history is completed. He does not seem to me to contract out from history. Neither, incidentally, do I think that Paul believes Christ's universality to be threatened by the unresponsiveness of the Jews. I do not think that this is what Rom. 9–11 is about. Paul seems to me to be entirely confident about Christ's universality. What does agonize him is the fact that the Jews seem to be failing of their destiny. But he believes that, before history is wound up, this will be changed. I could, then, I suppose, argue in the same way that history is still not complete, and that it is still possible to hope that Christ's universality will be vindicated by the time the whole story is told.

But Paul's historical perspective was very short, and I would be sorry, in fact, if my faith stood or fell with a hypothetical verdict at the (hypothetical) end of an indefinitely long drawn out history. Rather, I suggest that 'universality' needs to be carefully defined. It is not, in any case, a word that I am myself particularly anxious to apply to Christ; but if it be used of him, I suggest that it must be defined in such a way as to do justice to human freewill and to God's gentleness. If the Easter verdict is that to Christ there rightfully belongs the homage of all – so that to him every knee should bow and every tongue confess that Jesus Christ is Lord, to the glory of God the Father – is that verdict invalidated if, in the course of history, this acknowledgement is not universally forthcoming? The reason why the Easter verdict seems to me to be decisive is that I find it impossible to account for it except as an intimation traceable only to Christ himself. And the reason why I see no evidence in subsequent history for reversing that verdict is that the many rejections of that verdict and the many refusals of the universality of Christ that history contains appear to me (where I am in a position to judge) to spring from misunderstanding or worse; and that, conversely, where Christ's universality is acknowledged, there, in each successive generation, the marks of the Kingdom of God and of the aliveness of Christ are seen. In no generation since those earliest days have there been lacking some communities in which Christ's aliveness has been confirmed, even when the majority of men have been antagonistic or unresponsive. In short, I do not believe that I am evading history or failing to take it seriously when I still see the initial verdict as standing unassailed and refuse to measure it by man's failure to respond. Unless we believe that God is the sort of God to impose Christ's universality by force (and if he is, then the incarnation is no revelation of what he is like), its non-acceptance by some, or even by most, cannot, in itself, invalidate it. The problem of evil is notoriously insoluble. But it does not remove the (equally insoluble) 'problem of good'. Good Friday and Easter were not originally measured by majority response, and they stand in history, whatever the subsequent response. If not all are 'saved' in this life, it is not necessarily an admission of failure for the universality of Christ; nor is it a mere escape from history to hope that they will be saved in the beyond. Thus, I think I see what Dr Willmer means by his dilemma, but I question whether it is quite like that; and I hope that, in saying this, I am not betraying a complacency or insensitivity towards the agonies and the uncertainties of life, which, Heaven knows, are all too real.

Dr Willmer's other main question is whether I am not calling upon the universality of God 'to save the lack of universality of Jesus Christ'. This, I suppose, would be the same as an abuse of the Logos doctrine. But I do not think I am committing such an abuse. To believe that Christ is not merely one among other revelations but is the supreme (and, if you like, universal) revelation of what God is like, is not, so far as I can see, inconsistent with believing that the same God does reveal himself also in other ways, and that all genuine and sincere longing for God is rewarded by some vision of God. But it does, I think, mean believing that non-Christian religious experience is defective (even by the standards of human experience which, by definition, must in any case be defective when measured by divine and absolute standards). This must sound arrogant; but it is not necessarily so. It is true, as Dr Willmer observes, that Paul never gave up the distinction between Jew and Gentile. But it is also true that even Gentiles did, in Paul's eyes, become members of true Israel, 'God's Israel', by baptism into Christ or by grafting into the authentic olive tree. It was 'in Christ', and in Christ alone, Paul believed, that Israel's destiny lay. That is why, for Paul, baptism into Christ included and transcended circumcision. For Paul, Israel's future was full of hope, but the hope lay entirely in Christ, whose inclusiveness was, for Paul, axiomatic.

Thus, I do (I gratefully agree) adhere to the second alternative proposed by Dr Willmer – that of interpreting 'the phrase "God revealed in Jesus Christ" in such a way that Jesus Christ is the event of that revelation and the decisive criterion of what "God" means and so also of what the inclusiveness of God means'; and I welcome his penetrating insight, at the end of his comment, into the relation between Jesus and the Church: it is *both* that Jesus is *unlike* the disciple as having an 'achieved transcendence' and as being that which is proclaimed, *and yet also* that Jesus is *like* the disciple as being the process of transcendence and 'the Way and the Life to be shared by the disciple'; and that, accordingly 'we can never approach a Christian theology of other religions as though there is anywhere a possibility of getting beyond dispute: there is only the way of disputing creatively and recreatively rather than destructively'. If Dr Willmer and I differ, it may be because of his greater sensitivity in debate with other religions and also because of unexamined assumptions on my part in the realm of philosophy and truth-claims. This, I imagine, is the realm in which lies, at least in part, 'the really important matter of describing in detail the difference between good and bad disputing'.

Excursus: Obeisance (proskunein)

The New Testament incidence of the word *proskunein* (generally, 'to do obeisance'), is not a completely reliable guide, if one is looking for evidence as to when Jesus came to be worshipped like God; but it does provide a pointer. The Old Testament, for instance, although it uses *proskunein* = *hištaḥawôt* mainly for worship of God (or of false gods), does, on several occasions, use it for a gesture before a man. On the other hand, it seems to have been regarded as an exceptional and extravagant gesture when offered to a man. Jacob performs elaborate acts of obeisance before Esau ('he...bowed himself to the ground seven times, until he came to his brother', Gen. 33: 3); but then he is deliberately trying to propitiate him (32: 21, Eng. verse 20), and he even says (33: 10), 'I have seen thy face, as one seeth the face of God.' Similarly, in the book of Esther, it is the arrogance of an oriental potentate like Haman that expects inferiors to prostrate themselves before him, and is indignant when Mordecai refuses (Esther 3: 2); and, although Jewish exegesis made difficulties over this (see the texts quoted *in loc.* in the ICC commentary – I owe this observation to my friend Dr B. A. Mastin), Josephus and Philo were aware that it was a servile gesture if made towards a fellow-man. Josephus, *Ant.* x. 211, describes Nebuchadnezzar as falling on his face and hailing Daniel 'in the manner in which men worship God' (*hō(i) tropō(i) ton theon proskunousi*). Philo, *decal.* 64, says 'let us not do obeisance to those who by nature are brothers' (*tous adelphous phusei mē proskunōmen*); and in *leg. Gai.* 116, arguing against allowing divine rights to Gaius, he calls *proskunēsis* 'a barbaric custom'. E. Greeven, *TWNT s.v.*, vi. 763, who quotes these passages, quotes also one or two exceptions; but the tendency to regard the word as primarily suitable to worship seems clear.

So in the New Testament, there are passages affirming emphatically that *proskunēsis* is to be offered only to God: in Matt. 4: 9f., Luke 4: 7f., the temptation to do obeisance to Satan is repulsed by Deut. 6: 13 (worship God alone – though here the LXX does not use *proskunein*); in Acts 10: 26, Peter demurs when Cornelius does obeisance, saying, 'Stand up; I am a man like anyone else'; and in Rev. 19: 10, and 22:

9 the angel demurs to the seer's obeisance: 'it is God whom you must worship'. On the other hand, Matt. 18: 26 and Rev. 3: 9 use the word of a gesture to a fellow-man.

However, Matt. 18: 26 describes an abject gesture towards the creditor who has the debtor at his mercy (and 'through' whom God himself is perhaps intended to be seen – Greeven, *op. cit.* 764); and equally, Rev. 3: 9 describes the abject submission of the opponents to the faithful in Philadelphia. All the other occurrences in the New Testament are before Jesus; and, while it is rare in Mark and Luke, it is more frequent in Matthew. In Mark: 5: 6, the Gerasene demoniac and 15: 19, the mocking soldiers (as though before the deified Emperor?). In Luke: 24: 52 (*v.l.*), before the risen and glorified Christ. In John: 9: 38, when the man who had been blind confesses 'the Son of Man'. In Matthew: 2: 2, 8, 11, the magi; 8: 2, the leper; 9: 18 the ruler (= Jairus); 14: 33 (the disciples after the walking on the water); 15: 35 (the Syrophoenician woman); 20: 20 (the mother of James and John); 28: 9, 17 (resurrection stories).

In the light of this, one might argue (a) that *proskunein* was, indeed, for the most part reserved for worship of a divine being; and (b) that, while Mark virtually represents only supernatural powers according this honour to Jesus during his ministry, Matthew introduces it freely into the period of the ministry. But to put it so would be to ignore the fact that Mark and Luke, even when not using *proskunein*, allude to comparable gestures before the Jesus of the ministry: Mark 1: 40, the leper (described in Matt. as offering *proskunēsis* to Jesus) 'falls on his knees' (*gonupetōn*); and so with Jairus (Mark 5: 22), and the rich man (Mark 10: 17); and in Luke 5: 12 the leper falls on his face; and so Jairus (Luke 8: 41), and the Samaritan leper (17: 16) (cf. Rev. 5: 8, of worship before the Lamb). And in John, Mary falls at Jesus' feet (11: 32), and the opponents of Jesus fall to the ground (18: 6).

Broadly speaking, then, Jesus *is* represented as receiving the highest honours – though only very rarely during his ministry, except according to Matthew. Does this suggest that, already during his ministry, he had a 'numinous' presence which was occasionally recognized, and that Matthew has intensified and multiplied what was, nevertheless, there from the beginning? It seems to me that this is a plausible view.

Justin, *Trypho* 126, includes, among scriptural styles believed by Christians to be applicable to Jesus, *theos proskunētos* – referring presumably (since he attributes it to David) to Ps. 45: 12 or 72:11 or 97: 7. This shows how naturally *proskunein* did attach itself to God in the minds of Christian apologists.

See further M. P. Charlesworth, 'Some Observations on Ruler-Cult especially in Rome', *HTR* 28 (1935), 5ff.; and (on Dan. 2: 46), B. A. Mastin, 'Daniel 2 46 and the Hellenistic world', *ZAW* 85 (1973), 8off.

I. *Index of References*

D. THE DEAD SEA (QUMRAN) SCROLLS

E. RABBINICAL SOURCES

F. CLASSICAL AND HELLENISTIC AUTHORS AND EXTRA-CANONICAL CHRISTIAN WRITINGS

II. *Index of Names*